Wish-fulfilment in Philosophy and Psychoanalysis

Wish-fulfilment as a singular means of satisfying ineluctable desire is a pivotal concept in classical psychoanalysis. Freud argued that it was the thread that united dreams, daydreams, phantasy, omnipotent thinking, neurotic and some psychotic symptoms such as hallucinations and delusions, art, myth and religious illusions. The concept's theoretical exploration has been largely neglected within psychoanalysis since, but contemporary philosophers have recognised it as providing an explanatory model for much of the kind of irrational behaviour so problematic for psychiatry, social psychology and the philosophy of mind.

Although critically neglected in contemporary psychological and psychoanalytic thought, the concept remains clinically fundamental under different labels: it encompasses the processes of omnipotent phantasy, symbolic or substitutive satisfaction, actualisation in transference and acting out, symptom formation and defences such as projective identification. Wish-fulfilment can be shown to be a specifically psychoanalytic compartment of a common-sense psychological theory of action that illuminates not just clinical material but also the paradoxes of irrationality – such as weakness of will and self-deception – that preoccupy philosophers.

The first half of this book develops a comprehensive and novel theory of wish-fulfilment, explores its radical implications for the structure of mind, and locates it against the backdrop of both contemporary psychoanalytic and philosophical thought. In the second half, the book applies the theory to illuminate important features of self-deception and delusion, religion, insanity defences, creative writing and the exclusion of mind and intention in the biological drift of modern psychiatry.

The book will be essential to philosophers of mind, psychoanalysts, psychiatrists, psychologists, social theorists and students in these disciplines; as well as readers interested in understanding how the mind works in mental illness, self-deception, religion and creative writing.

Tamas Pataki is Honorary Senior Fellow in the School of Historical and Philosophical Studies, University of Melbourne. He is the author of *Against Religion* (2007) and co-editor with Michael Levine of *Racism in Mind* (2004).

Psychoanalytic Explorations series

Books in this series:

The Heart of Man's Destiny
Lacanian psychoanalysis and early Reformation thought
Herman Westerink

Wish-fulfilment in Philosophy and Psychoanalysis
The tyranny of desire
Tamas Pataki

Wish-fulfilment in Philosophy and Psychoanalysis

The tyranny of desire

Tamas Pataki

Routledge
Taylor & Francis Group

LONDON AND NEW YORK

First published 2014
by Routledge
27 Church Road, Hove, East Sussex, BN3 2FA

and by Routledge
711 Third Avenue, New York, NY 10017

Routledge is an imprint of the Taylor & Francis Group, an informa business

© 2014 Tamas Pataki

British Library Cataloguing in Publication Data
A catalogue record for this book is available from the British Library

Library of Congress Cataloging in Publication Data
Pataki, Tamas.
  Wish-fulfilment in philosophy and psychoanalysis : the tyranny of desire /
  Tamas Pataki. – 1 [edition].
    pages cm
  Includes bibliographical references.
  1. Desire. 2. Desire (Philosophy) I. Title.
BF575.D4P38 2014
150.19'5–dc23   2013047536

ISBN: 978-0-415-82292-3 (hbk)
ISBN: 978-0-203-55308-4 (ebk)

Typeset in Bembo and Gill Sans
by Sunrise Setting Ltd, Paignton, UK

For Michael P. Levine and John Johnston, who kept me in the game

Contents

Preface

But thought's the slave of life and life time's fool

Shakespeare, Henry IV, Part I

For much of the first long stint of my post-graduate efforts in philosophy, many years ago, I was in psychoanalysis with Dr. Clara Geroe, Australia's first Training Analyst, and like myself an Hungarian emigre. She was already old and very frail when analysis commenced and afflicted with what bureaucrats call time management issues. Patients arriving at the appointed hour could find themselves waiting in the corridor, or sent down for coffee, or secreted in the tiny office as others were anonymously exchanged between consulting and waiting rooms – Dr. Geroe was a great stickler for patient anonymity. Many times I would spend half an hour, an hour or more in the waiting room. But this was a boon because the room served in those days as the library of the Melbourne Institute of Psychoanalysis and thus I had at my disposal the journals and a fair collection of books in what was already a vast psychoanalytic literature.

My reading was desultory. D. W. Winnicott and Otto Kernberg and some of the now largely forgotten founders of psychosomatic medicine, Franz Alexander and Felix Deutsch, attracted me. Later Dr. Geroe directed my reading to Anna Freud, Heinz Hartmann and Margaret Mahler. Although *Civilization and its Discontents* had been an undergraduate text I didn't pay attention. My interests then were in philosophical logic and I deprecated the human sciences with the typical immaturity of the young logician. It was not till much later that I read Freud systematically.

I think that some of the themes that run through the book were already rattling around in my head as I read in the waiting room. Winnicott's explorations of phantasy, illusion and living a dissociated life were deeply impressive and had some affinity with my own experience. The significance of wishful phantasy and play was often discussed in sessions as I reported obervations on my young nieces. The insistent clinging to illusions, of believing that wishing can make it so (as I think Peter Pan said), and dissociation or splitting of the self – matters not unconnected as I came to see – puzzled me, as they puzzle me still. Other themes, however, have a different origin. The psychoanalytic material I was reading, though I found it immensely suggestive, lacked rigour and a concern for the conceptual clarity that was the hallmark (or at least the aspiration) of the Analytic philosophy, the conceptual or connective analysis, that was then my school. I do not mean that the psychoanalytic material lacked scientific rigour. There are many ways in science, and the psychoanalytic approach to studying humankind – principally the observations of two individuals in deep engagement over many years in relatively controlled conditions, the formulation and disconfirmation of theoretical hypotheses arising from many thousands of similar engagements, and observations of infant parent interactions – remote from the laboratory or the questionnaire room though it may be, is science. True, psychoanalysis was not making much of an effort to integrate its theories within the traditional divisions of the sciences, though there were isolated bold attempts by theorists such as Heinz Hartmann and David Rappaport to make it a General Psychology. But science was not, as I saw it, the problem. Lack of conceptual clarity and analysis was.

On the other hand, although conceptual clarity, untangling the knots of language, arriving at a perspicuous overview, were by the 1980s no longer everything, and ambitious theory construction was well underway, Analytic philosophers were making unusual progress in understanding the nature of mind and its place in a physical world by careful attention to a class of difficult concepts: *meaning* and *Intentionality* (in Brentano's sense), *desire, belief, deliberation, intention, decision, choice* and *action*. All these and many related concepts – *self, agency, rationality* - inhere in ordinary common-sense (or as we shall say, Intentional) psychology, are garnered on mother's knee, refined perusing Henry James, and used to make sense of other people and ourselves. And the trouble was that psychoanalytic theory at the time, though recognising that these concepts constituted the communicative medium of the clinic – of the 'clinical theory' - had little reflective interest in them; nor in coordinating its indigenous technical concepts such as *drive* and *phantasy* with the richer matrix of concepts of common-sense psychology. They were presupposed in the discourse but rarely investigated. Presumably, intention, deliberation, decision and so on were regarded as ego-functions whose investigation could be left to others. There was no sense – no sense that I could sense anyway – that the prevailing indifference to these concepts, sometimes clustered under the heading of 'action theory', hobbled psychoanalytic understanding. Of course there were exceptions to this innocence (as we shall see) but I am speaking here in general terms.

In 1990, after my supervisor at Melbourne University, Graeme Marshall, had turned my interest from the *Tractatus* to action theory, I had the good fortune to spend two semesters as a post-graduate student at the Psychoanalysis Unit in University College, London under the supervision of Professor Joseph Sandler. There I started reading Freud, and Sandler's and his colleagues' authoritative expositions of Freud, which were then being published as monographs. I don't think Sandler cared much for teaching, but his articles, especially a series in the 1970s on object relations and wish-fulfilment or 'actualisation' as he generalised the notion, were remarkable both for cogent argument and lucidity. It was then also that I first met Jim Hopkins and was introduced to his work and that of Richard Wollheim. The pervasive influence of these three authors on the present book will be evident to anyone who knows their work. It was, I think, Hopkins and Wollheim who first constructively brought to bear the Analytic philosophy of mind and action on psychoanalysis and showed that much of it is best understood as an extension of common-sense or Intentional psychology. This does not mean that substantive psychoanalytic claims about, say, castration anxiety or the role of early envy in the formation of borderline personality disorder, can be derived from reflection on common-sense psychology. They cannot. The Intentional approach or program (as I shall call it) that Hopkins and Wollheim instigated consisted in showing that many basic psychoanalytic concepts and psychoanalysis' causal, explanatory resources acquire their explanatory force or cogency from their being extensions of basic concepts and explanatory patterns of common-sense psychology. This seemed to me then, as it still does, the most promising approach to understanding much of psychoanalysis, and it is a premise that runs through this book like a thread.

But why should this be? Why should the extension of common-sense psychology be so important for understanding the psychopathology with which psychoanalysis and mainstream biological psychiatry concern themselves? After all, psychiatry now seems to have an organ (just like the other medical specialities), the brain, about which there is at last considerable knowledge; an organ that in mental illness, it alleges, malfunctions. And the languages appropriate for investigating and describing the brain are the various languages of neurobiology, not the Intentional idiom. Even neuropsychoanalysis or psychodynamic neuroscience, which appears to be the cutting edge of contemporary psychoanalysis, urges that the mind and the brain are one, and that psychoanalytic advance must make use of neuroscientific methods to 'determine the neural correlates of our basic psychoanalytic concepts' (Solms and Zellner 2012a: 51).

The answer will require discussion later but can be stated in relatively simple terms here. Even if some form of identity theory, or perhaps dual aspect theory, of mind and brain is true, it remains profoundly misleading to talk, as many do, of 'the mind-brain' or of the 'mind emerging from the brain' or of the major task of progressive psychoanalysis as finding neural correlates for mental states and processes in the brain (see e.g. Fotopoulou et al 2012). (A task, perhaps, but not a *major* task.) *Mind* is a concept with much wider extension than *brain*. In the first place there are many important mental states or processes which are neither identical with nor correlate with brain processes. *Self-esteem, self-understanding, envy, vindictiveness, candour, curiosity* and *forthrightness* are surely important Intentional concepts in psychoanalysis and, indeed, psychiatry – or should be. But there is clearly no prospect of finding anything like neural correlates falling under such 'thick' concepts. They spill over into behaviour, circumstance and the history of the individual to defy reduction or correlation. Not all that we regard as mental is centred in the brain. The mental is not a category correlative with the neurological by some kind of pre-established harmony. This should be obvious from a historical consideration of how mental concepts have evolved and accumulated; they were in use before anyone had the slightest inkling that they applied to the brain. (Of course, it could be *stipulated* that only those states can be considered mental that *do* have brain correlates; but that is a path to still further confusion.)

There is also a more general answer. It seems likely that one day neuroscientists will be able to produce a complete, exhaustive description of a person's brain in physical terms, the terms of neuroanatomy, neurochemistry etc. But no matter how complete that description, it will say nothing or next to nothing about the person's mind. It will say nothing of the content of their beliefs, desires, ambitions and fears; though it may say something interesting about their capacities for having these things. Why? Because the mind (usually) refers beyond itself; it requires that the brain be described in terms of what it is related to in the present and the past, in its historical and social relations. The Intentionality of mind (as philosophers say) cannot be captured in physical description of the brain alone; we cannot describe what is 'in' the mind without having to refer to what is outside the brain. To see this, consider sunburn, an unexpectedly much discussed topic in the philosophical literature. Imagine that sunburn is indistinguishable on physical examination from acid burn or toaster burn. Though their physical conditions may be indistinguishable there are critical differences between sunburn and the other burns that become evident in the way the conditions are treated. The sunburnt person will be told to avoid the sun, use lotions and so on. The reference to the sun is indispensable to an adequate characterisation of sunburn. So, too, the characterisation of beliefs, desires and other Intentional states require reference to objects (sensations and moods may be exceptions) which are generally located outside the brain, and so cannot be captured in a description of the brain. This is not an argument for anti-physicalism; the Intentional objects are generally physical or abstract. It is an argument for the indispensability of the Intentional idiom for describing mental conditions.

It is clear that if mental disorders are just disorders of the brain then it should be possible to describe them *completely* in neurobiological terms. No-one has a clue how to do this, and the argument above – controversial to be sure – suggests that it cannot be done for reasons of principle. A neurobiological description will always fall short of explaining what the illness is about, and most mental illnesses are about something. There are of course disorders of the brain that can be given full neurobiological descriptions (at least in principle); but they are neurological disorders not mental ones.

Years passed. I published a handful of papers on what, recognising the concept's singularity, I started calling 'Freudian wish-fulfilment'. Ideas and some passages from those papers reappear here, mostly in much revised form. I began to realise that the capacity for the full range of Freudian wish-fulfilment had interesting implications for the structure of mind. But then in the late nineties and during the last decade philosophical interest in psychoanalysis seemed to fade (or so it seemed from the Antipodes), mainstream psychiatry and the cognitive branches of clinical psychology continued to write psychoanalysis out of history, and psychiatry through the instrument of the Diagnostic Statistical Manuals persisted in diminishing itself by *reductio ad absurdum*. Religious extremism and the wars of religion broke loose and such philosophical interest as I had turned to understanding religion and racism; again, some of the work resulting reappears here in revised form.

But recently developments in these disciplines made me come to see the importance of re-asserting the Intentional program. Today it may seem that the rapid development of neuroscience, the neurobiological focus of contemporary psychiatry and neuropsychoanalysis, and the reductive trends in philosophy of mind, will completely overshadow the Intentional program. I think this would be unfortunate. It seems to me that when Freud at the foundation of psychoanalysis realised that neurophysiological concepts alone could get him nowhere in understanding the neuroses he encountered a limitation, not merely of the science of the day as he thought, but of *a priori* principle.

It seems important to do as much as one can to clarify the Intentional understanding of mind before our reductive propensities take over. That is one objective of this book, though of course its necessarily restricted choice of subject matter, if for no other reason, make it fall far short of this large ambition.

But there is another objective. For most of the history of thought, desire, longing, wishing, striving – the orectic aspects of mind – and their capacity to cause conflict and turmoil in the human breast have been at the centre of philosophical deliberation. Whether welcomed or deplored, ineluctable desire – I do not mean just sexual desire – preoccupied the minds of Plato, Augustine, Schopenhauer, Nietzsche and Freud. In classical psychoanalysis, the period I take as ending with the Hartmann era, desire conceived of as drive or wish in conflict with other drives, wishes or with mental structures, provided the prototypical explanation for the neuroses and related conditions. With the contemporary emphasis in psychoanalysis on object relations and environmental failure, that picture changed and the significance of conflict around infantile wishes receded into the background. (I exclude here the Lacanian and other schismatic schools.) In cognitively orientated clinical psychology and mainstream psychiatry desire and conflict caused by desire scarcely get mentioned (though the development of affective neuroscience by Panksepp and others is likely to change that situation). This is remarkable, a remarkable triumph, perhaps, of Puritanism in the social sciences. For it would be amazing if the orectic (desiderative, appetitive, wishful) and conative (willing, decisive) elements of mind, so conspicuous in every other sphere of life, vanished from the aetiology of psychopathology. A work on wish-fulfilment like the present one, which sees wish-fulfilment as a distinctive mode of orectically motivated action, will not concede this disappearance of desire.

I also hope that this book will make a contribution to Freudian scholarship. I chose to shape the book around Freudian concepts and used largely Freudian terminology. This is not without drawbacks because it requires a good deal of exposition and the presentation of textual evidence; but it also has major advantages. For one thing, although the different schools of psychoanalysis – the Kleinians, Lacanians, self-psychologists etc. – do not much read each other, everyone still reads Freud. Although not many philosophers interested in psychoanalysis read the psychoanalytic journals, or Fairbairn, Kernberg or Betty Joseph, they will read Freud (and perhaps Klein). But more to the point, although Freud did not know much philosophy he was philosophically astute, and when in the course of his work he confronted philosophical problems his solutions and strategies were ones that still command great interest. He is a contemporary, and in many ways the issues he grappled with are still being fought over, albeit over a larger terrain. Finally, it would seem to me a tremendous pity if we were to lose the extraordinarily rich heritage of psychoanalysis, its wealth of insight, apercu and theory in psychopathology; if we failed to acknowledge the important lines of research it started (and continues) in infant observation and developmental theory; and lost its illuminations in anthropology, the understanding of religion, art, insanity and ordinary, everyday life.

I have tried to relegate as much as possible of the technical and arcane scholarly discussion to footnotes but, inevitably, given the nature of the subject, some discipline-specific jargon and conceptions have had to remain in the text. To avoid repetition I have cross-referenced pasages by means of section number headings placed in bold. The reader who wishes a quick trip through the text could try **1.1 - 1.2, 1.4, 1.5, 2.3 - 2.4, 3.2, 4.2 – 4.6, 5.3 – 5.7**, and perhaps one of the chapters on applications, maybe **Chapter 7 or 8**.

Acknowledgements

I have profited greatly over the years from discussions with many people, including Edwin Coleman, Rai Gaita, Russell Grigg, Jim Hopkins, Jack Kirszenblat, Anne Manne, Graeme Marshall, Alex Miller and Glenn Newbery. I am deeply grateful to Jim Hopkins, Michael Levine, Agnes Petocz and Jintao Wang for illuminating discussion, advice and encouragement, over difficult times; and to Agnes and Michael especially for their very helpful comments on rebarbative early drafts of most chapters.

Various passages scattered throughout the book, mostly revised, have appeared in previous publications and I thank their publishers for kind permission to reprint them. Chapters 1 and 2: 'Intention in wish-fulfilment', *Australasian Journal of Philosophy* Vol. 74, No. 1, March 1996; and 'Freud, object relations, agency and the self' in *Psychoanalytic Knowledge* edited by M. C. Chung and C. Feltham, London, Palgrave: 2003. Chapter 3: 'Freudian wish-fulfilment and subintentional explanation' in *The Analytic Freud* edited by M. Levine, London, Routledge: 2000. Chapter 4: 'Intention in wish-fulfilment', *Australasian Journal of Philosophy* Vol. 74, No. 1, March 1996. Chapter 5: 'Freud, object relations, agency and the self' in *Psychoanalytic Knowledge* edited by M. C. Chung and C. Feltham, London, Palgrave: 2003; and 'Fairbairn and partitive conceptions of mind in *Fairbairn and the Object-Relations Tradition*, edited by David E. Scharff and Graham S. Clarke, London: Karnac Books: 2014. Chapter 6: 'Self-deception and wish-fulfilment' in *Philosophia* 25: 1-4, 1997. Chapter 7: *Against Religion*, Melbourne, Scribe Publications: 2007. Chapter 8: 'Some aspects of writing', *Quadrant* Vol. XLI, No. 3, April 1997. Chapter 9: 'Intention, excuse and insanity' in *Forensic Psychiatry: Influences of Evil*, edited by Tom Mason, Humana Press: 2006.

Part I

Theory

Chapter 1

Wish and wish-fulfilment

Hope deferred makes the heart sick, but the wish come true is a tree of life.

Proverbs XII, 12

1.1 Introduction: wish and wish-fulfilment

In 1899 Sigmund Freud wrote to his friend Fliess:

> My dear Wilhelm, … My last generalization holds good and seems inclined to spread to an unpredictable extent. It is not only dreams that are fulfilments of wishes, but hysterical attacks as well. This is true of hysterical symptoms, but it probably applies to every product of neurosis – for I recognized it long ago in acute delusional insanity. Reality – wish-fulfilment: it is from this contrasting pair that our mental life springs.
>
> (Freud 1950a: 277)

The generalisation did spread, and wish-fulfilment's scope acquired ambitious dimensions:

> … the principal function of the mental mechanism is to relieve the individual from the tensions created in him by his needs… But the satisfaction of… part of these needs… is regularly frustrated by reality. This leads to the further task of finding some other means of dealing with the unsatisfied impulses. The whole course of the history of civilization is no more than an account of the various methods adopted by mankind for 'binding' their unsatisfied wishes. Myths, religion and morality find their place in this scheme as attempts to seek a compensation for the lack of satisfaction of human wishes… [T]he neuroses themselves have turned out to be attempts to find individual solutions for the problems of compensating for unsatisfied wishes, whilst the institutions seek to provide social solutions for these same problems… [T]he exercising of an art [is] once again an activity intended to allay ungratified wishes – in the first place in the creative artist himself and subsequently in his audience or spectators.
>
> (Freud 1913j: 186–7)

Freud eventually concluded that dreams, daydreams, phantasies, neurotic and some psychotic symptoms – delusions, hallucinations – jokes and art, slips of the tongue, bungled actions, magical or omnipotent thinking and illusions such as religion, as well as forms of social organisation and moral institutions, were either wish-fulfilling or attempts at wish-fulfilment. When he wrote 'Reality – wish-fulfilment: it is from this contrasting pair that our mental life springs', Freud meant that wishes and 'reality' – or, rather, the agencies of mind representing 'reality' which oppose those wishes – may both be fulfilled in symptoms and their congeners.[1] So wish-fulfilment is usually a compromise: 'a symptom arises where the repressed and the repressing thought can come together in the wish-fulfilment' (1950a: 278). This is a startling idea. Symptoms are not only *caused* by conflicts between a person's wishes and the internalised demands of reality, but *are* the fulfilments or satisfactions – in a manner to be explored – of one or both.

Another novel idea emerges in the second passage quoted. The mind's task, the task of the 'mental mechanism', is the relief of tensions created by needs or drives **(see 2.2)**, expressed as desires or wishes. Ordinarily, when we strongly desire to perform an action or wish to obtain some state of affairs, we will act. But if prevented from acting by sleep, inhibition or social constraints, or because the desired end is unattainable, then sometimes we can produce transformations in ourselves – self-deceptive or consoling beliefs and phantasies, hallucinatory experiences, delusions or other symptoms – which manage to substitute for the real objects of those wishes and, in a manner, satisfy and temporarily terminate them. Here the mind has recourse to wish-fulfilment or, as Freud often says, 'substitutive satisfaction'. Evidently this conception of wish-fulfilment is quite singular and differs in important respects from the ordinary understanding of what it is for a wish to be fulfilled. I will henceforth refer to it as 'Freudian wish-fulfilment' or 'FWT'.

In the preceding passages I used 'wish' and 'desire' interchangeably, and this requires explanation. Even if wishing and desiring are taken as natural kinds (Schroeder 2004), or as having similar realisers in the brain (as assumed by most neuroscientists), there are important conceptual differences between them (and between wanting, longing, yearning, etc.). Moreover, the nature of 'the wish' in Freud's work has given rise to significant scholarly controversy and it will pay to insert a parenthesis here to settle this issue at the outset, as more important matters turn on it.

In its *conceptually central* uses, the wish-locution presupposes an acknowledgement that action is impossible, or close to being so: it indicates a mere expression of preference. 'How I wish I could have been there' or, even, 'I do wish I could go' do not place me in causal relation to action in a time frame but tell, instead, of my preferences. That is why one cannot desire or want what is known to be impossible, but one can certainly wish for it. I cannot knowingly desire to undo the past, but I may still wish that I had been born into wealth or gone to a better school. Nevertheless, because I want to adhere as closely as practicable to Freudian usage, I will use 'wish' and 'desire' interchangeably.

The German *wunsch* has a stronger causal affiliation with action than our 'wish' does, and neither Freud nor his translators distinguished systematically between wishing and desiring. Many of Freud's recent philosophical commentators, how-ever, have claimed to identify in Freud's account of wish-fulfilment a systematically quasi-technical use of 'the wish'. It is said that Freud distinguished between wishes and desires. Sebastian Gardner (1993: 124, 140) claims that the 'psychoanalytic wish' uncovered by Freud is a novel kind of mental creature, 'a sort of hybrid', different from both desire and ordinary wishes – though related to the ordinary kind of wish – and is 'necessarily engaged in the process of wish-fulfilment' (1993: 126). The difference he alleges is underlined in his claim that 'Freud did not envisage wish-fulfilment as a mode of satisfaction available to propositional desires' (1993: 123), though desires (according to Gardner) can exploit wish-fulfilment by regressing to a state of instinctual demand and give rise to a wish susceptible to wish-fulfilment (1993: 123). Richard Wollheim (1984: 85, 90ff) also recognises a quasi-technical notion of *wish* that acquires its significance in the context of the archaic operation of mind. Jonathan Lear says that 'a wish is a motivating force, but, unlike desire, its products are not actions. Freud implicitly recognises that a wish differs from a desire. For he characterises a wish by its role within the archaic functioning of the infantile mind' (1990: 75–6). Similarly, Brakel (2009: 139) thinks that 'wish' is a term of art for Freud and wishing, unlike desire, is exclusively satisfied by phantasy. Jim Hopkins, who does not usually put much weight on this distinction (1982: xix ff; 1995), did wonder, though, whether – in consequence of the irrationality and detachment from reality of the wishes fulfilled in dreams – Freud should not have 'introduced a special theoretical term – perhaps something like "night-time motive derivative" – instead of the common-sense term "wish" (1988: 44–5).

I think the attribution of these categorical distinctions to Freud is mistaken and leads their authors to distorted accounts of wish-fulfilment. Freud distinguishes amongst kinds of wishes in terms of their content and topographical location: whether they are conscious, preconscious or unconscious. But he does not distin-guish between ordinary and 'psychoanalytic wishes', or between pre-propositional wishes (or some hybrid of wish and desire) and propositional desires (Gardner 1993: 153–6). The fundamental distinction Freud makes is not between orectic kinds *wish* and *desire*, nor between an ordinary and a technical sense of 'wish', but between the kinds of process, primary or secondary, which can take both wishes and desires as their materials. This is easily demonstrable. First, Freud frequently uses 'wish' in an inclusive way to cover for all the conative and orectic states that set our minds turn-ing, as when he writes that 'nothing but a wish can set our mental apparatus work-ing' (Freud 1900a: 567). Second, in relation to the formation of the dream, Freud contends that there has to be at least one wish 'dating from earliest childhood' (1900a: 269) that is strong enough to instigate the dream (1900a: 553); these wishes, invariably associated with wish-fulfilment, have some of the properties attributed to them by the commentators. But Freud then goes on to claim that in dreams there is a *layering* of wish-fulfilments in which all manner of wishes and quite ordinary desires left over from the 'day residues' are also fulfilled – in the peculiar manner of FWT to be investigated presently (1900a: 550–72). Thus his 19-month-old daugh-ter Anna's spoken-out-loud dream consisting of a menu, to which her own name was attached: '*Anna F., stwawbewwies, wild stwawbewwies, omblet, pudden!*' (1916–17: 164) is directly instigated by unsatisfied desires of the previous day resulting from an enforced fast. Third, Freud conceived of daydream, art, religion, and other things as fulfilling wishes and desires equally. 'Only in art', he says, 'does it still happen that a man who is consumed by desires performs something resembling the accomplishment of those desires and that what he does in play produces emotional effects – thanks to artistic illusion – just as though it were something real' (1912–13: 90). What are those desires? Principally, they are commonplace (propositional) 'desires to win honour, power, wealth and the love of women' (1916–17: 376). Here 'wish' could be substituted without loss for 'desire', as could the reverse substitution in Freud's characterisation of religious ideas as 'illusions, fulfilments of the oldest, strongest and most urgent wishes of mankind' (1927c: 30). End of parenthesis.

Freudian wish-fulfilment is one of the fundamental but tacit working concepts of classical psychoanalysis. Although FWT pervades his work, Freud did not distinguish it as a fundamental tenet,[2] partly, I think, because he failed to recognise its singularity. Psychoanalysis is generally scant on rigorous conceptual analysis and that singularity has remained unappreciated. Several other specific reasons for the neglect may be noted. In some quarters a false dichotomy between drive theory and object relations or interpersonal theory is enjoined, as if object-relating somehow precluded mutual relations motivated by wishes. Since wish-fulfilment is part of an account of motivation naturally associated with drive theory, both motivational concepts – wish and drive – have suffered neglect. Generally speaking, the classical preoccupation with neuroses, considered largely as pathologies of desire and conflict, has given way in contemporary theory to concern with pathologies of developmental, predominantly cognitive, deficits due to environmental failures: failures in attachment leading to incapacity for 'mentalisation' (Fonagy *et al.* 2004; Holmes 2010); inadequate (pre-verbal) internalisation leading to faulty 'interactional structures'; Bowlby's (1971) 'internal working models' (IWMs); Stern's (1985) 'representations of interactions generalised' (RIGs); and the acquisition of unconscious pathogenic beliefs (Weiss and Sampson 1986). This attention to impaired (broadly) cognitive structures[3] and associated failures in affect regulation appears to have diminished interest in the active, desiderative, wish-fulfilling aspects of mind. Psychoanalysis appears now less concerned with the pathology of desire than of belief, or the various belief-like structures anteceding beliefs (IWMs, RIGs, procedural memories, etc.) that have been proposed; less concerned with the consequences of frustrated wishes than with deficits in cognitive functions. In this, of course, psychoanalysis has moved closer to schools of clinical psychology such as cognitive behavioural therapy that focus on the acquisition and role of cognitive structures and on rectifying faulty beliefs and interactional dispositions.

I believe that this emphasis on the (broadly) cognitive at the expense of the wishful aspects of mind is a mistake: neither the origins nor the persistence of pathogenic (broadly) cognitive structures can be understood independently of the orectic (desiderative, appetitive, wishful) and conative (willing, decisive, intending) aspects of mind. I hope to show why. In any event, the concept of wish-fulfilment has not vanished from psychoanalysis altogether. It retains a place in contemporary theory and practice, albeit under guises: as omnipotent phantasy; as underlying psychological defences that supervene on phantasy such as projective identification; in 'actualisation' (Sandler 1976) in transference, acting out, some aspects of symptom formation and the analysis of dreams; indeed, as active in much of the territory that Freud mapped out for it, but less explicitly.

It is evident that if Freud was even approximately right about the nature and scope of FWT, then it must also form an important compartment of any philosophy of mind that seeks to understand irrational action and belief formation in *Intentional or common-sense-psychological* terms.[4] And here I must insert another parenthesis, this time about terminology.

In philosophy the term 'intentional', as well as being used in the ordinary way to qualify action as 'purposeful' or 'meant', is also used in a technical sense which, following common practice, will be capitalised: 'Intentional'. The Latin root for this sense appears to be 'intentio', which in Scholastic use meant 'representation' (Kneale 1968), but – probably as a result of mistranslating Brentano's text, in which the term reappears in modern philosophy – Intentionality has come to denote the property of 'aboutness' possessed by most of the mental states which we use to explain human behaviour and, by extension, whatever bears sufficient similarity to such behaviour (Daniel Dennett's (1989) 'Intentional stance'). Belief, fear, desire, and so on, can have Intentional objects – for example what we think (that grass is green) or what we think about (grass, greenness); and since we can think about, fear, desire things that don't exist, Intentional objects need not exist or even be possible. Intentionality has been said to be the mark of the mental, but this is incorrect. Mental states such as bare awareness (Damasio 1999), moods and sensations fail to have Intentional objects: a headache, for example, is not about pain, it *is* pain. *It is very important in what follows not to confuse Intentionality with the notion of intentional or purposeful action.*

Intentional or common-sense psychology explains behaviour and relations between mental states by using Intentional idioms to attribute Intentional states and causal and conceptual connections between them. Other names for Intentional psychology include 'propositional attitude psychology', 'ordinary psychology', 'belief-desire psychology', 'folk-psychology', and 'theory of mind'. None of these names are entirely satisfactory. A choice has to be made, and I will mostly use 'Intentional' or 'common-sense psychology' as the most comprehensive terms. End of parenthesis.

1.2 The singularity of Freudian wish-fulfilment

FWT is conceptually complex. For the present, let's focus on its conceptual conditions and leave to the next chapter the issue of whether anything – dreams, symptoms etc. – actually satisfies it.

First, what is the *ordinary* understanding of what it is for a wish to be fulfilled? Suppose I wish I were in Spain and one evening I dream or hallucinate that I am in Spain; will my wish have been fulfilled in any ordinary sense? No, a person's wish that *p* is not fulfilled or satisfied in the ordinary understanding of these terms unless it becomes the case that p. For my wish to be fulfilled it is necessary that I get to Spain, that it be a fact that I am in Spain. Necessary, but not sufficient, for as well as being in Spain I must believe that I am in Spain; if I do not believe I am in Spain even when I am, I will continue wishing: my wish will not have been extinguished and therefore fulfilled.[5]

Here then are three marks of the ordinary, fully-fledged conception of what it is for a wish to be fulfilled: the wished-for state of affairs or action must obtain; the agent must come to believe that the wished-for state of affairs or action obtains; and the wish must be, at least temporarily, extinguished: the agent must cease (that) wishing.

There is a further condition. Suppose I wish to be in Spain and have somehow acquired the false belief that I am in Spain, though in fact I am not. One night, unawares, I am whisked off to Spain. I wake, still with my false belief. All three prescribed conditions hold: I believe that I am in Spain; I am in Spain; my wish to be in Spain is extinct. Yet this case is not an instance of ordinary wish-fulfilment. Why? The reason seems to be that it is a necessary condition for a wish being fulfilled in the ordinary way that its extinction be a causal consequence of the relevant disposition of states of affairs in the world. In the present case, although the wished-for state of affairs (my being in Spain) obtains, it is causally inert in relation to my belief and to the satisfaction of my wish. In the ordinary case, wish-fulfilling belief must be brought about in the right way.[6] Hence condition (iv) in the following summary:

(A) In the *ordinary sense*, any wish that p is fulfilled only if:
    (i) the wish is extinguished: the agent ceases to wish that p;
    (ii) the agent comes to believe that p;
    (iii) it is a fact that p: the wished-for state of affairs or action occurs;
    (iv) the wish is extinguished *because* of the occurrence or institution of p.

In contrast, it is distinctive of those phenomena identified by Freud as wish-fulfilling – dreams, daydreams, hallucinations and so on – that whilst conditions (i) and (ii) are necessary, conditions (iii) and (iv) are not. Characteristically in FWT either the wished-for states of affairs do not exist or come to pass or, if they do, they have no causal role in the extinction of the wish. The causal role must, therefore, rest entirely with (ii), 'coming to believe that p' (or with some mental state functioning terminatively in the manner of belief, if such there are).[7] Moreover, in nearly all cases of wish-fulfilment described by Freud, the agent *initiates* the wish-fulfilling process.[8] FWT cannot be something that adventitiously and entirely befalls an agent. Thus, Freud's patient Dora periodically succumbed to hysterical coughing and aphonia that were causally overdetermined; one such cause, according to Freud, was Dora's intention to separate her father from his mistress. Even if the symptoms were not manufactured intentionally – even if, say, they were produced subintentionally (by desire alone) or as the expression of affective processes – they could still have succeeded fortuitously in separating the lovers, and thus be wish-fulfilling in the Freudian sense. What would *not* count as wish-fulfilment in this sense is if, for example, a brick fell on the mistress's head. That would have served to satisfy Dora's wish to separate her father from his mistress but it would not count as an instance of FWT.

So a further condition recognising agency must be added to (i) and (ii). Since there may be degrees of intentional involvement it will be useful to mark the limits, from the (let's say) *maximally* intentional cases, such as compensatory daydreams, to the simplest cases where no intention (though perhaps just motivating desire or emotion) is at work, such as the hallucinatory wish-fulfilment in infant mental life posited by Freud. This can be done by distinguishing two forms of a condition which replaces conditions (iii) and (iv). The weaker form, (v(a)), is that the agent initiates the wish-fulfilling process, in a sense that does not entail but does not exclude intention. The stronger form, (v(b)), identifies the *maximal* cases of wish-fulfilment where a wish that *p* of an agent A is fulfilled – where the process that fulfils the wish can be truly described as intentional under such descriptions as 'A fulfilling A's wish that *p*' or 'A gratifying (consoling, appeasing...) A'.

Because I will insist that there are forms of FWT that causally involve intention, though in varying ways, we need a name for the position: *intentionalism* (not to be confused with 'representationalism') will serve. And because it is a feature of FWT that it is usually temporary, a stop-gap measure that breaks down in the face of ineluctable desire or need – long-standing delusions are perhaps exceptions – the conditions need to be suitably qualified. We then arrive at the following schema for Freudian wish-fulfilment.

(B) For any wish that *p*, it will be fulfilled in the manner of FWT only if:
      (i) the wish is (temporarily) terminated: the agent ceases to wish that *p*;
      (ii) the agent comes to (temporarily) believe that *p*;
    (v(a)) the agent initiates the wish-fulfilling process, in a sense that does not entail but does not exclude intention; or
    (v(b)) in maximal cases, the process that fulfils the wish can be truly described as intentional under such descriptions as 'A fulfilling A's wish that *p*' or 'A gratifying (consoling, appeasing...) A'.[9]

This conception, not of course expressed in these terms, is entirely original to Freud and, as we shall see, of great significance to the understanding of mind. However, it was muddied by him in three different ways. First, he regularly conflated the ordinary kind of wish-fulfilment with his novel discovery, FWT. Second, he conflated FWT with the conceptions of precursors, especially ancient oneiromancers, who had hit on wishful interpretations of dreams (**2.1**). But most importantly, if we distinguish between (i) a wish; (ii) a representation of a wish; (iii) the object or action or state of affairs whose occurrence would fulfil the wish; (iv) a representation of such an object, action or state of affairs; (v) a representation of a wish being fulfilled; and (vi) the fulfilment of the wish, the process (or, what is different, the end state) of the wish being fulfilled as this occurs (a) when the wish finds its true objects and (b) when the wish is fulfilled by some counterfeit, as in a dream or phantasy, then – amongst other conflations, such as between (i) and (ii) and (vi)(a) and (vi)(b) – Freud fails consistently to distinguish between (v) and (vi). Consider some typical statements:

(1) Of the famous Irma dream Freud says that 'its content was the fulfilment of a wish and its motive was a wish'. (1900a: 119)

(2) Hysterical acts are 'mimetic or hallucinatory representations of phantasies'. (Freud 1913: 173)

(3) Freud writes of a 'delusion having as content the fulfilment of the wish'. (1922b: 226)

(4) '*A dream is a (disguised) fulfilment of a (suppressed or repressed) wish.*' (1900a: 160)

(5) '*Dreams are not disturbers of sleep... but guardians of sleep which get rid of disturbances of sleep...* a dream does not simply give expression to a thought, but represents the wish fulfilled as a hallucinatory experience.... the dream does not simply reproduce the stimulus [the wish], but removes it, gets rid of it, deals with it, by means of a kind of experience.' (1916–17: 129)

(6) 'Every dream may be a wish-fulfilment, but apart from dreams there must be other forms of abnormal wish-fulfilments. And it is a fact that the theory governing all psychoneurotic symptoms culminates in a single proposition, which asserts that they too are to be regarded as fulfilments of unconscious wishes.' (1900a: 568–9)

(7) 'The motive force of phantasies are unsatisfied wishes, and every single phantasy is the fulfilment of a wish, a correction of unsatisfying reality.' (1908e: 146).

(8) 'Symptoms serve for the patient's sexual satisfaction; they are a substitute for satisfaction of this kind, which the patients are without in their lives. ... This symptom was fundamentally a wish-fulfilment, just like a dream – and moreover what is not always true of a dream, an erotic wish-fulfilment.' (1916–17: 299)

(9) Again: 'The symptoms of a neurosis are, it might be said, without exception either a substitutive satisfaction of some sexual urge or measures to prevent such a satisfaction; and as a rule they are compromises between the two.' (1940a: 186)

(10) 'Religious ideas... are illusions, fulfilments of the oldest and most urgent wishes of mankind.' (1927c: 30)

Scores of similar passages could be adduced, treating hallucinations, art and so on. Now, Freud says at least two quite different things about wish-fulfilling processes. In (1), (2) and (3) the processes are said to be *representations* of wish-fulfilment, or to have as their *content* representations of wish-fulfilment. But in the rest the processes are said to *be* wish-fulfilments. This is a distinction with significant difference. I suggest that Freud's considered view is that dreams, symptoms and some of their kin do not just represent the objects of wishes (e.g. a cake I crave) or, what is different, scenarios of wishes being fulfilled (my eating the cake); they actually fulfil them, though they do this in a qualified way (it is *as if* I had eaten the cake).

This understanding is supported by the fact that Freud frequently refers to wish-fulfilments as 'substitutive satisfactions', by which he appears to mean that they are real, albeit attenuated satisfactions of wishes, achieved by roundabout means. But we must see why this is a theoretical necessity in Freud's work and not just loose language. Representations of wishes being fulfilled, we shall find, only function as wish-fulfilling (FWT) in limited but important circumstances.

The idea that mere representation suffices for FWT fails to capture the specific roles that Freud assigns to the function of dreams and symptoms: for example, to preserve sleep or to circumvent realistic action. FWT involves less than full satisfaction (in the ordinary sense) but more than the mere representation of satisfaction: it involves, as well, *a cessation of wishing* or, in Jim Hopkins' term, a *pacification* of the wish (Hopkins 1995).[10] That the wishful representation alone cannot constitute FWT is evident from the fact, noted by Freud (1917d: 231), that a particular representation may at one time and not at another fulfil the wish it represents as fulfilled. Just as there is a difference between entertaining a thought and believing it, so there is between (merely) experiencing an imaginal representation of wish-fulfilment and taking it 'for real'. Freud notes also that dreams, though representationally intact, can fail to be wish-fulfilling when, as in some anxiety dreams, anxiety disrupts the dream and sleep is abandoned. Again, it is essential to distinguish between a delusional thought and a delusional belief with identical content. Freud considers the situation of persecutory or other irrational ideas entering consciousness 'without finding acceptance or belief' there (1922b: 228). The person who has a wishful phantasy or thought of killing his father, consciously or unconsciously, who represents to himself this wish fulfilled, may feel guilt at having evil thoughts. But this is a different matter altogether from the fully-fledged wish-fulfilling phantasy or delusion that he has killed his father.

The significance of termination (or pacification) in wish-fulfilment emerges clearly from an adaptational (Hartmann 1939; cf. Freud 1916–17: 366; 1924b: 185) perspective. There is little advantage to an incapacitated organism in merely expressing or representing wishes as fulfilled, in the absence of those conditions that can facilitate FWT: the organism that cannot change the world to accord with its desires still demands an end to the painful stimulus of ineluctable wish or desire and tries to terminate it, in default of realistic action. Dreams and the rest of the wish-fulfilling series aim to fulfil wishes in order to prevent or delay action, not *just* to represent them. Dreams are guardians of sleep. Symptoms are not merely representations but satisfactions achieved in roundabout ways (e.g. 1916–17: 350, 361), in the manner of FWT: they presuppose facilitating conditions **(2.3, 2.4)**.

Now the outline of the concept of FWT is traced, but we have no assurance either that the concept is coherent or that there are in fact mental processes or actions falling under it. The features of the concept were extracted from Freud's understanding of dreams, symptoms and their congeners, but of course Freud may have gone astray. It may be that *nothing* satisfies the concept whose features are set out in (B), just as nothing satisfies the concept *unicorn*. It may reasonably be objected that there simply are no psychological conditions under which any form of FWT can be efficacious; or, in particular, that the conditions for intentional and, especially, maximal cases of FWT cannot be satisfied. Showing that such objections can be answered, and how those answers illuminate much that seems puzzling in the life of the mind, are amongst our principal aims.

Having a handle now on the concept of FWT, I want to outline the book's argument. But FWT is entwined with several other puzzling concepts – with *belief*, with *mental dissociation* or *partition* and *unconscious intentionality*, amongst others – and they too require an introduction. The argument is not easily exposed. It will go best, I think, against the backdrop of its historical development.

1.3 A very brief history of our subject with polemical remarks

It is old wisdom, as the epigram shows, that frustrated desire can sicken and kill. When the seventeenth-century missionary Father Rageneau visited North America he found that the Huron people distinguished three causes of disease: natural causes; sorcery; unfulfilled wishes. Of the latter, some were known to the individual; others, called *ondinnonk*, were not, but could be revealed to him in his dreams. The wishes could, however, be concealed or implicit, and diviners were required to identify them. If the patient was mortally ill, the diviners would declare that the objects of his wishes were impossible to obtain. When there were chances of recovery, a 'festival of dreams' would be organised, a collection made amongst the group and the objects collected given to the patient during a banquet and public rejoicing. The patient would not only recover from his disease, but would sometimes come out a rich man.[11] Thus societies kinder and more enlightened than ours.

Ancient Greek and Hellenic philosophers wrote much about the pathologies of desire and divided selves (Sorabji 2006) and Augustine wrote brilliantly about the conflicted will. But in the long period of Christian totalitarianism that followed, philosophical interest in the appetitive roots of action, internal conflict[12] and the possibilities of self-division waned. Eros was deprecated and the immortality of the soul, implying indivisibility, precluded questions about self-division. It was not till the late Enlightenment and the Romantic age of heroic assertion and imperial conquest that philosophical interest turned once again to the motive power of passion and will, and their capacity to turn the self against itself. Arthur Schopenhauer, hugely influential in the last half of the nineteenth century, identified the will with the Kantian thing-in-itself, and so as noumenally constitutive of everything in the cosmos. In its personal expression the will is largely unconscious striving, without knowledge, aided by an intellect that is 'a mere tool in the service of the will' (Schopenhauer 1966: 205). 'In fact, the intellect remains so much excluded from the real resolutions and secret decisions of its own will that sometimes it can only get to know them, like those of a stranger, by spying out and taking it unawares; and it must surprise the will in the act of expressing itself, in order merely to discover its real intentions' (1966: 209).

Under the influence of Schopenhauer and the *Naturphilosophie* founded by F. W. von Schelling, the will came to be identified with a kind of universal Unconscious, and thinkers such as Carl Gustav Carus and Eduard von Hartmann developed highly elaborate and extravagant accounts of unconscious processes animating Nature as well as humankind. In the prevailing psychological schools of 'Voluntarism', *striving* or *willing* were regarded as the dominant principles of human psychology (Alexander and Seleznick 1966: 218 ff; Ellenberger 1970: ch. 5). American pragmatism has roots in these developments and William James and F. H. Bradley, the great proponent of Absolute Idealism, wrote extensively on the will, both of them in ways that still command interest. Towards the end of the century Nietzsche insisted, with unparalleled intensity and influence (though not plausibility), that the *will to power* is the fundamental motivation in human psychology and cosmos.

A little earlier, the Romantic psychiatrists Johann Heinroth (1773–1843), Johann Christian Reil (1759–1813) and Karl Wilhelm Ideler (1795–1860) expressed prescient insights. They recognised the paramount importance of passions and of inner conflict in the genesis of mental illness. Ideler emphasised the aetiological significance of sexuality and traced delusions back to childhood experiences. Heinroth expressed an acute awareness of the pathogenic role of guilt (sin, as he termed it). Like their precursors, the Magnetists, these alienists had an intuitive grasp of the significance of *the rapport*, of transference and suggestion, of unconscious motivation and the therapeutic import of 'unmasking' or revealing 'the pathogenic secret'; all of which, as Ellenberger remarks, became characteristic of the later dynamic psychiatry of the 1880s and 1890s, though their source had by then been forgotten (Ellenberger 1970: 277).

Sigmund Freud is usually appreciated as a scientist steeped in the spirit of the Enlightenment, educated in the reductionist biophysics principally associated with Herman von Helmholtz and his teachers Ernst Brucke and Theodore Meynert. Freud has testified to the importance of these men in shaping his work.[13] Yet in his authoritative study, Ellenberger (1970: 199) describes Freud (and Jung) as the late great epigones of Romanticism and this, thematically – as I have tried to adumbrate in my brief reference to Romantic psychiatry – is also true. Despite accepting the reductionist materialism of his teachers, which he never abandoned in principle, some of Freud's earliest defining doctrines and preoccupations were more in harmony with his Romantic predecessors than his contemporary scientific milieu. It is unlikely that there was direct influence: there is no evidence in his writings that Freud possessed anything like a *scholarly* knowledge of Schopenhauer, Carus, Nietzsche, Brentano, Kant or the Romantic psychiatrists but, of course, their popularised ideas were in the air, and so large a mind as Freud's could scarcely have failed to assimilate them.[14] It was with Bernheim in 1889 (in one of the last pockets of Romantic medicine), Freud tells us, that he 'received the profoundest impression of the possibility that there could be powerful mental processes which nevertheless remained hidden from the consciousness of men' (Freud 1925d: 17).

In the mid-nineteenth century Willhelm Griesinger declared that mental illness was a disease of the brain or central nervous system. That view soon prevailed in German psychiatry and shaped Freud's earliest approaches to mind (1950a). But during the late 1890s Freud's interest gradually shifted from his patients' central nervous systems to their early interpersonal experiences, and the manner in which these were distorted by their phantasies. Several features of Freud's early psychoanalytic work ran counter to the dominant scientific positivism and, specifically, neurological psychiatry of the late nineteenth century. Freud insisted on the importance of the emotions, and particularly sexuality, in the aetiology of psychopathology – a salient theme in Schopenhauer and some contemporary sexologists, but not in the milieu in which Freud worked. In his early writings Freud described mental conflict in terms of will (or intention) and counter-will, and hysteria as arising from an intentional or willed splitting of consciousness (Freud 1892–3: 122–28; 1894a). In contrast to the spirit of the biophysics movement, he insisted on the causality of mental states, especially the desiring, wishful aspects of mind, and on the consequences of their suppression. After 1905, Freud (1905d) attempted to underpin these motivational concepts with a biological concept of instinctual drive, but the relationship between these sets of concepts was neither clear nor unproblematic (2.2). Eventually Freud's apparently incompatible commitments to scientific materialism on the one hand, and to mental causation and the Intentional idiom indispensable for the expression of mental states on the other, created a schism in his theorising between a quasi-neurological framework, the 'metapsychology' that was the lingering ghost of his neurobiological tenets, and an augmented Intentional psychology. He realised that what needed to be said about the neuroses could be said only with the Intentional idiom.

> I have not always been a psychotherapist. Like other neuropathologists, I was trained to employ local diagnoses and electro-prognosis, and it still strikes me myself as strange that the case histories I write should read like stories and that, as one might say, they lack the serious stamp of science. I must console myself with the reflection that the nature of the subject is evidently responsible for this, rather than any preference of my own. The fact is that local diagnosis and electrical reactions lead nowhere in the study of hysteria, whereas a detailed description of mental processes such as we are accustomed to find in the works of imaginative writers enables me, with the use of a few psychological formulas, to at least obtain some kind of insight into the course of that affection.
>
> (1895: 160–1)

Freud never abjured the view that all psychological processes have a biological foundation and may eventually be described in purely physical terms, but in recognising the difficulties and struggling with his dual commitments he demonstrates greater philosophical acumen than many of our neuroscientific contemporaries. The shift from a neuroscientific perspective to a predominantly psychological and social one involved something so conspicuous that it is likely to be overlooked altogether: the overriding importance of other people! Freud's progressive realisation of the primacy of *object relations* in psychopathology and, later, in normal psychological development turned out to be a profound event in the human sciences.

Freud observed that object (interpersonal) relations, with the intense drama of sex, love, jealousy, begin in early childhood and that the child's earliest objects may be 'introjected' or internalised as 'imagos' into an 'inner world' of unconscious imagination or phantasy that is, however, not treated as imagination but as if it were real, as constituting a 'psychic reality'. Later, in his development of the 'structural model' of mind (Freud 1923b), he tried to show that through such internalisation and subsequent identification, objects could enter into the constitution of mind. Identification structured or partitioned the mind into separate agencies which then entered into relations in certain respects not unlike those between external agents (**5.3, 5.6**).

The idea that the mind may be divided to form separate selves or subpersonalities, like the idea of unconscious mentation, was also no novelty in the nineteenth century. Demonic possession as a clinical entity was gradually replaced by hysteria and multiple personality. The variety of hidden personalities which were manifested in certain conditions or evoked by therapeutic procedures eventually suggested to many investigators of the time that 'the human mind was rather like a matrix from which whole sets of subpersonalities could emerge and differentiate themselves' (Ellenberger 1970: 139). Jean Charcot introduced the idea that 'small, split-off fragments of the personality could follow an invisible development of their own and manifest themselves through clinical disturbances' (Ellenberger 1970: 149). Pierre Janet 'contended that certain hysterical symptoms can be related to the existence of split parts of personality (subconscious fixed ideas) endowed with an autonomous life and development' (Ellenberger 1970: 361). Tales, such as those of Dostoyevsky and Robert Louis Stevenson, of demonic possession, doppelgangers and split personalities abounded. Freud's views evolved against this background of conceptions of the unconscious and of divided minds. His special achievement in this connection was not only the particularly detailed and fruitful conception of the (topographical) Unconscious or the development of a structural theory of id, ego and superego that incorporated the features of that Unconscious; his major achievement was to link these two conceptions to the developmental and object-relational perspectives: to indicate some of the ways in which the intense need for objects in the course of individual development fundamentally modifies the structure of the mind. This is the model, in the barest possible outline, that stood at the centre of classical psychoanalysis.

By the 1970s it was obvious that fundamental parts of the Freudian edifice, especially the metapsychology intricately developed by his ego-psychologist heirs (e.g. Hartmann 1964; Hartmann, Kris and Loewenstein 1964; Rappaport 1971), were inadequate to the explanatory demands made on it. The structural model was too coarse-grained to accommodate new clinical entities such as narcissistic and borderline pathology; the superego underwent fission. In particular, the drive-discharge model of motivation (**2.2**), in which Hartmann had with deliberation placed his hopes (Hartmann 1948), failed to provide a plausible account of action. The ego-psychologists had hopes of creating a general psychology from psychoanalytic materials and confronted the fact that the ego had many functions that were autonomous, or relatively independent of drive activity: the ego perceived, deliberated, judged, decided and chose courses of action. But about such functions classical theory was largely silent. Hartmann complained that despite theoretical progress in other areas, there was 'still no systematic presentation of an *analytic theory of action*' (Hartmann 1947: 37). Melanie Klein, whilst formally accepting Freud's dual-drive model, shifted her interest to phantasy, and other object-relational thinkers retreated from drive psychology altogether. In effect, as the idea of a general psychoanalytic theory receded and object-relational conceptions of motivation remained opaque, interest in developing a systematic theory of motivation and action theory largely dissipated.

So it happened that for these and other reasons the 1970s witnessed a revival of interest in Freud's pre-drive account of motivation based on the wish and wish-fulfilment. This development can be observed in many articles of the period.[15] At the same time, significant developments in the Analytic philosophy of mind were taking place. The variety of broadly behaviourist approaches that dominated the middle third of the twentieth century lost their hold and renewed interest in motivation and action was initiated by the work of Wittgenstein, Elizabeth Anscombe (1957) and an influential series of papers by Donald Davidson (1980), amongst others (e.g. Goldman 1970; Kenny 1963). Eventually there appeared a promising survey of a stretch of conceptual terrain in which could be located, in reasonably systematic ways, the causal and conceptual relations between desire (wanting, wishing), instrumental belief, reasons for acting, deliberation, intention, choice, decision, and so on; some idea of how irrationality enters the picture, and of how some elements of action's antecedents may be physically realised.

Initially, Analytic philosophers showed little interest in psychoanalysis generally and wish-fulfilment in particular. Major figures such as Russell and Wittgenstein discussed Freudian doctrines but their engagement was superficial. Philosophers of science addressed methodological issues in psychoanalysis and swiftly determined it to be non-science, or worse (Karl Popper most famously – but see Hook 1959; Grunbaum 1984). Serious interest was slow in coming. As late as 1974, Richard Wollheim complained in the preface to his important anthology on Freud (Wollheim 1974a: ix) that Freud's ideas 'have barely impinged upon philosophers'. Then, as classical metapsychology collapsed, a number of psychoanalytically informed philosophers – pre-eminent amongst them Wollheim and Jim Hopkins – began to view psychoanalysis through the lens of Analytic action theory and explicitly articulated psychoanalytic concepts and causal structures as extensions of Intentional or common-sense psychology (Wollheim 1991, 1979, 1984, 1993a; Hopkins 1982, 1988, 1995). Their approach influenced important work in the philosophy of psychoanalysis but has not been as influential within psychoanalysis, philosophy or psychology disciplines in general as it should be.[16]

1.4 Some basic concepts for the philosophy of psychoanalysis

The general view taken by Wollheim and Hopkins, and of several philosophers who – albeit with significant variations – have followed them (e.g. Gardner 1993; Lear 1998a; Snelling 2000; Cavell 1993, 2006), can be summarised as follows:

(1) A significant part of psychoanalytic theory is an extension and deepening of common-sense psychology; this can be viewed in two parts:

(1(a)) some key concepts of psychoanalysis are extensions of common-sense-psychological concepts, e.g. *introjection* and *unconscious phantasy* are extensions – are based on our understanding of – *imagination*;

(1(b)) the forms of causal explanation used in psychoanalysis are in some cases the same as, and in others extensions of, those of common-sense psychology;

(2) the distinctive forms of causal explanation in psychoanalysis are Freudian wish-fulfilment (FWT) and phantasy (where phantasy is regarded as distinct from FWT);

(3) FWT involves modes of causal explanation that are non-intentional.

The view that the concepts of an extended Intentional or common-sense psychology suffice as materials for the explanation of neurotic symptoms (and their congeners), let alone for the major mental disorders, is not without critics.[17] I will come to them. I will later provide illustrations of the sorts of Intentional explanations referred to in the summary, and explain how I depart from the views summarised in the schema (1)–(3) above. But first I must set out and explain as plainly as I can some of the chief concepts of the Intentional framework of action theory employed in this book.

In Intentional or common-sense psychology we explain actions and mental activity, as well as dispositions and the occurrence of sensations, emotions and moods, using an immense variety of mental concepts – desire, belief, rage, joy, envy, disappointment, fear, fervour, worry, habit, cowardice, scrupulosity, generosity, malice, etc. It is necessary to recall how rich and heterogeneous this cluster of concepts is – evolved over millennia of human social life – and to resist the temptation to suppose that these concepts can be neatly reduced to, and behaviour explained in terms of, a few basic concepts such as belief and desire. Nevertheless, belief and desire are basic to the causal explanation of *much* action and mental activity, and for this reason, as well as for reasons of economy, the focus will generally be on them.

Not all explanation of action is causal. Sometimes action is explained by re-description. Money is seen to be changing hands and we explain that our friend is repaying a debt, bribing an official, buying a car. These re-descriptions are explanations, and useful ones. Psychology or neuroscience cannot displace such explanations because they presuppose concepts foreign to the sciences. The concepts of *debt, bribe* and *buying* supervene on conventions, practices and institutions that cannot conceivably figure as concepts of any possible psychology or neuroscience. However, we may become interested in *how* actions (the activation of the musculature, etc.) are performed, in what *manner* they are performed (resentfully, with trepidation) and *why* (because she wanted to clear a debt, to win) they are performed. Here the sciences spring into their own and, as regards manner and purpose, the causal explanations available to Intentional psychology are also invoked. The most basic pattern of explanation in Intentional psychology is that for intentional action. It seems to be a necessary condition of intentional action that it is performed for and from a reason.[18]

The condition has been challenged. It has been proposed that so-called *actes gratuit* are actions performed intentionally for no reason. This proposal would require that a person can intend, decide or choose to act without reason: that, for example, someone intentionally climbs a mountain for no reason. The claim seems to me incoherent, but even if it is not, it is likely to be empirically false and incompatible with a regulative principle of psychoanalysis: if there is no conscious reason for action in evidence, then there is an unconscious one.

Typically, a reason is said to consist of a desire and an instrumental belief that together rationalise and cause the action that is performed for the reason. My friend seeks out the fridge. She wants something to eat and believes that edibles are to be found therein. Her want and her belief cause her to seek the fridge, and make sense of her behaviour. This is the pattern of intentional explanation captured in the Aristotelian practical syllogism: a major premise states a want or desire, a minor premise states an instrumental belief, and the conclusion is an action (or, in some versions, an intention to act).

I will frequently refer to the 'subintentional' causation of acts, including mental acts, by wish or desire unfacilitated by instrumental beliefs or anything else. The term was introduced by O'Shaughnessy (1980). Such action has teleology but is caused non-rationally; that is, it is not performed for a reason or through an executive state such as intention, decision or choice. Perhaps wishful imagination, unconscious phantasy and some day-dreaming belong here **(2.6)**. Our Intentional framework also recognises other motives to action – I use 'motive' loosely to signify anything that instigates action and mental activity. There are forms of *expression* which have archaeology but no teleology, as when I clench my fists in (out of) anguish, or laugh, or shudder with fear. Explanation along these lines is Intentional, but neither intentional nor subintentional. So there are several forms of causal but non-intentional explanation, of which the subintentional and the expressive are examples.

Now we come to the extension of common-sense psychology in psychoanalysis. Richard Wollheim (1991: xixff; 1993a) has usefully (and I think more or less correctly) summarised the ways in which Freud built on and expanded the Intentional framework. I summarise his summary here and will elaborate on it selectively in later sections. First, *non-conscious* desires and beliefs operating as non-conscious reasons (Wollheim leaves it open whether the reasons are preconscious or dynamically unconscious) explain some intentional actions such as some parapraxes: the 'accidental' dropping of vases, the missing of crucial meetings, and the like (Freud 1901b). Second, unconscious desire and belief and a chain of association lead to what Wollheim calls a *displaced action*. Thus Freud's patient, the Ratman, wanted to kill his competitor, Dick (in German = fat), and embarked on a strenuous course of exercise to 'lose fat'. Through that chain of association, losing fat takes on the symbolic meaning of killing Dick. A third motive, the conjunction of desire and what Wollheim calls (infelicitously) 'instinct', results in processes designated *mental activity*. Wollheim includes (some of) the defence mechanisms in this category – such activities as disavowal, projection and repression. In such cases it *looks as if* an agent believed that initiating a defence mechanism would further her desire, but it is not plausible, Wollheim says, to posit instrumental beliefs (1991: xxxiii). (Wollheim next mentions the conjunction of desire and phantasy, but it is unclear how or in what instances he conceived of this motive's application, so I leave it aside.) Fourth, the operation of desire (in the absence of an instrumental belief and 'instinct') plus some precipitating factor leads to *expression*. 'Expression includes dreams, those neurotic symptoms which are not to be thought of as displaced actions and those parapraxes which are not to be thought of either as displaced actions or as actions with unconscious motivation' (1991: xxxv). Expression, Wollheim says, 'is clearly not action; it is also not activity' (1991: xxxv). Yet it is more in keeping with Freud's approach, he continues, to hold 'that the person would not have done what he did were it not for the gratification that ensued' (1991: xxxiv). I am not sure I understand Wollheim's thought here: he seems to be identifying a motive different from the ('archaic') expression of emotion noted above, as in smiling or shuddering, as well as the subintentional causation of action. In any case, I consider many of the phenomena Wollheim subsumes under 'expression' to have an intentional provenance, and will criticise this proposed extension below **(3.7)**.

The programme of explaining much of the psychoanalytic domain in the Intentional idiom is not an easy one and several authors, while committed to the programme overall, have seen a need to innovate, to introduce (to 'discover') new Intentional entities with special qualities apt for explicating wish-fulfilment and other 'psychoanalytic phenomena': for example, *the wish* and *phantasy*, understood as 'pre-propositional' by Gardner (1993) and Lear (1995, 1998a) and as technical terms by Brakel (2009); *propositional reflection* in Gardner (1993); and *neurotic belief* in Brakel (2009). I think that these innovations are unnecessary and I will argue for their dispensability in **Chapter 3**.

Wollheim's list is not complete. I will contend that ordinary intentional explanation (belief–desire explanation) plays a much greater role in unconscious intrapsychic activity, in the activity of the mental agencies in relation to each other, than Wollheim – and indeed most philosophers – would allow. But that is to come. Now (at last) I am in a position to outline the book's argument.

1.5 Four aporia and the outline of an argument

In his influential early formulations, Hopkins (1982, 1988) placed wish-fulfilment at the centre of an Intentional approach but explicitly contrasted the mode of action in FWT with intentional action. He conceives FWT subintentionally, as the result of imaginative activity animated by desire. He says: 'in rational action motives produce willed intentions and real actions aimed at satisfaction. Here [in dreams] they produce wishes and mere representations of satisfaction, on the pattern of wishful imagining' (1988: 41); this pattern is then enlisted in the explanation of complex obsessive symptoms as well as dreams (1982: xxiff; 1988: 55).[19]

Similarly, Gardner (1993) maintains that '[t]he fundamental idea on which a psychoanalytic extension of ordinary psychology hinges is that of a connection of content, driven by the operation of desire freed from rational constraints' (1993: 229; 88–9).

Hopkins was driven to the non-intentional analysis of FWT at least partly because he recognised that an intentional analysis entailed unconscious intentional activity, which he considered problematic. Specifically, there is the problem of identifying suitable practical syllogisms (1982: xix ff). To illustrate the problem, consider this clinical vignette:

> A patient, a successful scientist in his own field, came to analysis because (amongst other things) he had a severe work problem. He could, in fact, produce the work required of him, and had made several notable contributions in his field. He had previously had analysis for some years, and at the beginning of his current analysis it seemed that all the well known factors causing a work difficulty of the sort he had were present. His need to delay getting down to work till the very last minute was quite clearly an oedipal problem, in which he could not allow himself to feel that he had satisfied oedipal sexual and aggressive wishes by working well. It was also seen to be part of an anal-retentive tendency, which had persisted for most of his life, and so on. Analysis of his fear of success, of his need to hold on until the last moment, and of many other elements that were clearly related to his work problems did not do more than give him greater insight... Eventually... the significant function of his symptom became clear. By allowing himself to get into a state of anxiety, and by creating a feeling of great internal pressure as the time passed and his work was not done, he could recreate, to a degree which was almost hallucinatory in intensity, the feeling of being nagged at and even screamed at by his mother. It became clear that he used his symptom to re-experience an object-relationship, one in which a wished-for sado-masochistic relationship with his mother was actualised. However, what was present was more than the simple sexualisation of anxiety, but a real need to feel secure by re-experiencing the earlier relationship to the mother, even though he had to pay a rather painful price for this.
>
> (Sandler and Sandler 1978: 290–1)

The scientist is said to have 'used his symptom to re-experience... a wished-for sado-masochistic relationship with his mother'. It looks as if the Sandlers thought the scientist intentionally created his symptom to use it for a definite purpose. But how is that to be conceived? We may assume that the scientist has reason to want his mother's presence, to recreate the relationship to her – painful, to be sure, but satisfying his overriding need for attachment or security. In the light of this interpretation we can re-describe the anxiety he generates as representing (as *being experienced as*) mother's presence in near hallucinatory form. These assumptions yield the following syllogisms:

S wants mother's presence
S believes that by making himself anxious mother will be present

---

S makes himself anxious

S wants to experience mother's presence (something like her presence)
S believes that by making himself anxious he will experience her presence

---

S makes himself anxious

Other options of this kind can be fashioned, but none of them seem plausible because the instrumental beliefs in each case are mad. Who could believe such things? Difficulties of this kind have deterred even those receptive to the Freudian unconscious and to non-intentional types of FWT from countenancing a notion of FWT in which intention has a role, and *a fortiori* the notion of maximal FWT in which the wish-fulfilment itself is intended (see footnote 9; this case is discussed further in **3.2**).

Several philosophers, Sebastian Gardner (1993) most comprehensively, added to the difficulties by highlighting concerns about mental partition, or in his catchy phrase 'second-mind personology', that intentionalism appears to entail. To see the problem, consider a situation described by David Pears (1984: 79) in which a girl 'persuaded herself that her lover was not unfaithful ... (but avoided) ... a particular cafe because she believed that she might find him there with her rival ...' Let's suppose that consciously she was persuaded of her lover's fidelity, and her troubling belief that he was unfaithful was unconscious or otherwise dissociated. Then she harbours contradictory and segregated beliefs about her lover's fidelity. The more important point to notice, however, is that by intentionally avoiding the café she seems to be *actively protecting* herself against acknowledging a belief which she (unconsciously) already has; and *that* unconscious belief plays a part in motivating her protective activity. For the manoeuvre to succeed she must be unconscious of her *intentional* avoidance of the café; for her intention is predicated on a reason which contains the disavowed belief, and knowledge of it would unravel her purpose. The right hand cannot know what the left hand is doing. So the supposition of *unconscious intentional agency* seems to entail two perplexing conclusions: (a) that there is unconscious practical reasoning or deliberation leading to (unconscious) intentional action (i.e. there may be conscious knowledge that an action is performed but its grounds or causes are unconscious) and (b) a dissociation of self into at least two quasi-independent, self-like centres of agency. Gardner (1993) considers the notion of unconscious deliberation and intentional action problematic on its own terms, but he also contends that partition offends the view of persons as substantial unities embedded in ordinary psychology. 'This explains', he says, 'the importance of the issue of partition for the philosophy of psychoanalysis. At stake is the harmony between psychoanalysis and ordinary psychology: if psychoanalytic theory is partitive, its agreement with ordinary thought is questionable' (1993: 7).

We have, then, these two striking aporia: (a) the difficulty of constructing suitable practical syllogisms for unconscious intentional activity, and (b) the problem of mental partition or radical disunity. Implicit in (a) and (b) is another difficulty: (c) scepticism about the concept of unconscious intention and of unconscious ratiocination or deliberation. And there is a fourth difficulty, a venerable objection to psychoanalysis, particularly acute for our thesis: (d) Sartre's 'censor argument', according to which any attempt to introduce duality (or multiplicity) in mind by the interposition of a censor merely opens up an untenable duality in the censor, and institutes a vicious regress. My treatment of this fourth objection will be brief because, despite its venerability, it can be expeditiously dispatched **(4.7)**.

For these and other reasons, most philosophers have considered radical partition a price too high and have opted for non-intentional analyses of wish-fulfilment, phantasy and symptom formation.[20] The role of FWT in art, religion and prejudice they have largely ignored.

I take a different line. My overall strategy for establishing the relevance and good credentials of FWT is five-fold. First, the conception of FWT is shown to be coherent. Second, typical, albeit briefly described, cases – of phantasy, dream, symptom – are considered and shown to fit the models of FWT which reciprocally illuminate them. Third, the inadequacies of the subintentionalist and other competing accounts are exposed. Fourth, plausible motivational structures are developed together with an account of mental differentiation or dissociation that can accommodate FWT, including maximal FWT. Fifth, I demonstrate the relevance of explanation by means of FWT across a range of phenomena, pathological and normal, such as delusion, religion and art.

On the intentionalist view developed here, FWT involves a spectrum of techniques and processes with varying degrees of intentional involvement, including unconscious intentional involvement. The simplest forms, hallucinatory wish-fulfilment and most dreaming, involve only non-intentional mechanisms operating in mental conditions with little Intentional differentiation, but with propensity to *engrossment* in the salient objects of attention **(2.4)**. Freud has described the basic operation of this sort of FWT in a couple of famous passages and I will elaborate on his account **(2.3)**, endorse it with qualification and indicate its limitations. At the other end of the spectrum of FWT, however, are complex, reflexive processes in which phantastic (imaginal or plastic) representations, enactments, manipulation of other people or tendentious selections from available evidence are used intentionally and unconsciously for such purposes as fulfilling wishes or gratifying, consoling, protecting or appeasing oneself. Some compensatory daydreams are obvious examples of this kind, as are, less obviously, forms of wish-fulfilling symptoms, such as the anxious scientist's. I will suggest that Freud was an intentionalist about such cases, though the enabling conditions he described for the simpler forms of FWT – the operation of the primary process in the System Ucs. – do not allow for the explanation of the more complex forms involving action or enactment, the temporally extended projects of personality disorder, transference phenomena, religious devotion and other complex wish-fulfilling phenomena. To explain these phenomena requires that we enquire into the conceptions of unconscious agency (**4.2–4.6**) and the dissociation of the self that entails (**5.3–5.7**).

But first the alternatives to this novel and difficult account of FWT have to be addressed and dispatched. The entirety of **Chapter 3** is dedicated to that task. In the main, the approach is to demonstrate that the alternatives are inadequate to the clinical material which is the touchstone of adequacy. Some of the alternatives also suffer from internal incoherence and this, too, is exposed.

Chapter 4 sets out the case for unconscious intentional activity and shows that plausible practical syllogisms can indeed be constructed for the troublesome cases. The reflexive, maximal forms of FWT are located as members of a class of self-caring or self-solicitous activities such as self-consolation, self-appeasement and, in some of its forms, self-deception. These, albeit sometimes distorted, modes of self-caring may enter into auxiliary or superordinate relations. For example, self-abasement can be an instrument of self-appeasement, and self-deception is often in the strategic service of superordinate modes of self-solicitude such as self-consolation or self-justification. *Self-solicitude* will now emerge as the more encompassing class of which FWT is a member, but since the satisfaction of most needs graduates to the fulfilment of wishes and most self-solicitude presupposes the fulfilment of wishes, I will usually just refer to FWT.

Interestingly, the consideration of FWT leads to a new argument for the partitioning or dissociation of mind or self (greater exactitude is introduced in **5.6**). Successful FWT entails that the self be divided along certain lines. Thus partitioning appears not just as *deus ex machina* for curing the paradoxes of irrationality; the possibility of unconscious FWT *presupposes* partitioning of a kind for which there are already *established developmental grounds* (**4.6, 5.3**). The consolidation of certain kinds of internalised object relations produce forms of dissociation into agencies or person-like parts which on germane criteria are strongly partitive (**5.6**). This development, the consequence of ineluctable need for secure object relations and internalisation of maternal caring functions, the basic capacities for self-regulation, largely explains the range of reflexive, self-solicitous attitudes of which some forms of FWT, self-deception, *akrasia* are compartments. I will argue that the best way to figure these 'parts' or dissociated aspects of self is as 'personations' – persons enacting various roles in depth, mutually opaque, but with roles retaining sufficient threads of rational connection to preserve important elements of self-unity (**5.6–5.7**). These considerations usher in a welcome result for psychoanalysis: the description of some intrapsychic relations in language apposite for describing interpersonal relationships is vindicated.

That completes the outline of the major theoretical aims of this book and indicates our answers to the four perplexities that confronted us. Part II applies theory to a number of issues of social significance and illustrates and expands Freudian wish-fulfilment's remit. Self-deception and delusion are located in the context of FWT (**Chapter 6**) and the discussion of delusion provides further opportunity to provide examples of FWT in action. In **Chapter 7** I show how wishes associated with various character dispositions, particularly originating from narcissistic needs (for self-esteem, superiority, difference), find substitutive satisfaction in religious group identity and ideology. In **Chapter 9** on the insanity defence a novel argument sheds light on the operation of unconscious non-culpable intent in some cases of criminal insanity. In **Chapter 8** on writing as redemption I argue that writing can provide wish-fulfilling reconstructions of lost aspects of the self and of objects, but is ultimately an ephemeral and futile endeavour for that end. In the final chapter I briefly criticise the 'biological' trends in contemporary psychiatry that ignore, subordinate or deprecate the Intentional, orectic, wish-fulfilling and interpersonal sources of the troubles that afflict the majority of our kind. That is the outline of the argument.

1.6 The psychoanalysis of philosophy

I cannot leave this introductory chapter without a note on the psychoanalysis of philosophy. Philosophy, at least in certain registers, is a peculiar activity, and the lives, activities and doctrines of philosophers have attracted psychoanalytic curiosity and suspicion. I don't know about curiosity, but suspicion goes back at least as far as Thrasymachus, who thought philosophers unmanly. Nietzsche, who didn't like many people, was exceptionally mean about philosophers:

> They all pose as if they had discovered and reached their real opinions through the self-development of a cold, pure, divinely unconcerned dialectic... while at bottom it is an assumption, a hunch, indeed a kind of 'inspiration' - most often a desire of the heart that has been filtered and made abstract - that they defend with reasons they have sought after the fact. They are all advocates who resent that name...
>
> (Nietzsche 1966 [1886]: 202)

This kind of asperity is not often directed at historians or scientists. Freud had studied under Brentano briefly, translated Mill and obviously read some of the leading lights throughout his life, but there is little indication of systematic philosophical engagement, except perhaps on the mind/body issue on which he is acute. His comments on philosophers are generally disdainful, probably because he believed, wrongly, that philosophers as a tribe denied unconscious mentality. He detected unconscious motives. The 'intelligence is always weak', he wrote, 'and it is easy for a philosopher to transform resistance into discovering logical refutations' (1887–1902: 9/12/89).

Writers have been more popular subjects, but there is also a considerable psychoanalytic literature on philosophers, from Descartes to Sartre and Wittgenstein. But psychoanalysis is not at its best without a couch. The best analytic writing on philosophers comes from other philosophers, and there was an interesting, short-lived movement towards the middle of last century, inspired by Freud and Wittgenstein, that adopted a therapeutic approach to philosophy and its practitioners. There was already something of the therapeutic in Wittgenstein, though it is now largely neglected: 'A philosopher is a man who has to cure many intellectual diseases in himself before he can arrive at the notions of common sense' (Wittgenstein 1980:

44e). However, the idea that philosophers need psychological and not just intellectual therapy was only suggested by some of his students. John Wisdom wrote:

> There is therefore logical confusion and logical penetration at the back of metaphysics. But if we now ask, 'What drives people to pursue to such lengths questions of the sort 'Do we know this?' 'What right have we to make these statements?' and what preserves the power of those models which keep us for ever seeking but never finding the knowledge we seem to want, then it occurs to us to wonder whether the forces at work in this curiously unsatisfactory struggle which never ends up in success nor in failure aren't in part the same as those at work in those other struggles in which something is for ever sought and never found, struggles which in their turn are connected with an earlier time when there was something, namely the world of the grown-ups, knowledge of which we desperately desired and equally desperately dreaded.
>
> (Wisdom 1969: 281)

Morris Lazerowitz, Alice Ambrose (both also Wittgenstein's students), Charles Hanly and others wrote in a deliberately therapeutic vein (e.g. Hanly and Lazerowitz, eds, 1970). Ambrose noted the resistance of philosophers to the notion of the unconscious and held that philosophical theories are 'illusions soaked with unconscious thought... One can explain the manoeuvring with the terminology as a game played for the sake of the illusion created' (Ambrose 1970: 33). Of the psycho-biographies, one of the best is on Berkeley (Wisdom 1953). The book was most unfairly derided on publication and its author, J. O. Wisdom, suffered considerable opprobrium as a result. He summed up the value of analysing philosophers through their work in these words:

> Philosophy is the last refuge open to myth (though not necessarily every kind of philosophy is impregnated with it). Nonetheless, the analysis of a philosopher does not in itself refute the philosophy... The value of such analysis would seem to lie in several different consequences. (i) They give a new angle from which one can approach intellectual problems and contributions: one recognizes more easily a phantastic system for what it is, though more ready to see the grain of truth hidden in a system that might otherwise be written off. (ii) One is less concerned with arguments about the truth or falsity of such a system when it obviously depicts a phantasy. (iii) Such systems are seen to have a meaning and not to be nonsense as Logical Positivism has asserted. And (iv) the nature of the meaning brought out by the analysis may provide a good practical indication of whether or not there is something objective present.
>
> (Wisdom 1953: 230)

I won't pursue this line of thought, though I believe that the account of FWT provided here can throw considerable light on the way in which (some) philosophical doctrines can provide unconscious gratifications and, indeed, be motivated by the desire for those gratifications. Freud said that there was no appeal to a court above that of reason (Freud 1927c: 28). That is so, but it is not inconsistent with the need to maintain a lively sense of the extent to which even that court can be compromised by desire.

Notes

1 I will mostly use 'symptoms' to stand in for the class. In contemporary psychoanalytic nosology the emphasis is on character or personality disorder rather than on isolated symptoms, and the trend in the DSM classifications (APA 1994) to use syndromes or sets of symptoms to classify disorders, though largely ignoring aetiology, moves in the same direction. I use 'symptom' partly for simplicity and partly because the action theory that underpins much of the approach in this book is often concerned with causal relations between events such as those between forming an intention and performing a particular act or sequence of acts. Personality disorder may be viewed from this perspective as manifesting in a sequence of emotions, moods, actions or enactments strung out over a sustained period.

2 'The theories of resistance and repression, of the unconscious, of the etiological significance of sexual life and of the importance of infantile experiences – these form the principal constituents of the theoretical structure of psychoanalysis' (Freud 1925d: 40).

3 For a deft overview of the role of such unconscious representations see Eagle 2011: 126ff; on accommodating object relations with drive theory see Eagle 2011: 258ff; Maze 2009; Newberry 2010.

4 The partial integration of neuroscience, attachment theory and psychoanalytic studies of affect regulation exemplified in the work of Jim Hopkins (2012, 2013) and Panksepp (1998; Panksepp and Biven 2012), Schore (1994, 2003), Solms (Solms and Turnbull 2002), Fonagy (Fonagy et al. 2004) and others (e.g. Fotopoulou et al. 2012) is likely to refocus attention on Freudian wish-fulfilment (Hopkins 2012), for the following reason. Freudian drive theory is bound to make way for the type of affective theory of motivation charted by Panksepp (for efforts along these lines see Fotopoulou et al. 2012) in which primary subcortical emotional command systems – SEEKING, RAGE, CARE, etc. – constitute the basic motivational forces that stimulate or energise tertiary neocortical systems to produce purposeful action. This rather Humean account of motivation can be seen as having picked up the lead of the older orectic and conative faculties. It may be, as Panksepp contends, that the systems are, to begin with, objectless, but they cannot remain so if they are to function as motivational systems, and their functioning will be expressed on a personal level as wanting or wishing to do something. The theory cannot challenge our ordinary understanding of action using Intentional concepts. For if, say, I rage at X – I have come to the point of raging *at X* – I *will want or wish to do something to X*. It is the same with the other affective systems. Action, however, may be frustrated and it is then, as I suggested, that phantasy or other vehicles of FWT come to our aid.

5 There is a marginal sense in which the extinction of wishing is unnecessary to fulfilment, as when a person's wishes are fulfilled after they died, say in accord with a will. But we can leave that aside.

6 Imagine drugs could be administered to differentially obliterate particular wishes. Suppose that in a subject some wishes are differentially obliterated and that simultaneously the wished-for states of affairs occurred. We would not say of such wishes that they had been fulfilled. We could rightly speak of the elimination of these wishes and say that what the agent wished for had come to pass. But where the relation between the way the world is and the extinction of the wish is entirely adventitious, we do not have a case of fully-fledged wish-fulfilment.

7 It may be questioned whether 'coming to believe' that the wished-for state of affairs has come to pass is necessary, or even possible, in circumstances such as hallucinatory wish-fulfilment in the infant where propositional structures are absent. I think that this kind of objection supervenes on mistakes about the nature of *belief* that I discuss later **(2.4, 2.5)**.

8 The unconscious wish-fulfilment achieved through art or religious worship and ritual may be exceptions to this condition, though even here it seems likely that wish-fulfilment occurs only as a consequence of projective and introjective engagement with the work of art, religious conception or practice, in which unconscious wishes find or generate representations of their fulfilment and achieve FWT.

9 Examples may help. We can construct a wish-fulfilling series of increasing complexity as intention plays a greater role. In the simplest type of FWT a wish or desire instigates the process but intention plays no role in the satisfaction of the instigating wish: these are (see **1.4**) subintentional, expressive or related phenomena. In a second type, in which intention is not yet in play, a wish may be conceived to activate mental activity of the sort proposed by Wollheim (1993a), or by Johnston (1988) under the name of 'tropism' **(3.2)**, the operation of which leads to FWT. Perhaps defence mechanisms such as repression, avoidance and projection are examples. In a third type, representations or pictures of wished-for states of affairs – wishful phantasy or fond memory – may be generated intentionally, though not yet for the purpose of achieving wish-fulfilment. I may, for example, summon up remembrance of things past or review the nicer aspects of the holidays, but FWT can overtake this process if regressive conditions of engrossment **(2.3, 2.4)** or reverie impose, and wishful phantasy is mistaken for reality, albeit ephemerally. It is easy to see that children become engrossed in their play and wishful phantasies, but engrossment can occur later, too, when we are dozing, withdrawn or otherwise lost to the world. Much day-dreaming falls into this category. A fourth possible type – the maximal instances – presupposes a mind capable of intentionally providing for itself substitutive satisfactions. Some so-called 'lucid dreams', compensatory phantasy, neurotic and psychotic symptoms and various kinds of irrational behaviour and belief formation may be of this kind. In the other types, the relation between the wish and its expression in wishful phantasy (not wish-fulfilling phantasy) on the one hand, and the fulfilment of the wish on the other, was adventitious. There was a role for intention in the third type, but not for intended wish-fulfilment. In all these cases wish-fulfilment *befell* desire. The expressions of the wish or wishful phantasy were simply mistaken for what would satisfy the wish in the first and third types, and mental mechanism subvened to satisfy the wish in the second. In the fourth class the relations between wish, the *vehicle* of wish-fulfilment – whether phantasy, symptom or action – and the satisfaction of wish are not adventitious. Briefly, wish-fulfilment is itself either intended or is instrumental to another form of self-solicitude that is intended – and, as we will see, it must be intended unconsciously.

10 Hopkins, in earlier work (1988: 40), was wrong, I think, to impute to Freud the reasoning that 'Since the dream represents the wish as fulfilled, the dream can be regarded as wish-fulfilment'. See also Hopkins 1991: 97 and Cavell (1993: 44).

11 Abridged from Father Rageneau, *The Jesuit Relations and Allied Documents* (1897–99), quoted in Ellenberger (1970: 26).

12 It is the genius of Abrahamic religions to obscure self-knowledge by transforming internal conflict into dramatic engagement with illusionary figures. See **Chapter 7**.

13 Freud (1925d); Makari (2008). Freud performed neuroanatomical work in Brucke's laboratory for six years, made substantial contributions to neuropathology and worked at the Vienna General Hospital under the psychiatrist Meynert, who was influenced by both Schopenhauer and Wilhelm Griesinger. The latter is credited with establishing the dominance of the exclusively neurological or *Somatiker* approach in German psychiatry.

14 A large body of recent work depicts Freud as someone who sold out on science, developing psychoanalysis in an *a priori* fashion from philosophical and dated nineteenth-century scientific conceptions (Sulloway 1992; Kitcher 1992; Smith 2003; Brook 2003; Tauber 2010). This work, diverse in many ways, is remarkable for its indifference to the import of Freud's clinical experience. Kitcher (1992: 102–11), for example, argues that the superego concept was derived essentially from Freud's covert commitments in biology and anthropology, but Freud tried to conceal that and presented the superego concept as a clinical discovery. Yet entirely absent in her book is any clinically informed discussion of guilt, melancholia, negative therapeutic reaction, masochism or persecutory delusions; that is, all those conditions which would deeply impress a sensitive clinician, and whose manifestations cry out for a conceptualisation of intrapsychic relations of kinds like those of which the superego concept is an instance. Freud certainly knew the biology, neuroscience and anthropology of his day. But it is the most bookish of turns to suppose that the clinical phenomena he confronted daily played no, or only a negligible, part in the construction of theories designed to explain such self-reflexive phenomena.

Remarkable also is Tauber's (2010) portrayal of Freud as an engaged philosopher responding to the doctrines of Brentano, Kant, Schopenhauer, Lange and others. In Tauber's vision Freud is concerned explicitly to counter Brentano's denial of unconscious mentation while adopting the philosopher's thesis of Intentionality. Freud's conceptions of reason and freedom are 'ideas lifted directly from Kant', and 'the entire psychoanalytic edifice rested upon a version of Kant's philosophy of mind'. Indeed, 'Kant in striking ways served as Freud's philosophical North Star'. Freud is also 'profoundly indebted' to Schopenhauer and Nietzsche, a claim made by many others who have mined this field. On the biological conception of human nature Freud 'closely aligned himself with the Nietzschean-Schopenhaurian line'. 'The Schopenhaurian Will is the direct precursor of Freud's id' and 'Freud would later formulate this drive [Schopenhaurian Will to life'] into the various instincts'. And so on (2010: pp. 9, 19, 22, 123, 125, 156, 159). These claims are speculations based on superficial thematic affinity, and completely ignore the far-reaching impact of clinical encounter. The more cogent picture is that the philosophical themes detectable in Freud's work were common coin of educated folk in the last quarter of the nineteenth century. Freud was largely indifferent to traditional philosophical problems. Thus, he was committed to strong determinism and it is possible, as Tauber argues, to extract a view of rational autonomy in his later work when he turned his attention to ego autonomy. Tauber thinks that this view of rational autonomy or free will was adopted from Kant. But rather than demonstrating direct philosophical engagement, as Tauber supposes, Freud's attitude shows the opposite: the striking fact in relation to the incompatibility between psychic determinism and rational autonomy is that he made no attempt to resolve it. There is little evidence that Freud even felt the philosophical tension. Such insensitivity may be a vice, but it is beside the point to complain, as Tauber does (138), that Freud failed to 'explicitly develop psychoanalysis as a moral enterprise'. Few things could have been further from his mind.

15 See e.g. Gill and Holzmann 1976; Sandler 1976; Sandler and Sandler 1978; Holt 1976; Schafer 1976; Wollheim 1979.

16 Gardner 1993; Cavell 1993, 2006; Lear 1998a; Petocz 1999; Levine (ed.) 2000; Chung and Feltham (eds.) 2003)

17 Note that the claim is not about specific clinical findings – about castration anxiety, envy and so on – being extensions of common-sense psychology; it is about the extension of basic Intentional concepts – wishing, imagining, and so on – and explanatory patterns in the context of an evolving theory.

18 The 'for and from' locution is intended to eliminate the possibility of deviant causal chains: one has reasons for doing X, one does X because of those reasons, but not *for*

those reasons. I have reasons for killing my uncle. On my way to murder him I acciden-tally run over a pedestrian who, unknown to me, happens to be my uncle. Here my reasons had a causal role in the killing of my uncle, but not in the *right way*. A common expedient for circumventing the problem is to insert an executive state, an intention, decision or choice between the having of reasons for action and the performing of it.

19 In later papers Hopkins recognises that FWT requires not only the representation of a wish fulfilled but also its pacification. It is, he says, 'a form of wishful thinking or imag-ining, in which a wish or desire causes an imaginative representation of its fulfilment, which is experience- or belief-like' and yields 'pacification without satisfaction' (1995: 461, 471). In Hopkins (2012) essentially the same formula is repeated for dreams but now is applied only to pathological *thoughts*, not to actions.

20 Against partition see Thalberg 1974; De Sousa 1976; Davidson 1982a; Moore 1984; Johnston 1988; Gardner 1993; Graham 2010. Davidson, it is true, argued for segregating constellations of propositional attitudes, but he did not hold that these constellations constitute independent centres of agency: 'such constellations', as Hopkins (1995: 473) says, 'do not *have* motives; rather they *are* (groups of) motives'. To my knowledge, only David Pears (1984), Rorty (1988); Pataki (1996b, 2000, 2003) and Boag (2005) have, though along different lines, argued for a conception of mind whose parts satisfy, at least transiently, sufficient conditions for independent agency. Petocz (1999: 164) is also recep-tive to mental plurality. Within psychoanalysis, on the other hand, it is commonplace to hold that the mind is constituted by independent agencies. Freud, Fairbairn (arguably), M. Klein, Winnicott, Bion, Ogden, Symington, S. Mitchell have all explicitly embraced partitive conceptions of mind. Of course, a roll-call doesn't settle anything about the adequacy of partitive conceptualisation, but it can suggest that the observed clinical phe-nomena do press strongly in its direction. For the non-intentional reading of FWT within a broadly common-sense-psychological framework see Wollheim 1991, 1979, 1984, 1993c; Hopkins 1982, 1988, 1991, 1995, 2012; Moore 1984; Eagle 1984, 2011; Johnston 1988; Lear 1998a; Gardner 1991, 1993; Cavell 1993, 2006; Marshall 2000. McLaughlin (1988) and Brakel (2009) possibly also belong here. R. K. Shope (1967, 1970) had earlier argued that psychoanalytic explanation was non-intentional. Woll-heim's account of the motivational structures found in symptoms and their kin allows for instances of intentional activity, as in his notion of 'displaced action', but essentially comes down on the side of the subintentional and expressive at the expense of the intentional. Some early attempts to explicate enactments (obsessive acts in the main) as intentional are discussed in Hopkins (1982: xxiff).

Chapter 2

Freud's conception of wish-fulfilment

Extension of a concept in a *theory* (e.g. wish-fulfilment dreams).

Wittgenstein 1967: 499

2.1 Freud's originality

I have repeatedly insisted that Freud's conception of wish-fulfilment is entirely singular. How is it then that in successive editions of his seminal dream book (1900a: 96ff) Freud accumulated references to thinkers who, he claimed, anticipated his wish-fulfilment theory of dreams? It goes without saying that the wishful character of some dreams could hardly have escaped earlier thinkers. Anyone who recalls and thinks about their dreams will know that they often take up scenes of quotidian life and paint them in pleasing colours. But Freud and the commentators who agreed with him were wrong to assimilate his views with the alleged forerunners. It will shed some light on FWT to briefly notice why.

E. R. Dodds (1951: 119) observed that the notion that some dreams were meaningful and wish-fulfilling was common among the Ancients. There are indeed ancient records of dreams interpreted along wishful lines. The interpretation of Alexander the Great's Satyr dream is mentioned by Freud (1900a: 131). In Hunt's (1989: 89) summary it runs: 'Impatient and uncertain in the midst of his long siege of Tyre, Alexander dreams of a satyr dancing on a shield. Aristander, his astrologer and dream interpreter, suggested persevering in the attack (which was successful) on the basis that the Greek "*Tyr Sa*" means "Tyre is yours"'. (This rebus interpretation would have delighted Freud.) Penelope's famous eagle dream in the *Iliad* is interpreted as wishful by the disguised Odysseus himself (Hunt 1989: 88). Similarly, the dreams sought with votive offerings in the temples of Asclepius in which 'the dreamer's parent or some other respected or impressive personage, perhaps a priest or even a god, reveals without symbolism what will or will not happen, or should or should not be done' (Dodds 1951: 107) have an obviously wishful tincture since, naturally, the dream visitors had the dreamer's interests at heart. However, in all these cases, although there is wishful content it is more accurate to say that the dreams are either wishfully *prognostic* or *instructive*, directive in the latter case of what ought to be done, rather than as wish-fulfilling, as being *substitutive satisfactions*, in the Freudian sense. It could hardly be supposed that the votaries of Asclepius would undergo the privations to which they were subject for the transient satisfactions of the dream as Freud understood them.

Schopenhauer's insights on the activity of will **(1.3)** are remarkable and some passages come close to articulating Freudian wish-fulfilment of the maximal kind **(Chapter 5)**. Wilhelm Griesinger has a most suggestive passage cited by Freud, relating dreams and mental illness,[1] which is worth reproducing.

> Agreeable, ravishing heavenly dreams [are rare in health, but to] the individual who is distressed by bodily and mental troubles, the dream realizes what reality has refused – happiness and fortune. The starving Trenck, during his imprisonment, often dreamed of rich repasts; the beggar dreams that he is wealthy... So also in mental disease... we see clearly how supposed possession and imaginary realizations of good things and wishes, the denial and destruction of which furnished a moral cause of the disease, constitute commonly the chief subjects of the delirium of insanity: for example, she who has lost a darling child raves of a mother's joy, he who has suffered loss of fortune imagines himself rich, the disappointed maiden is happy in the thought that she is tenderly loved by a faithful lover.
>
> (Griesinger 1867: 108–9)

These are good observations by the father of neurological psychiatry and they must have worked on Freud. But, as with the insights of Schopenhauer and other nineteenth-century philosophers, they remain isolated, and Griesinger makes no attempt to explain them in the context of either a psychological or a neurological theory. Griesinger neglects the desiderative or wishful aspects of mind, as does mainstream psychiatry today. Similar remarks could be made about all the authorities Freud cites. He mistakenly sought consilience with earlier thinkers, hoping to corroborate his wish-fulfilment theory, but in fact no writer appears to have anticipated his singular conception.

2.2 Drive and wish

Both classical psychoanalysis and contemporary neuropsychoanalysis place great store on the significance of the motivational concept of *instinctual drive* (*Triebe*). Drive is supposed to provide the biological bedrock that links mind to body, psychoanalysis to the hard sciences.[2] Given the fundamental importance of the conceptions of instinctual drive and wish in various phases of Freud's work, it is odd that he nowhere provides a perspicuous statement of the relations between them. In the *Project* (1954) he briefly mentions endogenous sources of stimuli, the precursors of drives, giving rise to wishes or wishful states. But his main concern there is with explaining the way in which the mental apparatus deals with irruptions of *external* stimuli and the reaction to them. The relations between reactive wishes to remove external disturbances and continuous endogenous stimuli, prefiguring the drives as later conceived (excepting perhaps ego-drives), are rather opaque.

After *Three Essays on the Theory of Sexuality* (1905b) Freud addressed motivation increasingly in terms of the vicissitudes of drives, presumably under the influence of Darwin and of his own conviction of the importance of sexuality with its obvious biological connections. This is not the place to enter the labyrinth of psychoanalytic drive theory. Our aim is to determine how much can be achieved in understanding psychoanalysis using an extended Intentional psychology, and that psychology sheds little light on sub-personal processes such as drives. It will suffice to observe that drives are inconsistently characterised throughout Freud's work: sometimes as somatic entities, sometimes as psychological entities and sometimes, rather unhelpfully, as borderline entities. And there is little guidance on how wish and wish-fulfilment on the one hand, and drive and drive discharge on the other, are related **(4.1)**. Some of the things Freud says, and some authoritative recent expositions, treat drives as the psychical representatives or mental representations of bodily states (Solms and Zellner 2012a: 50–2). I think that the weight of textual evidence tilts against this interpretation. True, some passages are favourable: 'an "instinct"', Freud writes, 'appears to us as a concept on the frontier between the mental and the somatic, as the psychical representative of the stimuli originating within the organism and reaching the mind, as a measure of the demand upon the mind for work in consequence of its connection with the body' (1915c: 121–2). But elsewhere, and especially in late articles (e.g. 1926f: 265), drive is somatic substratum giving rise to psychical processes:

> An instinct can never become an object of consciousness – only the idea that represents the instinct can. Even in the unconscious, moreover, an instinct cannot be represented otherwise than by an idea. If the instinct did not attach itself to an idea or manifest itself as an affective state, we could know nothing about it. When we nevertheless speak of an unconscious instinctual impulse or of a repressed instinctual impulse, the looseness of phraseology is a harmless one. We can only mean an instinctual impulse the ideational representative of which is unconscious, for nothing else comes into consideration.
>
> (1915e: 177)

A reasonable supposition is that Freud came to conceive of wishes as the psychical representatives of instinctual drives, the latter conceived as somatic motivational states, 'metabolic and endocrinological imperatives of the body' (Solms and Zellner 2012a: 49). This accords well with Freud's definition of the 'instinctual representative' as 'an idea (Vorstellung) or group of ideas which is cathected with a definite quota of psychical energy (libido or interest) coming from an instinct' (Freud 1915e: 152). Fortunately, we do not have to decide this issue, nor do we have to wait on the neuroscientific determination of the relations between drive, primary affective processes and higher tertiary functions of the brain (Solms and Turnbull 2002: ch. 4; Solms and Zellner 2012b). Whatever the outcome of this scientific work, it can be no more inconsistent with our common-sense psychological view of wishes and their fulfilment than can quantum mechanics with the existence of furniture.

2.3 The basic model of Freudian wish-fulfilment

In **1.2** we articulated the conceptual structure of FWT, the conditions that any process or activity has to satisfy to be considered an instance of FWT. But *are* there any such processes or activities? The features of the concept were extracted from Freud's understanding of dreams, symptoms and so on but, as we said, Freud may have got it wrong and nothing satisfies the concept, just as nothing satisfies the concept *unicorn*.

The simplest candidate for being a form of FWT, hallucinatory wish-fulfilment or gratification, is exposed in an important passage in *The Interpretation of Dreams*:

> A hungry baby screams or kicks helplessly... the excitation arising from the internal need is not due to a force producing a *momentary* impact but to one which is in continuous operation. A change can only come about if in some way or other (in the case of the baby, through outside help) an 'experience of satisfaction' can be achieved which puts an end to the internal stimulus. An essential component of this experience of satisfaction is a particular perception (that of nourishment, in our example) the mnemic image of which remains associated thence forward with the memory trace of the excitation produced by the need. As a result of the link that has thus been established, next time this need arises a psychical impulse will at once emerge which will seek to re-cathect the mnemic image of the perception and to re-evoke the perception itself, that is to say, to re-establish the situation of the original satisfaction. An impulse of this kind is what we call a wish; the re-appearance of the perception is the fulfilment of the wish; and the shortest path to the fulfilment of the wish is a path leading direct from the excitation produced by the need to a complete cathexis of the perception. Nothing prevents us from assuming that there was a primitive state of the psychical apparatus in which this path was actually traversed, that is, in which wishing ended in hallucinating. Thus, the aim of the first psychical activity was to produce a 'perceptual identity' – a repetition of the perception which was linked with the satisfaction of the need.
>
> (1900a: 565–6; cf. 1950a: 317ff)

I don't propose to treat in detail the (quasi-)neurological or metapsychological details and speculations underwriting this model,[3] important though they are. Instead I will provide a rough gloss and then expose Freud's mature characterisation in the Intentional idiom. On the rough gloss wish-fulfilment involves a regression: when a wishful impulse's immediate access to satisfaction is blocked, as it is in the helpless hungry infant and the sleeper, a topographical regression of psychic energy ('quantity') to the perceptual system of the mental apparatus ensues, and a reactivation of a memory of satisfaction as a hallucinatory experience provides a 'perceptual identity' with the original satisfaction. A memory of a previously satisfying experience is thus 'mistaken' for a perception of the wished-for object, and wish-fulfilment (or discharge) is achieved. On the standard psychoanalytic premises the 'mistaking' of the wishful phantasy for the state of affairs that would in fact satisfy the wish is attributed to regression to that special mode of mental functioning, the primary process, whose key characteristics include mobility of cathexis and 'the replacement of external by psychical reality' (Freud 1915e: 187). So far as it goes this is acceptable, but it leaves the primary process as an unanalysable feature of mind and it may rightly be wondered whether there are not more basic materials that enter into its construction.[4]

Freud himself realised that characterising wish-fulfilment as the revival of a memory-percept in a primitive mode of functioning would not quite deliver the necessary result (1900a: 555, fn. 1; 1917d), and he supplements the mechanical process with an Intentional explanation. Dreams, he points out – which are hallucinatory and share the basic structure of infantile hallucinatory wish-fulfilment[5] – are mostly not just thoughts or sensory images, 'their ideational content being transformed from thoughts into sensory images *to which belief is attached* and which appear to be experienced' (1900a: 535; see also 50; italics added). In a later work he emphasises that hallucination cannot consist merely in the regressive reactivation of memories or sensory images: hallucination 'brings belief in reality with it' (1917d: 230).

> If the secret of hallucination is nothing else than that of regression, every regression of sufficient intensity would produce hallucination with belief in its reality. But we are quite familiar with situations in which a process of regressive reflection brings to consciousness very clear mnemic images, though we do not on that account for a single moment take them for real perceptions. Again, we could well imagine the dream-work penetrating to mnemic images of this kind, making conscious to us what was previously unconscious, and holding up to us a wishful phantasy which rouses our longing, but which we should not regard as a real fulfilment of the wish.
>
> (1917d: 231)

In Freud's most considered account, then, *belief* converts the wishful phantasy which pictures fulfilment into the 'real fulfilment of the wish'. And how does belief do that? Here Freud harks back to an old tradition: when an idea isn't contradicted, it's accepted (1900a: 50–2, 535; 1917d).[6] When nothing in the mind 'contradicts' or is incompatible with a particular idea or perception, because all incompatible ideas or perceptions have been excluded or 'decathected' – have Cs. and Pcs. attention withdrawn from them – then 'reality testing' is inoperative, and the particular idea or perception is 'believed'. This is the recurrent condition of the neonate, Freud supposes, and of the dreamer.

> The state of sleep does not wish to know anything of the external world; it takes no interest in reality... Hence it withdraws cathexis from the system Cs. as well as the other systems, the Pcs. and the Ucs., in so far as the cathexis in them obey the wish to sleep. *With the system Cs. thus uncathected, the possibility of reality testing is abandoned; and the excitations which, independently of the state of sleep, have entered on the path of regression will find the path clear as far as the system Cs. where they will count as undisputed reality.*
>
> (Freud 1917d: 234. Italics added)

This metapsychological description can be recast cogently in the Intentional idiom. Desires (or wishes) press to action or the generation of mental states and dispositions. We are familiar with the way in which they stimulate imagination and generate phenomenal content. As Freud put it: 'every desire takes before long the form of picturing its own fulfilment' (1916–17: 372). This statement is too strong, but it is not far from the truth, and in the infant or regressed mind with fluctuating capacity to distinguish between different mental states – between, for instance, internally generated experiences like phantasy and perceptions, and (what may in part underlie the latter condition) its propensity to be *engrossed* – it may be very close to the truth.[7] When the wish has brought about the representation of the state of affairs that would satisfy it, the first step towards perceptual identity is achieved. When, in addition, there is a poverty of engagement with the external world and with other sectors of the internal world or psychic reality, as we may presume is the case in unintegrated infantile states, sleep or psychosis (Freud 1924b, 1924e), or when the sheer fascination of an idea captures the mind in engrossment, the process of achieving perceptual identity is completed. In these conditions wishful representations brook no contradiction and succeed in presenting themselves as irrecusable *agent's evidence*[8] on which critical occurrent beliefs are based: the agent acquires a belief that what was wished has come to pass. It is undeniable that there are circumstances in which a heightened degree of engrossment in events, internal to mind or external,[9] succeeds in excluding not only the contingently distractive, such as disturbing noises, but also incompatible beliefs, and that these states can generate transient wish-fulfilling beliefs. Consider the common experience of enjoying a sexual phantasy or compensatory day-dream of which we, ourselves, are the authors; or the pretend-games of young children. Engrossment deprives us of the occurrent knowledge of our authorship. It is an ephemeral deprivation but it is enough. So, as a consequence of the agent's acquired belief that the conditions it has wished for have come to pass, the wish is, albeit temporarily, extinguished and wish-fulfilment is attained. It is a sinister feature of our lives that we become so engrossed in certain roles that we become oblivious to the consequences of what we do **(5.7)**.

2.4 Engrossment and belief

I have employed two concepts both of which may be regarded in this context as problematic: *engrossment* and *belief*. 'Engrossment' is not a Freudian term, though I will argue directly that it corresponds to a Freudian idea that illuminates the circumstances in which FWT occurs. Then I will try to allay some difficulties with the other problematic concept: *belief* as it occurs in psychically primitive, pre-linguistic circumstances.

The intuitive conception of engrossment I invoked above attracts several immediate objections. I want to use these objections to see if something determinate and useful can be extracted from the conception. First, it may be objected that the notion of engrossment in wishful phantasy is unnecessary to achieving wish-fulfilment because the operation of a-rational primary process, or one feature of primary process – 'the *equation* of psychic reality with external reality' or *psychic equivalence* (Fonagy *et al.* 2004: 255–61; note the difference between this and Freud's formulation in **2.3**) – is sufficient. Second, it may be objected that engrossment cannot explain *unconscious* FWT (and, as we shall see, there certainly are such cases), because engrossment is a vicissitude of conscious attention. Accounting for unconscious FWT would entail positing unconscious engrossment, a condition that is incoherent. Third, even if sufficient for simple intrapsychic cases such as dreams or omnipotent phantasy, engrossment cannot explain the more complex cases of FWT exemplified in symptoms, enactments, art and religion: *what*, one might ask, is the object of engrossment in such cases, and *who*, or what element of self, is engrossed? Although Freud applied his conception of wish-fulfilment to a very broad range of phenomena, he did not provide a metapsychological extension that covers all of them. It is difficult to see how the basic model of hallucinatory wish-fufilment, at least as turning on the relation between engrossment and belief expounded here, can explain FWT in symptoms and, especially, the more complex expressions of self-solicitude. In these cases there is action, often intentional action, and therefore practical reasoning – but we have no guidance on how the conditions of engrossment can so engulf an agent as to issue in FWT. These are serious objections. How are we to proceed?

Following Freud, we accepted that there are circumstances in which symptoms, phantasies, enactments, and so on, could be wish-fulfilling in the manner of FWT. These vehicles function as evidence – agent's evidence – that, under conditions of engrossment, manage to monopolise the agent's available evidence and generate (often) contrary to fact wish-fulfilling beliefs. There may be conditions other than engrossment in which such vehicles claim the mind, but engrossment seems to be the most significant of these and appears to be present in all or in most cases of FWT. Four features of engrossment require consideration.

(1)   engrossment is a vicissitude of attention;
(2)   engrossment excludes the incompossible;
(3)   engrossment extends into the internal world;
(4)   engrossment tends to generate belief.

In claiming that engrossment is a vicissitude of attention I do not mean to imply that attention is a discrete activity apart from and on all fours with the perceptual modalities, including that of inner sense.[10] On the contrary, attention is a vicissitude of the perceptual modalities and is inconceivable without them. But there is a particular intimacy between engrossment and attention lacking between engrossment and perception *per se*. Engrossment befalls perception when perception, including inner sense, is in the attentive mode. Attention and engrossment always imply what perception always does not: selection, focalisation and exclusion (James 1890: I, 404). It does not follow that attention's objects are restricted to the particular. One can attend to, and become engrossed in, the lecture and the play. Attention, though it implies a narrowing, does not imply a narrowness of mind. It is consistent with, and may presuppose, concurrent mental activity. When listening attentively to music we may have an experience of absorption and timelessness. But one can be engrossed in activities like playing chess or playing a role on the stage, and these things obviously involve a good deal of thoughtful activity. Although there is some philosophical resistance to the idea, it is quite natural and correct to figure a person as attending to, and becoming engrossed in, their internal world of episodic memory, phantasy and daydream. If engrossment is a vicissitude of attention it follows that we can attend to, and not only *have*, such inner experiences.[11]

Essential to the engrossed attention is its exclusion of everything not germane to the attentional project. That is a constitutive condition of engrossment. When engrossed we become, in the first place, dead or deaf to those parts of the world not included as objects of attention; in the second place, we are immersed in forgetfulness of self. There are, of course, degrees of engrossment, and it may befall one or it may be willed, as in the effort of concentration. I call everything with which engrossment has to contend *incompossible*. Where one is engrossed there must be not only the exclusion of what is incompossible with it in the external world but also the exclusion of what is incompossible with it in the internal world. This may be illustrated by example. Suppose our friend dreams that she is about to be murdered by X and wakes in terror, believing (or dream-believing) that she was about to be murdered. For that to occur, other beliefs incompossible with the transitory (dream) beliefs, for example that X is in fact dead, must be rendered ineffective.

Attention can be directed at creatures of the internal world, such as daydreams and images, and we can be engrossed in them. It now remains to be shown that attention can be directed to items of which one is unconscious – unconscious phantasies, internal or virtual objects, and the like. And if the latter may be objects of attention, it follows they may be objects of engrossment. It is easy to show, though it may at first sight appear contradictory, that attention can be directed at objects of which there is no conscious awareness; that attention may operate unconsciously. Some of the relevant phenomena have been known for centuries. Here is an early example from William James: take a hypnotised subject,

> Make him blind to one person in the room, set all the persons in a row, and tell him to count them. He will count all but that one. But how can he tell which one not to count? In like manner make a stroke on a paper or blackboard, and tell him it is not there, and he will see nothing but the clean paper or board. Next (he not looking) surround the original stroke with other strokes just like it, and ask him what he sees. He will point out one by one all the new strokes, and omit the original one every time, no matter how numerous the new strokes may be, or in what order they are arranged. ... Obviously he is not blind to the kind of stroke in the least. He is blind only to one individual stroke of that kind in a particular position on the board or paper – that is to a particular complex object; and paradoxical as it may seem to say so, he must distinguish it with great accuracy from others like it, in order to remain blind to it when

the others are brought near. He discriminates it as a preliminary to not seeing it at all.

(James 1890: I, 212)

The subject attends to an external object that, consciously, he neither experiences nor can avow. (This is reminiscent, of course, of recent work on 'blind-sight'.) But what about attention directed at something in the unconscious *internal* world? I think that with a slight modification the Freudian conceptions of *cathexis*, and especially *attention cathexis*, can shed light on this question. 'Cathexis' is a neologism coined by Freud's English translator, James Strachey (from the Greek 'catecheis', 'to occupy') as a translation for *Besetzung*, which means occupation. The conception does much work in Freudian metapsychology, and something like this notion does seem necessary to account for the mind's preoccupation with its objects. In Freud's mature scheme, ideas, representations of objects and the self, as well as functions, can be cathected with libido, aggression or neutralised energies. Cathexes can emanate from the id, in the form of instinctual cathexes, or from the ego, as interest or attention. In the earlier topographical model Freud makes use of Ucs., Cs. and Pcs. cathexes, the last two corresponding to ego-cathexes.

In the *Project* (1950a), cathexes are conceived as literally charging or investing neurones with psychic energy. This notion carries over to the later models of mind where cathexes attach themselves to representations and functions and are intended to account for their salience or significance. This is, of course, problematic, but there is a way of conceiving of cathexes which discards the energic dimension, and to which Freud himself was drawn. In general, he regards attention and interest as types of cathexis. Thus he writes that 'the system Pcs ... has at its disposal for distribution a mobile cathectic energy, a part of which is familiar to us in the form of attention' (1900a: 653). But occasionally he uses the terms almost interchangeably. Freud considers the event of persecutory ideas entering consciousness 'without finding acceptance or belief' there. The important factor in these cases, he says, is quantitative: 'the degree of attention or, more correctly, the amount of cathexis that these structures are able to attract to themselves' (1922b: 228). It is inviting to investigate whether attention and its vicissitudes, preoccupation and engrossment, can do the work which the concept of *cathexis* had been called upon to do. Consider this critical passage on repression:

It must be a matter of withdrawal of cathexis; but the question is, in which system does the withdrawal take place and to which system does the cathexis which is withdrawn belong? The repressed idea remains capable of action in the Ucs., and it must therefore have retained   its cathexis. What has been withdrawn must be something else. Let us take the case of repression proper ('after-pressure'), as it affects an idea which is preconscious or even actually conscious. Here repression can only consist in withdrawing from the idea the (pre)conscious cathexis which belongs to the system Pcs. The idea then either remains uncathected, or receives cathexis from the Ucs., or retains the Ucs. cathexis which it already had. Thus there is a withdrawal of the preconscious

cathexis, retention of the unconscious cathexis, or replacement of the preconscious cathexis by an unconscious one.

(1915e: 180)

Freud goes on to point out that withdrawal of Pcs. cathexis is inadequate to explain
either primal repression – where a Pcs. cathexis was never in question – or the
maintenance of repression, which requires 'the assumption of an anticathexis, by
means of which the system Pcs. protects itself from the pressure upon it of the
unconscious idea'. The anticathexis, we learn, is a 'substitutive idea' to which 'the
Pcs. cathexis which has taken flight attaches itself' (1915e: 180).

My suggestion is that this energic model of repression can be reconstructed, in
Freudian spirit, by discarding the notion of Ucs. cathexis (of cathexis emanating
from the Ucs.) and substituting preconscious and conscious *attention* for Pcs. and Cs.
cathexis, respectively. Then, in repression, conscious attention is withdrawn from
ideas (primarily self and object representations and phantasies). Preconscious attention is generally not entirely withdrawn, although it may be, if the repression is
entirely successful. The degree of preconscious – that is, descriptively unconscious –
attention attached to the repressed, or, perhaps better, the *disposition* to attend, then
determines the repressed's influence. For unconscious phantasies and internal
objects could have no causal influence on action unless they were in some degree
noticed or *registered* by the unconscious executive agency **(4.2)**, the unconscious ego
(in the main corresponding to the Pcs). So the relationship between ego and its
internal world can be described as being based on the ego's unconscious preoccupation with its internal objects and phantasies.[12] It is not implied that the latter rivet
the attention, although they may do so in madness; however, they can remain
objects of preoccupation, much as do objects of the external world to which we are
disposed to attend at every turn and which, in love and neurosis, can become very
intense objects of preoccupation indeed.

This perspective finds support in clinical material. In emphasising the role of
unconscious preoccupation with internal objects it spells out one of the essential
conditions involved in maintaining an unconscious relationship with internal
objects. Preoccupation is a vicissitude of attention. If there were no such preoccupation there would be no dynamic point of view. If we did not attend to our internal objects we would not fear them or react with anxiety to their return; we would
not be sustained by, identify with or be torn away from the external world by them.
The postulation of an inwardly directed preconscious attention appears to be an
inescapable consequence of the acknowledgement of engagement with an unconscious world of internal objects and phantasy.

The censorship between the Pcs. and the Cs. (Freud 1915e) takes on added significance in this view, for we are positing a preconscious involvement with the
repressed and other Ucs. material that precludes easy access to consciousness. But
this, too, is in accord with the unconscious ego's role in protecting consciousness
(Sandler 1976; Weiss and Sampson 1986). The anticathexis retains a role similar to
its earlier one: it can now be seen as a substitute to which the attention attaches itself
as a defence against unwanted preoccupation, rather in the way in which people

seek distraction in external things, in books or driven activity, to avoid confrontation with internal turmoil. Many of the classical defence mechanisms can be reinterpreted as vicissitudes of attention, as the unconscious ego exploiting its control over attention. Apart from repression, consider aversion or avoidance, isolation, denial and manic defence. The earliest defences, such as the infant's 'turning away', obviously exploit attention and engrossment. An infant struggling with envy or jealousy may turn away from the provocative object and become engrossed in another activity or driven play.

If an Intentional revision along these lines can be sustained then engrossment may be considered to extend into the unconscious internal world. That we become engrossed in conscious daydreaming and other imaginative activities is undeniable. In relation to unconscious phantasies and internal objects, we cannot rely directly on introspection. However, two considerations bear on the claim. The first, just discussed, is that for unconscious wishes, beliefs, phantasies and internal objects (the contents of the dynamic unconscious) to influence action they must be 'noticed' and be objects of engrossment or preoccupation by the executive agency, otherwise they could make no difference. The second is that, indisputably, there is unconscious FWT, and the latter mostly, perhaps invariably, involves engrossment. It follows that there must be unconscious engrossment. This will be discussed in detail later (**4.4–4.6**) but as one type of example consider the unconscious identifications with parents or powerful figures (Superman, gods) that serve children as defensive, wish-fulfilling measures, or the grandiosity of narcissistic characters which supervenes on unconscious identifications (with the idealised self and objects) to create the wish-fulfilling illusions of power, beauty and invulnerability (Kernberg 1975).

Let me briefly recapitulate in broad strokes. The ego attends to the external world consciously and preconsciously. It can attend inwardly to its own internal world of conscious images, feelings and so on, as well as to unconscious internal objects and phantasies. Attention suffers similar fates in both worlds. It can become preoccupied and it can become engrossed.[13] Intense preoccupation with the internal world accounts for the influence of unconscious ideas and fixations (or at least some of the things which have been called fixations), and the return of the repressed – for it is the ego's devotion to its internal objects that persistently revives them. This picture of the ego is of a central agency capable of scanning both its internal and external worlds consciously and unconsciously, developing interests and preoccupations in both. It is a notable feature of this picture that the source of attention, the dark point from which attention emanates, and thereby the locus of agency, has been largely displaced from the conscious to the unconscious ego (**4.2**). We have arrived at this picture by systematically replacing the quasi-mechanistic concept of cathexis with our enhanced but less speculative concept of attention.

Utilising a conception of *unconscious attention* may seem counter-intuitive but like *unconscious wish*, *unconscious intention* and *unconscious belief* it appears indispensable for understanding clinical features of many cases (**4.1ff**). Kaplan-Solms and Solms (2000: 157–9) discuss a clinical experiment conducted by V. Ramachandran on an anosognostic patient with paralysis and neglect of her left arm. She persistently denies the paralysis. Curiously, the neglect disappears completely when cold water is poured into her left ear, but then returns again once the caloric stimulation wears off. The patient then insists that she can use her arm normally. Ramachandran concludes that 'at some deeper level she does indeed have knowledge of the paralysis' but represses it. Kaplan-Solms and Solms elaborate:

> We would have to say that *unconsciously* [such patients] ... *do* perceive, attend to, and remember that they are paralysed... We take it that it is now generally accepted that human perceptual and memory functions are largely unconscious. It is however more questionable whether there is such a thing as unconscious attention. Many people – Freud included – would say that it is precisely the function of attention which renders unconscious mental processing conscious... Be that as it may, the important point is that Ramachandran's experiment demonstrates that unconsciously these patients do perceive and remember that they are paralysed, notwithstanding the fact that they are unable to direct their conscious attention to these facts.

If the patient perceives her infirmity, that it is an infirmity, then she must indeed be able to attend to it, even if she has no conscious awareness of it. Their conclusion is sound, and the authors need not be concerned by Freud's apparent demurral. For Freud, attention has indeed a special relation to consciousness: 'Becoming conscious is connected with the application of a particular psychical function, that of attention – a function which, as it seems, is available only in a specific quantity' (1900a: 593). But this proposition does not imply that everything attended to becomes conscious: attention is a necessary but not a sufficient condition of consciousness.[14]

It is possible that some such notion as engrossment fixing an agent's beliefs and governing their actions will receive corroboration from neuroscience. In a far-reaching paper, Hopkins (2012) has shown that repression and Freudian wish-fulfilment can be neatly explained by the so-called Bayesian brain's exclusionary function in the management of conflict directed at maintaining homeostasis. The general idea is that the Bayesian brain's main functions are prediction of sensory experience and avoidance of conflict with the current dominant model that the brain is using to make sense of experience. To do this the brain suppresses/represses material inconsistent with that model but keeps it alive as a potential correction to its current state. (We might say that the material remains unconsciously cathected or attended.) Thus 'we can start to understand the Freudian unconscious as the natural product, in our conflicted species, of the management of conflict by the Bayesian brain' (2012: 262).

Confronted with an internal stimulus such as a desire conflicting with the dominant model in circumstances where action is impossible (as in sleep), the brain, governed by the imperative of conflict avoidance, may rapidly repress the desire and produce in its place 'an internal representation of the experience of satisfaction the desire predicts' (2012: 258). This, as Freud supposed, would seem tailored by the ego to enable sleep undisturbed. In other words, 'it is done as the Bayesian brain would do, if, as seems possible, it was acting in the interests of homeostasis to keep motivational arousal from causing what it (as ego) calculated would be an uneconomic interference with sleep' (2012: 258). But from the point of view of rational consciousness, 'this neurologically intelligible way of managing conflict related to internal sensory input appears as a kind of *perfect and all-encompassing miniature hallucination*, in which the deluded dreaming subject utterly obliterates both what is happening in his mind and how things are in the world. ... his dreaming brain (as ego) is producing a *double denial of reality...*' (2012: 258). Thus the exclusionary, homeostatic function of the brain produces an experience which, in the case of dreaming or daydream, essentially corresponds with imaginative engrossment as we have conceived it. But, we would add, the efficacy of engrossment is indexed to the degree of belief with which the imaginative experience is entertained, the extent to which the experience can transfix the subject.

It seems to me that whilst (something like) unconscious engrossment in latent content is necessary to make sense of certain clinical material, the concept as surveyed so far will be inadequate to the more complex cases involving intentional FWT. *Engrossment* is itself a complex concept, a family of concepts. Engrossment as a spectator in a game of football is unlike engrossment as a player in a game of chess or engrossment of an actor performing a role, and both are different from engrossment in a daydream. I think, however, that Freud – Freud's views as interpreted here – cannot take us further in our account of FWT. We will need to take it further, and the thread of argument will be resumed **(4.5, 5.7)**.

2.5 An aside on belief

Whereas the notion of engrossment appears promising in primitive contexts such as hallucinatory gratification but problematic in complex cases such as obsessive acts, the notion of action being temporarily terminated or pacified by wish-fulfilling beliefs is promising in complex cases but problematic in primitive ones.[15] Freud clearly links FWT to belief: to achieve 'real' wish-fulfilment, a wishful phantasy must attract belief. It is because hallucination presupposes belief – the sensory elements of hallucination become irrecusable agent's evidence – that terminating beliefs are generated and wishes are fulfilled in the manner of FWT. However, the notion of beliefs operating in dream or infant experience, exclusive of language and holistic constraints, is widely considered problematic. Moreover, empirical research in infant development raises questions about the capacity of infants to own Intentional states such as beliefs, to differentiate them from other Intentional states and to make Intentional attributions to others.[16]

As regards the empirical studies, it must be observed that significant disagreement about *when* infants acquire Intentional capacities is the rule. Some authorities maintain that Intentional attributions are made almost from birth. Others (Stern 1985; Tomasello 1999) maintain that rudimentary Intentional attributions start in the last quarter of the first year. Gergely appears to hold that whilst infants can interpret goal-directed and rational behaviour teleologically in the second half of the first year (in Fonagy *et al.* 2004: 33, 146–7), the Intentional stance proper arrives only at the end of the first year, and false belief attribution not until three or four years.[17] These issues of timing, about when infants can attribute Intentional states to others (and presumably themselves), are important but not decisive for the concerns at hand. Even if feelings, beliefs and intentions are not discriminated as distinct types in the infant's mind or attributed to others (are not 'mentalised'), it does not follow on all cogent accounts of the relevant concepts that the infant cannot *have* feelings, beliefs and intentions. From the fact that infants don't have conscious access to their own inner states it doesn't follow that they cannot act on them. If it did, the entire psychoanalytic edifice based on unconscious motivation would be in jeopardy.

The conceptual difficulties are not so easily allayed. The case against attributing propositional attitudes to non-linguistic creatures, mostly prosecuted against animals (Davidson 1975, 1982b), spills over naturally to infants (Cavell 1993) and to the System Unconscious or id (Gardner 1993). The case turns mostly on the import of meaning holism – the notion, roughly, that to possess one concept or belief (or other Intentional attitude) requires the possession of many others. For instance, to believe that the cat is on the mat presupposes a network of beliefs about cats, mats and the relation *on*. So mental holism appears to preclude infants – and therefore, on the usual premises about the infantile character of the unconscious, the unconscious as well – from sharing in the propositional network, including beliefs.

This objection, and several related ones, were expressed forcefully by Donald Davidson (1975, 1982b; Cavell 1993, chs. 1 and 8). I think they are unsound and may quickly be disarmed. A dog chases a cat, but barks up the wrong oak tree. What does the dog believe? If the dog believes that the cat went up the tree then, according to Davidson, it must have many other general beliefs: 'without many general beliefs there would be no reason to identify a belief as a belief about a tree, much less an oak tree. Similar considerations apply to the dog's supposed thinking about the cat' (Davidson 1982b: 98–9).

The conclusion, *mutatis mutandis*, applies to infants also. On the face of it, it is highly counter-intuitive. It is hard to see how, in Davidson's view, infants ever break into the charmed circle of propositional attitudes. If to hold one belief presupposes holding many general beliefs, how do they acquire any beliefs at all? Beliefs are not acquired in large packages. 'Da-da gone' surely expresses a belief even if 'cat gone' means nothing to the child who verbalises it. Moreover – back to dogs – even if they don't have *our* concepts and beliefs, it doesn't follow that they have no concepts or beliefs. We may not know under what doggy concepts dogs identify items in their environment and predicate things of them, but we know that they do these things because we know that dogs classify, recognise and organise their environment. We cannot express their beliefs *oratio recta*, but we can do so *oratio obliqua*, as when we report some statement without knowing the exact words the original speaker used. Our attributions of content may be shaky, but it doesn't follow that the attribution of believing – of the dog's capacity to believe – need be. There are congeries of concepts which hang together with belief. Creatures with beliefs show recognisable expectancy and disappointment and (as Davidson notes) surprise. Dogs have expectations and show disappointment and surprise and something for all the world like puzzlement. They operate on evidence and make mistakes. Infants obviously have expectations, operate with instrumental beliefs about how to achieve goals and end their desire-driven behaviour when they believe they have gained their ends.

Another argument (Davidson 1982b) contends that in order to have a belief it is necessary to have the concept of belief, but to have the concept of belief presupposes the concept of false belief. Certainly having the concept of *belief* involves the concept of *false belief*. The central meaning of 'I believe that *p*' is something like 'I hold *p* true but accept that it could be false'. But it does not follow that a creature cannot have beliefs without having the concept of belief, any more than that it cannot have rheumatism without having the concept *rheumatism*. Children under the age of three or four do not perform well on false belief tests, and so presumably don't operate with the concept *false belief* (Perner 1991), but it is evident that they have rich caches of beliefs before then. The possession of beliefs *cannot* be contingent on the possession of the concept *false belief*.

Davidson's third argument is: 'without speech we cannot make the fine distinctions between thoughts that are essential to the explanations (of human action) we can sometimes confidently supply' (Davidson 1975: 15). The belief that the cat is up the oak tree is not the same as the belief that the cat is up the tallest tree in the garden, even if that oak is the tallest tree. How, in the absence of language, are such distinctions to be descried? The point is sound, but does not impugn the capacity of animals or infants to have beliefs; it impugns *our* capacity to identify and articulate them. But this is a common restriction on communication, when we can only report what a speaker says *oratio obliqua*, not having access to precisely what is said. Indeed, infant belief may have, and could be expected to have, precisely that quality of indeterminateness that Davidson thinks is fatal to their doxastic capacities.

The tradition Davidson represents descends principally from Bertrand Russell's interest in the logical form of certain non-extensional molecular propositions which he designated 'propositional attitudes' (Russell 1921b). Believing, knowing and fearing he regarded as different attitudes to propositions. Propositions, though, are problematic entities and have been variously construed as the meanings of sentences, statements (what is said), truth-bearers, abstract objects, sets of possible worlds and other things. These abstract construals have problems with individuation, though, and one inviting solution is to relate them in some perspicuous way (such as identity) with concrete citizens such as sentences. Then the beliefs, the propositions you hold true, are precisely expressed by the sentences you hold true. But beliefs don't seem to *be* mere relations to public sentences. So the next step in this line of things is to regard beliefs as sentences or sentence-like representations in the head (where beliefs seem to belong), or as structured brain states, or as mental states reducible to or supervening on such brain states. This approach seems to account for the content of belief (at least narrow content) but it doesn't yet tell us what belief is, how to distinguish it from other Intentional attitudes such as fearing or knowing; beliefs have distinctive causal and logical properties the other states don't. To achieve *that* distinction requires functional elaboration: beliefs are brain states with certain kinds of inputs and outputs, they are caused by certain kinds of experiences and are apt for producing actions and inferences and so on. There are many variations on this theme, and they constitute, perhaps, the standard approach today.

I believe that the entire approach described in this thumbnail history is misconceived, and the concerns it generates about pre-linguistic belief are largely misplaced. That is not easily shown, of course, and it would be fruitless to attempt a refutation here. Instead I will sketch an alternative way of viewing belief, one that is more plausible and congenial to our psychoanalytic concerns. It begins with the observation that *belief* is a family resemblance concept. Opinion, expectation, conviction belong in the doxastic family but are of quite different types. Empirical belief differs in important respects from belief in logical or mathematical propositions. Empirical beliefs are analytically connected to a range of other primitive concepts: accepting evidence,[18] initiating and terminating intentional action, expectation of consequences; mathematical propositions and tautologies are not.

The analytic relationships of empirical beliefs are preserved if we think of beliefs, as F. P. Ramsey did, as maps by which we steer, on which we act (Ramsey 1931; Armstrong 1973). This is the core idea embedded in some of the cognitive conceptions of the developmental researchers, in the 'internal working models' of the attachment theorists (Bowlby 1971; Cassidy and Shaver 1999), of Stern's (1985) RIGS and, indeed, in aspects of Freud's idea of an internal world (1924b). But we need not think of these maps as located entirely in us; they may include features of the environment. An important distinction for the analysis of FWT, depending as it does on terminating or pacifying beliefs, is between a map on which we are prepared to act and to cease acting (if our aims have been achieved) and one that we merely entertain − a distinction corresponding to believing a proposition and merely entertaining one. The belief-map may be figured as a state of the brain with dispositional or causal properties, but equally − or perhaps better (for our purposes here this is not crucial) − it may be conceived as a global state whose content is revealed by counterfactual analysis (a position providing better accommodation for externalist views of mental content). The counterfactual analysis has been worked out cogently by Lynne Rudder Baker (1995). Belief, Baker maintains, is

> a global state of a whole person, not of any proper part of the person, such as the brain.... Whether a person S has a particular belief ... is determined by what S does, says, and thinks, and what S *would* do, say, and think in various circumstances, where 'what S would do' may itself be specified [I]ntentionally. So, whether... 'S believes that p' is true depends on there being relevant counterfactuals true of S.
>
> (Baker 1995: 153–4)

It is evident how the analysis of *belief* along such lines allows for infant (or non-linguistic and unconscious) belief (Baker 1995: 189). We may infer an infant's beliefs and express them *oratio obliqua*, more or less, based on our knowledge of his perceptual field, gestures, intentional actions, expectations and terminations of action patterns. Thus, when an infant makes a proto-declaration to mother of pointing and wanting, we infer that he *believes* that mother can respond to his wishes and satisfy them, that he *expects* that she will look at his gesture, and we predict that he will cease his efforts once he *believes he possesses* the object of his desire. Notice: 'believes he possesses': the infant may have what he wants but not know or believe that he has – if, for instance, he is in a terrible rage, or too envious to acknowledge the gift.

Such counterfactual analyses are not unproblematic,[19] but they offer one promising avenue for philosophically explicating what we know already to be true: that infants at a very early stage have beliefs, desires and intentions and that the concepts of unconscious belief, desire and intention are not undermined by alleged criteria of propositionality or semantic opacity. If that is right, then it would seem that we do not require such apparent artifices as 'experience or belief-like' states to account for the pacification or termination of wishes (Hopkins 1995) or 'pre-propositional states' such as the *psychoanalytic wish* and *phantasy*, as construed by Gardner (1993: 110ff; also Lear 1995) to go yeoman for them. We will revisit this issue in more detail **(3.4, 3.5)**, but now a related matter requires attention, in preparation for the next chapter.

2.6 Belief and phantasy

On Freud's official view, the imaginative activity of phantasying proceeds from children's play:

> With the introduction of the reality principle one species of thought activity was split-off; it was kept free from reality testing and remained subordinated to the pleasure principle alone. This activity is phantasying which begins already in children's play, and later, continued as daydreaming abandons dependence on real objects.
>
> (Freud 1911b: 222)

In play the child 'likes to link his imagined objects and situations to the tangible and visible things of the real world. This linking is all that differentiates the child's "play" from "phantasying"' (1908e: 144). Since playing is an intentional activity – the child determines objectives and has beliefs about how to achieve them – it follows on this account that phantasying is also intentional.

But there are passages in which phantasy is clearly conceived to antedate play: 'Unconscious phantasies have either been unconscious all along and have been formed in the unconscious; or – as is more often the case – they were once conscious phantasies, day-dreams, and have since been purposely forgotten and have become unconscious through repression' (1908a: 161). Elsewhere, Freud is at pains to distinguish 'freely wandering phantastic thinking' from intentionally directed reflection (1921b; Kris 1952: 311). Phantasies formed in the unconscious can scarcely be derivatives of play, and freely wondering phantastic thinking is the opposite of purposive or intentional activity. Freud is inconsistent, and there has been little consistency over the nature of phantasy (or fantasy) in the subsequent psychoanalytic literature.

Freud also thought that phantasies can be actualised plastically or projected into the motor sphere. Thus, hysterical 'attacks are nothing else but phantasies translated into the motor sphere, projected onto motility and portrayed in pantomime' (1909a: 229). These attacks are 'mimetic or hallucinatory representations of phantasies' (1913j: 173). From here it was a short step for Melanie Klein to understand phantasy not as a derivative of play, but as underlying play: play is an expression of unconscious phantasy. Phantasy was the deeper thing, and Kleinian theorists (Isaacs 1948; Segal 1964) came to figure it as the primary expression of drives.

In a further development of Kleinian thought, phantasy is linked to personality structure. Thus Segal:

> The structure of the personality is largely determined by the more permanent of the phantasies which the ego has about itself and the objects that it contains. The fact that structure is intimately related to unconscious phantasy is extremely important: it is this which makes it possible to influence the structure of the ego and the superego through analysis.
>
> (Segal 1964: 20)

'Structure' refers, roughly speaking, to the more or less stable, organised and coherent configurations of mental processes and contents which account for the stability and continuity of personality. That being so, there are evident difficulties with Segal's formulation. What is a permanent phantasy? It may seem that Segal's thought here is that such phantasies are *beliefs* – about internal objects and so on. At least some important elements of personality structure are determined by beliefs. But phantasying is an *activity* and believing is not; they are of different kinds – so a connection between structure and phantasy along these lines is not viable. It may be, though, that by 'permanent' Segal intends to mean 'recurrent'. But in that case phantasies would seem to require some kind of causal or dispositional grounds, and so do not so much determine structure as manifest it. It is perhaps for this reason that Richard Wollheim introduced the notion of *dispositional phantasy*, along with occurrent phantasy, in *The Thread of Life* (1984: 142ff). A dispositional phantasy is a disposition to phantasise or to act out in ways written into the disposition. But then dispositional phantasies are radically different from the occurrent type: unlike occurrent phantasies, they have no phenomenology and are not activities. Since a dispositional phantasy is just a disposition to phantasise occurrently or act in determinate ways, it is more economical to explain (occurrent) phantasying and action in terms of beliefs and/or desires, in the same way that we would the occurrence of most other action. Once apprehension about unconscious belief is dispelled, so too is the need to burden the concept of *phantasy* with the tasks that *belief* performs so well.

2.7 Some grounds for intentionalism

Let's now resume the discussion interrupted at the end of **2.3**. That Freud regarded some wish-fulfilling processes as brought about intentionally is fairly evident. In one of his earliest psychoanalytic papers he writes:'*the splitting of the content of consciousness is the result of an act of will on the part of the patient.* By this I do not, of course, mean that the patient intends to bring about a splitting of consciousness. His intention is a different one; but, instead of attaining its aim, it produces a splitting of consciousness' (1894a: 46–7). It is not entirely clear here whether Freud thought that the process on which splitting supervenes is unconscious but, reflecting on this view many years later, context makes it clear that that is exactly what he had in mind. Breuer, he writes, preferred at the time a physiological theory to account for splitting, but he on the other hand 'was inclined to suspect the existence of an interplay of forces and the operation of intentions and purposes such as are to be observed in normal life' (1925d: 23).

Freud invoked unconscious intentions to explain the wish-fulfilling phenomena of symptoms (1916–17: chs. XIX–XIII, esp. 298–9; 1909a: 231); paraptaxes (1901b *passim*); phantasies (1908a: 159, 164; 1909a); play (1908e: 146; 1911b: 39); and art (1908e *passim*). He presents daydreams and masturbation phantasies (1912f; Stoller 1979) as crafted products intentionally manufactured for the purpose of gaining satisfaction that consists not (or not only) in the physical discharge but also in the latent, unconscious content of the underlying wish-fulfilling phantasy. There is no suggestion in his work that unconscious intentions *qua* intentions operated in ways radically different to conscious ones. Indeed, he frequently enjoined the homogeneity of conscious and descriptively unconscious mental types:

> All the categories which we employ to describe conscious mental acts, such as ideas, purposes, resolutions and so on, can be applied to them [unconscious mental acts]. Indeed, we are obliged to say of some of these latent states that the only respect in which they differ from conscious ones is precisely in the absence of consciousness.
>
> (1915e: 168)

In his later, structural model, Freud assimilates hallucinations to phantasy and emphasises the ego's intentional role in their construction (1924b; 1924e). The dream too is described 'as a piece of phantasy working on behalf of the maintenance of sleep' (1923b: 151): the ego responds to disturbing demands by 'what appears to be an act of compliance: it meets the demand with what is in the circumstances a harmless fulfilment of a wish and so gets rid of it' (1940a: 170). This late, undeveloped intentionalism in dream theory remained unreconciled with the earlier reflex arc model of dream formation, though even in the earlier model there were suggestions of intentional process. Freud noticed that dreams could be shaped in response to events in therapy; in particular, disconfirming dreams were produced by patients to frustrate therapeutic developments and an avalanche of dreams, or their drying up altogether, could be used for the purpose of resistance (1911e). The analysand's dreams participate in the analytic dialogue.

In later editions of *The Interpretation of Dreams* Freud included striking examples of intentional control over the shape of the dream (1900a: 570ff):

> ... there are some people who are quite clearly aware during the night that they are asleep and dreaming and who thus seem to possess the faculty of consciously directing their dreams. If, for instance, a dreamer of this kind is dissatisfied with the turn taken by the dream, he can break it off without waking up and start it again in another direction – just as a popular dramatist may under pressure give his play a happier ending.[20]

Finally, consider Freud's remarks on the evocation of hysterical symptoms. He first recognises precipitation by economic and associative factors, but then adds that they can also be evoked

> (3) in the service of the primary purpose – as an expression of the 'flight into illness', when reality becomes distressing or frightening – that is, as a consolation; (4) in the service of the secondary purposes, with which the illness allies itself, as soon as, by producing an attack, the patient can achieve an aim that is useful to him. In the last case the attack is directed at particular individuals, and can be put off till they are present, and it gives an impression of being consciously simulated.
>
> (1909a: 231–2)

The description of neurosis as consoling flight into illness is certainly suggestive of intentional strategy, and it could hardly be plainer that this was his view of the secondary purpose. It is true, as Gardner (1993: 192) points out, that the secondary purpose is preconscious and does not shape the symptom, but this does not alter its unconscious strategic character. The secondary purpose is descriptively unconscious, subject to the potent censorship between the Pcs. and the Cs. systems (Freud 1915e: 196), perhaps permanently inaccessible to the patient, probably running counter to the patient's conscious intentions, and an intentional cause of the precipitation of the symptom.

It seems plain that, at least after the innovations of *The Ego and the Id*, Freud was an intentionalist about much of the psychoanalytic domain, and that he was an intentionalist about some forms of wish-fulfilment even before then. But intentionalism is not an easy doctrine to uphold.

Notes

1 Aristotle recognised a common origin for dreams, the hallucinations of the sick and the illusions of the sane. But unlike many of his contemporaries, he denies that dreams are god-sent: 'if the gods wished to communicate knowledge to men, they would do so in the daytime, and they would choose the recipients more carefully' (Dodds 1951: 1120).

2 Alan Schore writes: 'Psychobiological and neurobiological studies from the last decade or so thus strongly indicate that the concept of drive, devalued over the last 20 years, must be reintroduced as a central construct of psychoanalytic theory' (2003: 198). A similar view is adopted in the work of Mark Solms (Solms and Turnbull 2002) and has

affinities with the affective neuroscience of Jaak Panksepp (Panksepp and Biven 2012) and others.

3   For the model: Freud 1950a: Part I; 1900a: 575ff; 1917d: 234ff; Holt 1989: ch. 4. For a recent elaboration see Carhart-Harris and Friston 2012.

4   That the primary process is a basic postulate of psychoanalysis, recently reaffirmed in Brakel (2009), that this is the a-rational way the Ucs. (and later the id and parts of the unconscious ego) works, may well be true, but it doesn't follow that the process is immune to further analysis, in such terms as we will consider.

5   The dream is often distorted by the primary process, censorship and other factors operating during the dreamwork. Some of that distortion is directly attributable to what Freud refers to as 'mechanical or economic factors'. He principally has condensation in mind (but also, at times, fixed symbolism): 'although condensation makes dreams obscure, it does not give one the impression of being an effect of the dream-censorship. It seems traceable rather to some mechanical or economic factor' (1916–17: 173). The censorship, mainly utilising displacement (1916–17: 174), results in omission, modification, fresh grouping of the material. There is also secondary revision, an attempt to order the material into something coherent. Interestingly, these factors are not included in Freud's discussion of the basic model of hallucinatory gratification; perhaps because Freud considered the censorship and the secondary revision as intentional activities, as actions performed for reasons.

6   William James cites Spinoza as the source. James asks us to consider a new-born mind presented with an imaginary visual impression of a candle:

> What possible sense (for that mind) would a suspicion have that the candle was not real? What would doubt or disbelief imply? When we, the onlooking psychologists, say the candle is unreal, we mean something quite definite, viz., that there is a world known to us which is real, and to which we perceive the candle does not belong … By the hypothesis, however, the mind which sees the candle can spin no such considerations as these about it, for of other facts actual or possible, it has no inkling whatever. The candle is its all, its absolute. Its entire faculty of attention is absorbed by it.
>
> (James 1950, II: 288)

He goes on: 'The world of dreams is our real world whilst we are sleeping because our attention then lapses from the sensible world. Conversely when we are awake the attention usually lapses from the dream world and that becomes unreal' (1950, II: 294).

7   There is continuing debate about the age at which infants can reliably distinguish amongst different mental states, recognise them in others ('mentalisation'), or distinguish between psychic and external reality. See Fonagy et al. (2004, chs. 4–6) for detailed discussion of a range of views. However the timing issue is resolved, it is certain that even in the older infant and adult there are intermittent recurrences of confusion between different Intentional states and inner and outer experience.

8   I use the term in a technical sense to denote that portion of available evidence which an agent *does* accept as evidence irrespective of whether it *should* be accepted; indeed of whether it really is evidence as canonically understood. See **3.2**, especially fn. 2, for further discussion.

9   Ernst Kris relates the following story: 'From a remote country place, where he has passed his life, a farmer comes to town and visits a theatre. The implications of dramatic art are unknown to him. The play is an inspiring one: A great hero is seen at the height of his glory; a group of his alleged friends are threatening to destroy his life and career. They claim that he is usurping the government and planning to violate the constitutional rights of the people - although he has no such intention. The farmer is on the hero's side;

the man's greatness and frankness attract him. At the moment when the conspirators are preparing to murder the hero, the farmer, who cannot bear to see the victory of traitors over the genius, decides to interfere. He gets up from his seat and shouts through the hall: "Look out, they are armed!" And thus the great scene of Casius' first stroke against Caesar is suddenly interrupted.' (Kris 1952: 39–40).

10 The notion of *inner sense* is, of course, philosophically controversial but, as with the notion of *inner world* – that is, of imagination, unconscious phantasy and internal objects – I assume their good credentials here without argument. These concepts are indispensable to psychoanalysis and, in my view, entirely defensible.

11 It seemed evident to James and Freud that attention can be directed to images, dreams and the like. Freud writes of the dream that 'it succeeds in drawing attention to itself and in being noticed by consciousness' (Freud 1900a: 574) and that 'it has been shown that part of the attention which operates during the day continues to be directed towards dreams during the state of sleep' (1900a: 505). Brian O'Shaughnessy maintained that we cannot attend to images and thoughts. All that is mental, he says, is 'necessarily not a possible immediate object of the attention. And does that not seem obviously true? For example: is it not certain that I cannot notice and hence cannot attend to my thoughts and mental images?' (O'Shaughnessy 1980: II, 158). It does not seem obvious to me. There is a sense of *noticing* which is more or less the same as that of *perceiving*, but images can be perceived; how else could we register their presence? Is it that we cannot notice images because their presence is too obvious; or is it because we cannot just realise that they are there, because we are the authors of their being? Perhaps. But even if it were true that I do not notice my images in the way in which I notice you out of the corner of my eye, it doesn't follow that I cannot attend to them, any more than that I couldn't attend to you – because I couldn't notice you (or realise that you were there) – because you were standing in front of me, on my toes. It seems to me that we do notice or realise that we have images, just as we can gradually notice that we are in mental pain, angry or sad, or become aware of a phantasy loitering in the back of our minds.

12 How do we reconcile this with the proposition that the id can only wish? It is interesting to briefly speculate about this. It seems clear that FWT occurs in the unconscious ego or the system Pcs. where attention and engrossment can penetrate. Our conjecture is that attention and engrossment extend only to the edges of the id and do not penetrate it. A wishful phantasy topographically located in the id cannot be an object of engrossment and cannot therefore function as wish-fulfilling. That is why the id can only strive and can find no satisfaction internal to it.

13 Brian O'Shaughnessy writes: 'being one person, we can only really orient ourselves in one direction at a time. This is a tautology. ... [H]ow could one be lost in two activities simultaneously? ... For while one broad river-bed can support two quite distinct rivulets, there can of absolute necessity be but one thinking process supported by a single mind. ... [T]he 'mere difficulty' is not a result of the finite amount of attention available to all of us, but is a direct consequence of the fact that, since each of us is no more than one person, we can be given up wholly to no more than one action at a time' (1980: II, 25–6). It does not seem a tautology to me. I agree that one cannot be *engrossed* in more than one act at a time, though not for the reason that this is a condition of personhood: it is a condition of being engrossed. But it does not follow from the impossibility of being engrossed in more than one act at a time that a person cannot perform more than one mental act at a time. Can't I listen to you while making unconscious assessments of your character? And perhaps it is not quite so plain that 'each of us is no more than one person ... given up wholly to no more than one action at a time' **(5.6–5.7)**.

14 The introduction of the triad of unconscious attention, engrossment and unconscious FWT raises difficulties. In the case of unconscious FWT it would seem that there must be, in some sense, a concurrent presentation of latent content to be the object of

engrossment. The difficulty then is to grasp the sense in which latent content is present in the mind. Freud wondered about the way in which latent dream thoughts attended the mind during dream formation (1900a: 280ff). He was inclined to think that the great bulk of latent dream thoughts *were* present, either before or during the formation of the dream. But the sense in which dream-thoughts were arrayed was left unexplained. Perhaps we could take a cue from Kleinian theory, in which 'unconscious phantasies are ubiquitous and always present in every individual' (Segal 1964: 12). Unconscious phantasies, being ubiquitous and suitably imbricated with conscious thoughts and perceptions, provide the required objects of attention and engrossment. But this still leaves a puzzle about the dispersal of attention. It seems to imply an orientation of conscious and preconscious attention in opposite directions, and is that not absurd? I do not think so. The view would be absurd if it entailed a dispersal of engrossment; if there were engrossment in manifest content and external environment at the same time as engrossment in unconscious phantasies. But we are not committed to such a view. Only a division of attention is required, and there is clinical material, especially relating to states of withdrawal, which strongly suggests that some such dispensation of attention occurs. Engrossment in unconscious phantasy and the partial withdrawal of attention from the external world may account for that peculiar complexion of *distrait* which accompanies aesthetic absorption and hysterical states and certain kinds of daydreaming; the kind of dissociation, perhaps, for which Breuer was prompted to coin the term 'hypnoid' (Freud and Breuer 1895d). It may indeed be a condition of at least certain kinds of withdrawn states that there is concurrent engrossment in an unconscious phantasy together with a restricted awareness of the environment.

15 The role of belief in causing action has attracted much more attention than its role in terminating action. My interest was stimulated by Bertrand Russell's (1921b) work on behaviour cycles.

16 There are other grounds for dispute. R. R. Holt denies that anything as complex as the process of wish-fulfilment can take place in infants: 'without stable objects, in an amorphous world of swirling flux, it is hard to imagine that anything we could call ideation goes on' (1989: 268). Other researchers, he adds, reject 'the possibility of early infantile hallucination on the additional grounds that it implies the capacity to conceive or represent an absent object without some kind of action on it' (1989: 271). More recent studies suggest that the infant's experiential world isn't quite the swirling flux Holt imagines, and that the capacity to cognise and to re-cognise objects appears very early. But they also suggest that the young infant is more attuned to attending to the external world than its internal states and that clear differentiation between such states is a relative latecomer (Stern 1985; Fonagy *et al*. 2004: 219ff, 260ff). Still, a conception of early hallucination that involves *non-volitional* sensory presentations attracting belief − or, expressed in different concepts, the early operation of omnipotent phantasy or psychic equivalence − is not precluded by the empirical data. Moreover, even if the prospects for early infantile hallucinatory gratification are dim, the Freudian form remains a useful concept to illuminate later hallucinatory experience.

17 Fonagy *et al*. 2004 distinguish between the teleological, where reference is made 'to future states (goals) as explanatory entities in the interpretation of behaviour based on the principle of "rational action"' (2004: 33) and the Intentional stance. This is, I think, unfounded, as reflection on their examples quickly shows (2004: 355).

18 The idea that there is a *logical* connection between agents-evidence and belief is congenial to the account of pathology I am developing, as the manufacturing of evidence − through phantasy, enactment − to ground wish-fulfilling beliefs (**3.2**). In some respects the account is similar to McDougall's (1986: 166) view that psychological symptoms are attempts at self-cure: all the neurotic scenarios she describes (1986: 255ff) may be seen as attempts to create evidence for wish-fulfilling conclusions. But even if there is not a

logical connection between agents-evidence and empirical belief, it may *in fact* be that in pathology we try to prove things to ourselves by manufacturing evidence that grounds wish-fulfilling, action-terminating beliefs **(4.1)**.

19 In particular, the causal role of belief requires explication. I agree with Baker exactly when she notes that 'although some philosophers hold that causal explanations explain by citing underlying physical mechanism... intentional [i.e. Intentional] explanations generally do no such thing; explanations that do cite underlying physical mechanisms are a special case, useful in some physical sciences, but by no means exhaustive of causal explanations' (1995: 123) and also that 'Even if beliefs were constituted by brain states it would not be by dint of their being so constituted that they are causally explanatory...' (1995: 136–7). These issues, however, lie beyond our remit.

20 I have many such dreams, and apparently these 'lucid dreams' are quite common. The dream researcher Harry T. Hunt concludes that 'the very existence of lucid dreams... seems to show just that expansion of awareness, increased self-reflectiveness and directed volition that is supposedly impossible in dreaming' (Hunt 1989: 71). Weiss and Sampson (1986) emphasise the intentionalism in Freud's later work. Of dreams they write: 'the dreamer exerts control over his unconscious mental life. He regulates the production of dreams in accordance with the criteria of safety and danger... The ego produces dreams in an attempt to deal adaptively with its problems, including those that arise from the demands on it of the instincts, of conscience, and of current reality. It produces dreams as part of its task of self-preservation' (1986: 117). In fact, that dreams are intended communications to oneself or the analyst, or can be, has been noted by many clinicians in the Freudian and Jungian traditions. Charles Rycroft (1979) quotes Calvin Hall as saying that 'the dream is a letter to oneself'. Well, why send letters to oneself? If the dream is wish-fulfilling then we can see why one might be interested in self-communion: the dream can provide a form of self-consolation. The dream may be likened to an answer to the child's request 'Tell me a story', and may be influenced by that story-telling institution which consoles the child for the impending loss of his objects in sleep. The dream keeps the child – and the adult – in touch with objects, including him or her self, and tries to paint them into gratifying scenarios.

Chapter 3

Problems with non-intentionalism

In his opinion it was perfectly possible to fulfil the desires commonly supposed to be the most difficult to satisfy under normal conditions, and this by the trifling subterfuge of producing a fair imitation of the object of those desires.

Huysmans 1959: 35

3.1 Reprise

In the preceding chapters I argued that the Freudian conception of wish-fulfilment (FWT) differs significantly from the ordinary conception of what it is for a wish to be fulfilled; that there are various forms of FWT distinguished by degrees of intentional involvement and enabling conditions; and that it appears to have been Freud's view that some forms of FWT are brought about intentionally: not only do reasons (as composites of desire and instrumental belief) or executive states such as proximate intention or decision play a role in bringing about the processes or actions partly constituting FWT but, in maximal cases, FWT (or, more broadly, self-solicitude) is itself intended. I argued that Freud did not distinguish carefully amongst the varieties of wish-fulfilment and that he provided only one explicit model for the enabling circumstances in which FWT is achieved, viz. the model of hallucinatory gratification. This model, or a more sophisticated neuroscientific version of it, may be apt for the explanation of some dreaming and primitive hallucination but cannot accommodate the full range of wish-fulfilling phenomena Freud identified – pathological enactments, religiosity, art, and so on. Whether understood in terms of drive discharge or on the Intentional model developed in the previous chapter, the Freudian account of hallucinatory gratification is inadequate as an explanation of the more complex varieties of FWT.

The view that intention plays a role in some forms of FWT I dubbed 'intentionalism', and the view that there are maximal cases of FWT I dubbed 'maximalism'; and evidence was reviewed for believing that Freud was, at least, an intentionalist. Whether or not the evidence for Freud's intentionalism is compelling, I think that intentionalism, and indeed maximalism, is true, and this and following chapters will present reasons for thinking so. However, intentionalism about FWT, as about self-deception and other forms of irrationality, is, as I have said, not easy. Initially the route to intentionalism will be the *via negativa*. I will begin by exposing some general limitations of all non-intentionalist alternatives and then argue against specific details of the most persuasive non-intentionalist accounts known to me. Clearly, this approach is limited. Even if non-intentionalist accounts fail, from that failure intentionalism is only one of several possible conclusions: the futility of the Intentional programme is another. In the absence of a positive, Intentional account of wish-fulfilment, our understanding of agency in psychoanalysis is seriously deficient. A positive account will be developed in **Chapters 4** and **5**.

3.2 Some general problems with non-intentionalism

The favourite non-intentional motive – I use 'motive' loosely to denote anything that motivates action or mental activity – invoked to explain the instigation of FWT is subintentional causation, understood as the causal expression of desire without facilitation by instrumental beliefs or anything else **(1.4)**. Hopkins (1982), Wollheim (1991), Gardner (1993), Johnston (1988), Cavell (1993), Lear (1998), and others consider subintentional explanation as more or less paradigmatic for all psychoanalytic explanation. Hopkins seems to invoke subintentional causation when he describes wish-fulfilment as engendered by 'an exercise of will of a kind prior to that in intentional action' (1982: xxii) and compares it to the activity of imagination. Similarly, Gardner states that '[t]he fundamental idea on which a psychoanalytic extension of ordinary psychology hinges is that of a connection of content, driven by the operation of desire freed from rational constraints' (1993: 229, 88–9). Gardner concedes that in a case history there are 'many [intentional], strategy-suggestive phenomena, some of which are genuinely strategic'. But '[t]he crucial point is that these do not stand at the core of psychoanalytic irrational phenomena…' (191).[1] In **1.4** we saw that there are other non-intentional motives enlisted in the explanation of wish-fulfilment. There are forms of expressive action not involving desire; those, for example, which have an archaeology but no teleology, as when one smiles. And Wollheim (1984; 1993a: 97) identified a group of 'mental activities' which involve desire but, instead of combining with belief to initiate intentional action or operating subintentionally, combine with a 'mechanism' he calls 'instinct' to produce action which is not, or not always, rationalised; that is, performed for and from a reason. There are other variations on this general theme that we will have to address.

On the face of it, the non-intentionalist approaches are advantaged in being able to dispense with the fraught apparatus of unconscious deliberation or practical reasoning, unconscious choice, decision or judgement and the formation of unconscious intentions. They thus resist the 'over-intellectualisation' of the unconscious and the threatened dissociation of mind which, as indicated in **1.5**, such unconscious activity appears to entail. Non-intentionalists can go along with the idea that dreams, symptoms and so on are wish-fulfilments, and recognise that FWT involves the acquisition of wish-fulfilling beliefs. They depart, however, from Freud – Freud as here interpreted – and from ourselves, in denying that the agent has an intentional hand in the acquisition of at least some of those beliefs. In my view, the explanatory scope of these approaches is so restricted as to kill the broader aspiration of rendering wish-fulfilment central to psychoanalytic explanation. They fail also to accommodate the clinical material that is the touchstone of adequacy.

A good place to begin is Mark Johnston's (1988) important attempt at subintentional explanation of self-deception and wishful thinking. Johnston is principally concerned with the threat of homuncularism (second-mind personology) posed by 'over-intellectualised' (intentionalist) accounts of these irrational phenomena. By 'wishful thinking' he means much the same as we mean by 'wish-fulfilment'. He writes:

> The recognition of subintentional mental processes points the way out of the so-called paradoxes of self-deception and avoids an implausible homuncularism. The sub-intentional mental process involved in wishful thinking and self-deception is an instance of a non-accidental mental regularity: anxious desire that p, or more generally anxiety concerning p, generates the belief that p. Deeper morals about the nature of mind emerge from the recognition of such non-accidental, purpose serving mental regularities – mental tropisms, as I shall call them.
>
> (1988: 66)

> The suggestion is then that we should understand wishful thinking, not as the actual or potential outcome of practical reasoning occurring in the unconscious or some homuncular part of the mind, but as a mental mechanism or tropism by which a desire that p and accompanying anxiety that not-p set the conditions for the rewarding (because anxiety reducing) response of coming to believe that p . . . This treatment of wishful thought and, by implication, self-deception as the nonintentional outcome of a mental tropism is a rebuff to those who would represent such phenomena as intentional.
>
> (1988: 73)

Johnston says that tropisms abound: amongst other things he lists 'division, denial, repression, removal of appropriate affect, wishful perception, wishful memory, and wishful thought' (1988: 65). Evidently, Johnston's notion of tropism, subintentional causation under another name, is more ambitious than O'Shaughnessy's original account on which desire may manifest as a 'feeling-like' or 'wanting to', say, move a leg (to a more comfortable position), and such like things. Johnston has a much richer agenda for tropism or anxious desire: it can manufacture beliefs, indeed very complex beliefs. This is a bold proposal going far beyond the claim that anxious desires activate defence mechanisms such as splitting or repression, or the other processes on Johnston's list.

How is anxious desire supposed to create beliefs? Johnston's answer is straightforward: 'This is the way our minds work; anxious desire that p simply leads one to be disposed to believe that p' (1988: 85). This is an unilluminating explanation, but its chief problem is that it is probably false. There seems to be a decisive objection: an agent cannot be disposed to a change in (empirical) belief without an appropriate accommodation in their *accepted* evidence – 'agent's evidence', as I have called it **(2.3)**. That is because (empirical) belief and (agent's) evidence appear to be internally related.[2] If anxious desire is to generate belief it must do so by first creating the 'agent's evidence' which grounds that belief. Johnston is aware of this objection and adopts a heroic measure to circumvent it. He argues that severing the conceptual link between belief and evidence does not materially erode either concept. Call ungrounded belief '"quasi-belief" if you must', he says, 'but recognize its similarity on the output side to the best grounded beliefs' (1988: 73). I think that this claim is contestable a priori, along the following lines. To assert that one believes that *p* (or that one knows that *p*) is to express an implicit presupposition that the assertion is backed by evidence, that there are reasons supporting the belief. The claim that one *believes* that *p*, but for no particular reason or grounds, that one just does, is incoherent. (How could the doxastic condition be distinguished from merely entertaining that *p*?) Even religious beliefs are not exempt from the requirement of implicit grounds – even if they're not remotely plausible. This is one reason, I think, why FWT involves the creation of 'evidence' in phantasy, enactment and symptom.

The argument can be reinforced by clinical example.

> You will find if you get to talk with the exhibitionist, that his purpose in displaying his genitals is not to seduce a woman into making love with him but rather to shock her. If she is upset – is embarrassed, becomes angry, runs away – and especially if she calls the police, he has, he feels, absolute proof that his genitals are important. When you learn that he is likely to exhibit himself following a humiliation earlier in the day, you will be alert to the hostile components he experiences in his excitement. For him, this sexual act serves as a kind of rape – a forced intrusion (at least that is the way he fantasizes it) into the woman's sensibilities and delicacy. If he cannot believe that he has harmed her, the act has failed for him ... His idea – his fantasy – of what is going on includes, then, the following features. He has done something hostile to a woman; he has been the active force, not the passive victim as he was earlier in the day when someone humiliated him. He has converted this trauma to a triumph, capped by his success in becoming sexually excited ... He seems to be running great risks: he may be caught and arrested, his family and job put in jeopardy. But the true danger that perversion is to protect him from – that he is insignificant, unmanly – is not out there on the street but within him and therefore inescapable. It is so fundamental a threat that he is willing to run the lesser risk, that of being caught.
>
> (Stoller 1979: xii)

This man is reeking of 'anxious desire'. Why doesn't anxious desire just install the wish-fulfilling beliefs (that he is important, manly, etc.) and save him from this perilous charade? It is precisely in these 'hot' instances that one would have expected anxious desire to be most active in disposing its subjects to wish-fulfilling beliefs. If tropisms have the capacity to directly create these beliefs then it is extraordinary that they should not do so in a case which cries out for their subvention. But suppose that they *did* subvene. That would have the consequence of depriving this enactment, which is in many ways typical of a significant class of irrational actions in the psychoanalytic domain, of a role in the circuit of motivated wish-fulfilment. *The intervention of tropisms would make such actions as the exhibitionist's superfluous to his wish-fulfilling endeavours.* And this circumstance generalises and raises the question of why there are symptoms at all – or, at least, symptoms other than delusions constituted by quasi-beliefs putatively caused by tropisms. We *know*, however, that such symptoms are not superfluous, even if we don't know exactly how they further those endeavours.[3]

Why does the exhibitionist go through with his performance? Maybe he gets a 'kick' out of it, or something of that sort. But that just raises further questions about why he gets a 'kick' out of such things, what drives him compulsively, and so on. The deeper answer, I suggest, is that he requires evidence (though not of course under the description 'evidence') from which he can conclude that he is manly, triumphant, and so on. There is no short-cut to belief. To effect his wish-fulfilling strategy the evidence of the charade has to be manufactured, even if it hurts. Of course, what he accepts as evidence would hardly be taken as evidence for the truth of his conclusion in the normal course of events – not even by the exhibitionist, if you asked him. It is certainly unobvious how frightening a strange woman by exposing himself can provide efficacious evidence for undoing a humiliation or narcissistic hurt. His actions seem bizarre. However, that appearance can be dispelled by attending to the unconscious significance of his actions, to the 'unconscious evidence', the way his actions are *seen-as* unconsciously **(4.5)**. Then it transpires why a minor humiliation should provoke this sort of exhibition; why the object of aggression generally has to be a woman; why the urge to act seems so irresistible; and so forth. There are good reasons to believe that the underlying humiliation he is trying to undo occurred in his infancy, was inflicted on him probably by his mother or experienced in relation to her, and was most likely at a time when he believed or wished to believe that his penis was a potent instrument (Stoller 1979). The exhibitionist doesn't consciously know it, but – jumping ahead of our argument – his unconscious strategy is to console the humiliated 'child within', himself conceived under a certain aspect, by presenting *it* with the evidence deemed necessary to undo the original humiliation (which is the fundamental meaning of later humiliations); that strategy is caused and rationalised by beliefs and desires preserved from the past **(5.7)**.

This explanation is incomplete, of course, and I harbour no expectations at this stage of converting the sceptics. But whatever the difficulties with this intentionalist account, they should not obscure the obstacle examples such as that of the exhibitionist present for tropistic or other forms of subintentionalism.

The subintentional story can be given a more sophisticated turn that provides a role for wish-fulfilling vehicles – symptoms, enactments and their kin. Perhaps what occurs in such cases is not that anxious desire or tropism subintentionally implants wish-fulfilling beliefs, but that it subintentionally generates symptoms and other vehicles which then serve as agent's evidence for wish-fulfilling beliefs. This is a cogent conception.

> A patient suffered from pain in the lower abdomen. The pain repeated sensations she had felt as a child during an attack of appendicitis. At that time she had been treated with unusual tenderness by her father. The abdominal pain expressed simultaneously a longing for the father's tenderness and a fear that an even more painful operation might follow a fulfilment of this longing.
> (Fenichel 1972: 220)

Accepting the interpretation, we are to imagine the patient's longing for her father's tenderness as capable in some way of causing the abdominal pain which then functions as evidence, as a kind of reminder, of the father's tenderness. This symptom – let's assume it's a hysterical conversion – presents difficulties for intentionalism and invites, on the face of it, something like the tropistic account. In considering the exhibitionist we had no difficulty identifying the action-events which constituted the exhibitionist's enactments. Our problem was to identify unconscious reasons that could rationalise and cause the events as intended symptoms. The exhibitionist unbuttons his raincoat and exhibits himself. When we understand that he wants unconsciously to undo a narcissistic hurt and believes unconsciously that by exposing himself he can do so – or wants and believes things of that sort – and when we are justified in supposing that this belief-desire set was efficacious in bringing about his actions, then we can re-describe them as (unconsciously) undoing or restoring his self-esteem. But in the conversion symptom it is difficult even to identify a candidate for being an action-event. Perhaps then the patient's longing, her desire for father's tenderness, acts directly to produce a painful innervation, through a causal link of the sort that non-intentionalists have posited between desire or emotion and symptom. Recall Dora's symptoms of cough and aphonia **(1.2)**. It is possible to construe Dora's symptoms, used in hysterically identifying with Frau K. and keeping her away from Dora's father, as created through a voluntary pathway, for example constantly clearing her throat, nervous cough, etc. But in the present case it is difficult to see how the abdominal pain can be an intentional action – basic[4] or instrumental. It may be that a subintentional causal pathway to the symptom, as yet unknown, can serve to re-evoke the wish-fulfilling memories of the father's tenderness.

The subintentional story is at its most plausible in this type of case, though even here its advantage over intentional construals is not assured. The mechanisms of hysterical conversion are still obscure (PDM Task Force 2006: 115–19), and it is not evident that the conjectured subintentional mental mechanics are less problematic than possible intentional structures exploiting some unexplored voluntary pathway. The suggestion that desires or wishes directly animate hysterical conversion symptoms still seems problematic, notwithstanding conditioned associations between desire and affective states and certain somatic conditions.

Let us, however, concede this type of case to the non-intentionalists, for the argument above is not decisive and there is no plausible intentionalist alternative to offer. Our aim, however, is not to show that non-intentionalism is empty but that it is insufficient, that its scope is limited. When it comes to the more complex and significant cases of FWT, especially the putatively maximal cases like the exhibitionist, even the more sophisticated non-intentional story founders.

Simple instances of the more complex motivational structures are exemplified in the familiar erotic or masturbatory phantasy. These are usually intentionally crafted products following in their main features personal templates that have a long history of elaboration (Freud 1912a: 99–100; Stoller 1979: ch. 4). The fact that engrossment in such phantasies generates excitement indicates that transitory wish-fulfilling beliefs are also being generated. That is because the significant feature of such activity usually is not the physical but the psychological climax: the phantasy comes to a desired conclusion, and the agent believes it, even if only transiently. The FWT may not be discernible in the manifest content of the phantasy, as it usually is not in the dream or daydream; it may be only the unconscious content which yields its real significance. The agent consciously knows that what is enacted in phantasy is unreal – that deprivation is what animates the FWT in the first place – but circumvents that knowledge in engrossment. The intent in the manifest content of the phantasy is usually perspicuous – to bring about pleasure by imagining a wish-fulfilling scenario, or something like that. But the FWT that supervenes on the phantasy's latent or unconscious content would seem to require either the operation of unconscious intent as the cause of it or, at least, an unconscious understanding or 'reading' of the conscious phantasy that provides unconscious satisfaction in the manner of FWT. In either case subintentional mechanics seems to have no point of application. But the matter is perplexing and calls for more light to be shed (**4.4–4.6**).

Consider again the anxious scientist introduced in **1.5**. At times he has a need to experience the presence of his mother. We do not mean mother in the flesh. Even if she were alive – it is not disclosed whether she is or not – her physical presence is unlikely to allay the grown man's anxiety. The mother he longs for ministers to the infantile needs that persist in him and characterise the distraught 'child within'; the good mother whose representation he can draw upon as an 'internal object', a kind of benign presence. Notice that despite the intensity of his desire to re-experience her presence (to cling to her) no apposite wish-fulfilling belief gets subintentionally inserted into his mind. No anxiety-reducing tropisms abound here. Instead, like the exhibitionist, he has to embark on a complex undertaking which creates the feeling of intense pressure and being nagged at, 'almost hallucinatory in intensity', which unconsciously signifies her presence. There is a heavy price to pay but, as W. R. D. Fairbairn pointed out long ago, even children dreadfully abused by their mothers will cling to them: a bad object, he observed, is better than no object. Notice also that the anxiety and panic that he works himself into is not the product of a single stroke. Instead there probably is endless procrastination, pencil-sharpening... a veritable programme of postponement. In other words, the mother-invoking strategy invades nearly every corner of his life and intentional projects: *a thousand acts pointing in the same direction*. It seems evident that the process of creating the hallucinatory experience of mother, which is the vehicle for the wish-fulfilling belief that she is present, is not just an adventitious consequence of the scientist's procrastinations, but the result of an intentional wish-fulfilling *strategy*. For it seems inconceivable how, on the alternative subintentionalist account, a vast array of subintentional mechanisms or tropisms could be strung together in the service of the one unified purpose. How could subintentional mechanism have come to infect the thousand acts that contrive themselves into the achievement of that purpose?

This is a serious problem for all forms of non-intentionalism. Their incapacity to account for the complexity of this sort of enactment or symptom imposes important limits on their scope, and their difficulties will soon be multiplied. I do not dispute that there are subintentional (and expressive and related) mechanisms or that they may account for primitive phenomena like hallucinatory gratification and perhaps some symptoms (such as the hysterical pain considered above) and defence mechanisms. However, I claim that they cannot explain most of the diverse phenomena considered under the heads of self-deception, *akrasia* and the pathologies encountered in the psychoanalytic clinic.

3.3 More problems for non-intentionalism

I have drawn attention to difficulties with non-intentionalist accounts of wish-fulfilling symptom formation that seek to establish a direct link between desire and wish-fulfilling belief or belief-like states such as the quasi-beliefs proposed by Johnston: they can neither explain the unconscious intentionality (the 'intellectualisation' of mind) that manifestly underlies complex cases of FWT, nor indeed the formation and *role* of the symptom. Subintentional accounts such as these render the symptom superfluous. Moreover, I have indicated that the conceptions of *unconscious intention* and *deliberation* may prove indispensable for an account of FWT that does not exclude the complex cases: denying that the complex cases are instances of FWT is, of course, one option, adopted for instance by Gardner (1993) **(3.8)**. The conceptions of unconscious intention and deliberation will be examined and put to good use in the next chapter. But first we turn a critical eye to some other non-intentionalist accounts accepting the broadly Intentional programme for psychoanalytic explanation. Later we turn to accounts of psychopathology that reject Intentional characterisation entirely or in part.

3.4 Wish-fulfilment without belief

Sebastian Gardner's (1993) original project to provide an essentially Intentional or common-sense psychological but non-intentional metapsychology for psychoanalysis is one of the most detailed and rigorous attempts to have emerged, and I will describe it in some detail. In this account, infantile hallucinatory wish-fulfilment and dreaming are presented as paradigms of wish-fulfilment (1993:120); it is unclear whether they are intended to exhaust it. It is important for Gardner's project to distinguish propositional attitudes, intentional action and rational (reason-giving) explanation, on the one hand, from what he refers to as 'psychoanalytic states' (unconscious wish and phantasy), 'activity' and non-rational modes of explanation, on the other. Gardner contends that psychoanalytic states are pre-propositional: they 'are not to be thought of as sub-classes of non-psychoanalytic states – they are not species of beliefs and desires, or combinations of such – for their associated way of mental processing differs fundamentally from that of the propositional attitudes' (1993: 116). The pre-propositional states, he claims, link causally but non-rationally with other mental states and action in ways represented, but undeveloped, in common-sense psychology. It follows that there is a 'radical heterogeneity' between unconscious and conscious motives, on which Gardner insists for a variety of reasons (1993: 111, 153–6): conscious motives (desires, beliefs) are governed by holistic constraints – concepts and propositions have meaning or content only within a network of rationally connected concepts and propositions – and are linked essentially to language; unconscious motives or psychoanalytic states, on the other hand, are not so governed and link to infancy, the pre-linguistic (1993: 154–5) **(2.4)**. Gardner's chief concern is that if there were unconscious propositional attitudes, and therefore unconscious rational causation, that would entail unconscious intentional action and strategy, which in turn threatens an intolerable sub-systemic or 'second-mind' personology; something he believes he can thoroughly discredit (1993: 76–7, 114). Gardner knows that Freud specifically enjoined the homogeneity of unconscious and conscious mental states **(2.6)** but explicitly rejects this fundamental claim. Homogeneity, he argues, tempts rational explanation, but rational explanation is marginal to psychoanalysis. The familiar rational or belief–desire model cannot account for the operation of hallucinatory wish-fulfilment, or defences like repression, the formation of neurotic symptoms or 'acting-out', by which Gardner means enactment or action symptoms such as compulsive acts.[5]

According to Gardner, then, unconscious wishes and phantasies are not propositional attitudes but are better figured as 'Inner Pictures' or unconscious mental images (1993: 156). Moreover, psychoanalysis forces us to recognise that there are two types of agency or exercises of the will: *action* and *activity*. Activity is 'due to desire's *giving expression to its intrinsic tendency to cause the realisation of its conditions of satisfaction*'(1993: 118); it is short of intentional action but more than brute sub-rational association, which is best explained at the sub-personal level. For Gardner the notion of 'the operation of desire freed from rational constraints' is crucial (1993: 229; 88–9). Most 'psychoanalytic phenomena' can only be explained as such activity or the effects of activity: psychoanalytic explanation is not modelled on the practical syllogism but is essentially subintentional (1993: 186–9).

Now, can activity or subintentional causation, construed as a direct relation between (pre-propositional) wish and the representation of its fulfilment, explain processes like the dream or infantile hallucinatory wish-fulfilment? I think that some of these processes must indeed be construed subintentionally – but not in

Gardner's fashion. On his construction – presented as an exposition of Freud's view – the wish directly causes a representation of its object; this representation is a sensory or imaginative experience that subsequently brings about a 'subjective event', an 'experiential registration of satisfaction'; *this* experience then 'puts the feeling of need in abeyance, and terminates the subject's action disposition to fulfil the goal set by its motivational state' (1993: 125). Wish-fulfilment and rational satisfaction are both held to involve an experiential registration of satisfaction, but the latter is more complex: there, the registration of satisfaction is preceded and in part caused by the belief that the relevant action has been performed, and it is followed by the belief that the desire prompting the action is satisfied. However, on Gardner's account belief can play no role in the allegedly pre-propositional process of hallucinatory wish-fulfilment. How, then, does the 'wish-fulfilling representation' cause the registration of satisfaction and the consequent cessation of wishing? Gardner's answer is that 'a sensory experience takes over the causal role' of the beliefs operative in rational satisfaction: the 'simplest assumption' is that 'in wish-fulfilment, the experiential registration [of satisfaction] is the direct effect of a sensory experience, and that, once it [i.e. the registration of satisfaction] has been produced, the cessation of trying and temporary abeyance of the action-disposition follow…' (1993: 125).

Against the backdrop of Freud's exploration of hallucinatory wish-fulfilment and dream formation **(2.3)** we can discern conclusive objections to this spare reconstruction. The first observes that the alleged event of the experiential registration of satisfaction crucial to this account, whilst it is conceivable in some infantile hallucination, is *absent* in the dream and most related wish-fulfilling activity. The reconstruction therefore leaves wish-fulfilment in the dream, and many of its kin, unexplained – a serious matter in this line of things. On reflection it is evident that the *experience of satisfaction* referred to by Freud in the key passage (reproduced in **2.3**) on which Gardner has erected his account is only a contingency attaching to a suitable perception in the special case Freud is there examining, the hungry baby's situation (cf. Freud 1950a: 318). That an experience or registration of satisfaction cannot be essential, even in hallucinatory wish-fulfilment, is especially evident in its clinically significant *negative* forms, such as the denial or hallucinating away of persecutory objects (Klein 1975b: 64–5). In such instances the experience of satisfaction can have no representational content whatever if the denial is to succeed, but an experience of satisfaction without representational content is, for all but perhaps the most primitive cases, incoherent. As regards dreams, Freud nowhere states that they involve an experiential registration of satisfaction (something quite different from the representation of the wish being satisfied), and indeed most do not, though some, of course, may be pleasant. Freud takes (successful) dreams to be experiences to 'which we attach complete belief' (1900a: 50; 535), and belief to suffice for termination or pacification. Gardner's pre-propositional account, unlike Freud's, is fatally restricted. In endeavouring to make do without belief it leans upon a phenomenology of satisfaction untypical of FWT.[6]

The second objection concerns the alleged causal connections between the 'wish-fulfilling representation' (better: the representation of the wish being fulfilled or of the object that would fulfil the wish), the putative registration of satisfaction, and wish-fulfilment. Even if there *are* experiences of satisfaction, as Gardner's account proposes, we are owed an explanation of how *representations* of wish-fulfilment can generate them and how they produce wish-fulfilment. As we saw **(2.4)**, Freud distinguished between wishful phantasy – the representation of the wish fulfilled – and *real* wish-fulfilment involving termination (Freud 1917d: 231). This distinction underlies those between delusional thoughts and delusional beliefs; wishful phantasy and wish-fulfilling phantasy; phantasy and omnipotent phantasy. Between these pairs there is a gap that Freud bridged by invoking *belief*: merely having a wishful phantasy does not pacify in the way that 'believing it to be real' does. But having prescribed an austere pre-propositional framework for psychoanalysis, Gardner is unable to provide the materials for spanning this gap.

The passage from the production of a wishful representation to the alleged experience of satisfaction, and thence to wish-fulfilment, requires explanation. It may be thought that at least the latter passage from the putative experience of satisfaction to wish-fulfilment is unproblematic. It is not. To see this, suppose that our friend is thirsty and wishes to drink. Then she is injected with a substance that terminates her thirst and provides an experience of satisfaction. Her thirst will have been quenched and she will be satisfied – but has her wish to drink been fulfilled? No, it was *relinquished*, but not fulfilled.

3.5 Wish-fulfilment and 'belief-like' representations

In early articles, Jim Hopkins (1982, 1988) held that it was sufficient for wish-fulfilment that a wish cause a representation of the wish fulfilled (or being fulfilled, or the wished-for object). In later articles Hopkins (1994, 1995) recognises that FWT requires not just the representation of a wish fulfilled but its temporary termination (or, in his term, pacification). Freudian wish-fulfilment is 'a form of wishful thinking or imagining, in which a wish or desire causes an imaginative representation of its fulfilment, which is experience- or belief-like' and yields 'pacification without satisfaction' (1995: 461, 471).[7] Belief, in this view, is a limiting case of experience- or belief-like representation (or *b-rep*, for short). Condensed into a formula, Freudian wish-fulfilment was expressed as follows:

> A's desire that P -[causes]→ A's b-rep that P -[causes]→ A's desire that P is pacified.
>
> (1995: 472)

In a recent paper Hopkins unpacks the account of b-reps.[8] In action caused by wishing to drink, we have:

> A des P [A drinks] → P [A drinks] → A experiences, believes P [A drinks] → A's des P pacified.

And in the dream:

> A des P [A drinks] → A dream-exps, bels P [A drinks] → A des P temporarily pacified

And in (one of the Ratman's compulsive) symptoms:

> A des P [A's father tortured] → A imaginarily exps, bels P [A's father tortured] → A's des P temporarily pacified.

Notice that in these instances pacification does not rest, as in Gardner's construction, upon a supposed 'experiential registration of satisfaction', an affective experience caused by the perception of satisfaction, but on the actual experience of the desire being satisfied in the case of action, and on dream and imaginative experiences (or perceptions) in the other cases. Even so, I think that the strategy of introducing these commodious disjunctions, in which representations like dreams and symptoms function as b-reps, as intrinsically pacifying entities, cannot succeed – except in the case where belief is the limiting case.[9] It may be possible to provide just enough of the argument to indicate why this is so. B-reps, on Hopkins' account, are radically disparate. The class is intended to include fully-fledged beliefs, quasi-beliefs, dream-beliefs, imaginal representations and experiences. Plainly, I have no quarrel with the notion that fully-fledged beliefs and dream-beliefs (which in my view are genuine but transient beliefs) can pacify desire. But this species of b-rep is precluded from a story of wish-fulfilment in which b-reps are directly caused by desires: producing fully-fledged belief in the absence of a concurrent accommodation in (agent's) evidence is something that desire cannot directly do, or so we have argued (3.2). The conceptual credentials of a *kind of empirical belief* unsecured in relevant evidence, and therefore potentially in conflict with evidence accepted as such by its owner, are dubious at best. That's why concepts of attenuated belief like *quasi-belief* were invented. Quasi-beliefs are supposed to have the convenient properties of being pacific, of bearing no conceptual ties to relevant evidence, and of being potentially the direct effects of desires. But, as we saw above, if quasi-beliefs could be manufactured as envisaged, they would leave us wondering why patients bothered to produce symptoms in the first place. They would obviate the very processes they are invoked to explain.

So we turn to b-reps as terminating imaginative representations and experiences, such as dreams, phantasies and symptoms. Such experiences are phenomenologically nothing like beliefs or quasi-beliefs. Beliefs and quasi-beliefs do not have a phenomenology[10], though of course states associated with them such as pleasure or terror do. The similarity which qualifies imaginal or experience-like things as b-reps presumably must therefore be a similarity in causal powers, such as the capacity to pacify wishes, terminate action or generate further beliefs. But then the onus remains, as it did on Gardner's account, to explain just how such representations can have these convenient, *intrinsic* belief-like powers: otherwise the conspicuous gap between wishful representation and wish-fulfilment simply remains unbridged.

The concept of *belief-like representation* embraces the benefits of *belief* without wanting to pay the costs.

We are driven to conclude that the conception of b-rep does not advance our understanding of wish-fulfilment. This is because the b-reps which are imaginal or experience-like cannot by themselves deliver pacification, and the b-reps which are merely belief-like – without experiential content – leave unilluminated what most needs to be illuminated: the role of dream, symptom and their congeners in the cycle of wish-fulfilment.[11]

3.6 Increasing complexity: enactment

These attempts to explain the mechanics of primitive wish-fulfilment are neither faithful to Freud's richer account nor successful. Yet the same austere, non-intentional machinery is pressed into service when it comes to the more complex cases of wish-fulfilment, those in which, *prima facie*, intention is manifest or projected into action.

Consider Freud's patient, 'the table-cloth lady' (1916–17: 261–4; 1907b). Several times a day she would rush from one room to another, stand by a particular table with a stained table-cloth, adjust it, ring for the maid, ensure that the maid saw the stain, and then send her away. This behaviour was inexplicable until she recalled some events of her wedding night. Her husband had been impotent and rushed many times from his room to hers, without success. In the end, in an attempt to conceal his shame from the hotel staff, he stained the nuptial bed sheet with red ink, though in the wrong place. The recollection made the lady's obsessive enactment-symptom intelligible. It could now be seen as a kind of pantomimic undoing or correction of the wedding night, in which (on one plausible interpretation) she identified with her husband, and the maid was cast in the role of confirming witness: he was *not* impotent, he had no need to be ashamed: 'It represented this wish, in the manner of a dream, as fulfilled in the present day action; it served the purpose of making her husband superior to his past mishap' (1916–17: 263).

In an early consideration of the case, Hopkins (1982: xxivff) argued that although it is natural to assume that behaviour like the table-cloth lady's can be explained on the pattern of intentional action, it is implausible to do so. The overriding difficulty he identified is the (apparent) impossibility of locating credible instrumental beliefs that can yield, together with the lady's wishes, a practical syllogism whose conclusion is the obsessive action-symptom. Could she believe, for example, that her enactment can undo the past, or make her husband potent, or get herself or the maid to believe that he is? Without some such instrumental belief there can be, on the standard account, no reason that can cause and rationalise her action. Intentional actions are performed for and from a reason, but here there appears to be no credible reason articulated as the premises of a practical syllogism for the lady's behaviour. The solution, according to Hopkins, is to see that wish-fulfilment in such a case is achieved not on the pattern of the practical syllogism, but through the non-intentional activity of imagination producing representations of gratified desire (1982: xxv; Cavell 1993: ch. 9).

> Wish-fulfilment may seem most like action where it is effected by bodily or intentional activity… Someone may indeed imagine himself to be performing one kind of action [vindicating husband] by actually performing another [showing maid spot]; his imagining, that is, may consist partly in his doing something which symbolises, resembles, or otherwise represents (to him) what he imagines doing. That imagining may govern someone's intentional actions in this way, however, does not show that the imagining itself is intentional. Characteristically, it seems, the action will be intentional but the imagining not. This is because imaginative activity seems not to be governed by belief and desire in the way intentional action is.

There seem to be at least two ways of understanding this passage as it applies to our example. On the weaker reading, the lady's performance, under the description of calling the maid etc., is intentional and, given the various symbolic correspondences between components of the performance and the relevant events of the wedding night, she comes unconsciously to imagine – perhaps to believe – that her husband has been vindicated. On this interpretation the imagining and the consequent fulfilment of her wish supervene on an intentional performance. Before raising an objection to this account, let's notice some of the case's formidable complexity.

Notice that the example involves an indirect or symbolic fulfilment of an unconscious wish. The table, the stain, the maid are stand-ins for the *mise-en-scene* of the wedding night. How is that symbolic fulfilment achieved? To sharpen this question it may help to first define indirect or symbolic wish-fulfilment by briefly contrasting it with two other vicissitudes of wish or instinctual drive with which it is sometimes confused. Freud was aware that wishes could be relinquished and replaced by others in such a way as to satisfy their subject without providing wish-fulfilment. He refers on occasion to the *plasticity of instinct*: 'the sexual instinctual impulses in particular are extraordinarily *plastic*, if I may so express it. One of them can take the place of another, one of them can take over another's intensity; if the satisfaction of one of them is frustrated by reality, the satisfaction of another can afford complete compensation' (1916–17: 344). Sometimes a desire for a Drumstick (a kind of ice-cream) has to be relinquished and you make do with a Cornetto (very much like a Drumstick). Were this an instance of wish-fulfilment, then the original desire for the Drumstick would have to be pacified. But that need not happen for you to be satisfied, and it is not entailed in the plasticity Freud describes. Nor is symbolic wish-fulfilment the same as *sublimation*. In an early formulation Freud describes sublimation of libido as consisting 'in the sexual trend abandoning its aim of obtaining a component or reproductive pleasure and taking on another which is related genetically to the abandoned one but is itself no longer sexual and must be described as social' (1916–17: 345). In this process the originary wish is neither relinquished nor fulfilled, but transformed. In successful sublimation the resulting wishes do not retain the significance of the older ones: the new activity is not a *symbol* for the older one; the meaning connection is broken altogether and the originary wishes are not being pacified.[12] (Symbolism is discussed further in **4.5**.)

In contrast to these two vicissitudes, in symbolic wish-fulfilment the originary wish is neither relinquished nor transformed, but fulfilled in the manner of FWT, which entails its being pacified. So the question now is: how can the maid-fetching performance, conceived 'in the manner of a dream' as symbolic or disguised imaginative representation, fulfil in this way the lady's more or less unconscious originary wish that her husband be vindicated?[13] If we take the view that the symptom is wish-fulfilling merely by virtue of it being a wishful representation (Hopkins 1982: xxi) then the answer appears straightforward: the enactment is a disguised symbolic wishful representation of the undoing of the events of the wedding night. But that view of wish-fulfilment has been shown to be mistaken, for representation alone, as repeatedly stressed, does not suffice for pacification and, therefore, for Freudian wish-fulfilment. In the present example we need to understand not just how the symbolic representation of the lady's originary wish is constructed, but how that wish is pacified. Insisting that the performance is belief-like, a b-rep, won't rescue this account – for the reasons affirmed above, but also because if there is to be pacification of the originary wish, if *that* wish is to be caused to cease to operate temporarily, then the performance-as-belief-like-representation must somehow be understood by the lady as the state of affairs which is the satisfying condition of the wish. It must be for the lady *as if her husband had been vindicated*, a complex mental state that would seem to involve at least an *unconscious belief* that he *had* been vindicated (or was potent, or whatever). Without supplementation by some such notion of unconscious understanding (of symbolic relations), or *seeing-as* (**4.5**), it is quite mysterious how the performance symptom could acquire its pacific powers.

I think that *with* such supplementation (which may be implied in the passage under consideration) we do arrive at a form of wish-fulfilment – the lady does something: it is seen or understood unconsciously as a wished-for state of affairs, the undoing of the wedding-night debacle, which then pacifies her wish. But even so the account remains deficient, for the wish-fulfilment is adventitious: the lady does something which happens in the circumstances to pacify an unconscious wish. What we do not yet have is an understanding of why she did what she did. But clearly both Hopkins and Freud believe that the wish-fulfilment in a case like this is more than adventitious in the described sense.

So we abandon this account and turn to the second, stronger reading of Hopkins' passage. Hopkins in fact says more than that wish-fulfilling imagination supervenes on the performance; he says that the imagining *governs* the performance, and the kind of imagining appropriate here is (subintentional) expression of desire. The performance – the symptom – is conceived as a product of desire expressing itself subintentionally in plastic imagination. On this account we have the requisite causal link between the lady's wish and her action, but also an insurmountable difficulty. Although an action-event may be intentional under some descriptions and not others, it cannot be intentional under a description and *also* be caused subintentionally. This much seems clear about intentional action: it is action performed for and from a reason, standardly understood as a belief–desire pair.[14] Subintentional action is caused by desire, understood in a broad sense, alone. Subintentional causation brutely precludes intentionality: for if a putative example of a subintentional action-event were re-describable as intentional, and therefore as having a reason or intention amongst its causal conditions, it would not be subintentional. So if the performance *is* the imagining, and if the imagining is subintentional, the product of 'an exercise of will of a kind prior to that in intentional action' (1982: xxiv), then the performance cannot be intentional. But the performance seems to be intended and, as the passage makes clear, Hopkins thinks that it is.

3.7 The omnipotence of thought

Can a different conception of imagination, or a different, deeper conception of wish-fulfilment, rescue Freud's wish-fulfilment thesis? Richard Wollheim (1991: xxixff; 1993: 99ff) classified a number of ways in which Freud deepened and elaborated the standard explanatory schemas for action that I summarised in **1.4**.

Can any of these explanatory models (other than the subintentional one) shed light on the table-cloth lady's enactments? In the 'displaced action' model a desire and belief jointly rationalise some action but that action is not what the person does; instead another action, reached by a chain of association, is performed. Wollheim's example is from an episode in the Ratman's life (Freud 1909d). The Ratman wishes to kill a rival, Dick, but instead of homicide embarks on a furious programme of exercise to lose weight or fat – 'Dick' in German. He has a motive to kill Dick but his behaviour is transposed into the physical exercise, a symbolic killing (Wollheim 1991: xxxi, 90–1). Wollheim leaves it open whether the latter is an action *tout court* – that is, is intentional. And he seems to hold that the Ratman would not actually think of himself – at any level – as killing Dick (1991: 90). But if this is so, then for reasons already considered, it is difficult to see how the displaced action could pacify the Ratman's originary wish and be wish-fulfilling, though this is a characteristic which Wollheim would wish to preserve. It is difficult to see how the unconscious originary wish could be fulfilled if he does not think of his action at least unconsciously as providing conditions satisfying his wish.

Perhaps one of the other models may circumvent this difficulty. Much that Wollheim says – about the links between expression, acting-out and wish-fulfilment – suggests that he would classify such cases as the table-cloth lady's performance as examples of *expressive action*. Expression, as Wollheim conceives it, is the result of desire operating without facilitation by belief or instinct; it is a mode of subintentional agency, a kind of eruption of desire 'indicative of what moves the person'. It is responsible for producing dreams, some parapraxes and neurotic symptoms, and acting-out (1991: xxxv). Expression, in this scheme, covers a broad range of behaviour, not all of it wish-fulfilling. But Wollheim's conception is different to the subintentional cases considered so far in that expression's capacity to produce wish-fulfilment is not intrinsic to it but depends (as may displaced action) on a special condition of the mind functioning in omnipotent mode.

The notion of omnipotent functioning undergoes evolution over time in Wollheim's thought and I will consider only some phases of it. In a creative paper, Wollheim (1979) recalls a neglected strand in Freud's thinking about the power of wishes. This strand subtends from Freud's account of 'the omnipotence of thought' (Freud 1909d; 1912–13). It is not entirely clear whether Wollheim conceives of the omnipotence of thought as supplementing or as undergirding FWT (1979: 54–5).[15] The latter reading, on which FWT is explained by the omnipotence of thought – and, later, elaborated in the context of a 'corporeal' or 'archaic theory of mind' (1984, 1993) – is vulnerable to criticism in ways that the first is not. Here I consider only the reading on which the omnipotence of thought is taken as more basic than, as explaining, FWT.

Freud had observed that certain patients imputed to their thoughts and wishes exaggerated powers and efficacy. If the Ratman

> thought of someone, he would be sure to meet that very person immediately afterwards, as though by magic. If he suddenly asked after the health of an acquaintance whom he had not seen in a long time, he would hear that he had just died, so that it would look as though a telepathic message had arrived from him. If, without any really serious intention, he swore at some stranger, he might be sure that the man would die soon afterwards…
>
> (Freud 1912–13: 86–7)

Freud linked this disposition to the magical thinking of children and 'primitive man', and gave it a name: 'the principle of the omnipotence of thought' (1912–13: 85). The person governed by this principle is best understood, Wollheim suggests, as subscribing to a primitive theory or as holding a belief: *if I think (imagine, wish, believe) that* p, *then* p. In a mind so affected, imagination does not function as imagination; instead 'the person believes that what he imagines is also real' (1979: 56). Wollheim states that the holding of such a belief can explain wish-fulfilment as a systematic phenomenon. At least part of what this seems to mean is that in a mind operating under the impression of the omnipotent belief, the passage from 'I wish (imagine) that p' to '(I believe) that p' is systematically facilitated: wishing that p becomes inseparable from believing that p. But then, 'How does the person come by such a useful belief?' (1979: 56). Wollheim, like Freud, links the provenance of the belief to narcissism. Freud wrote:

> Primitive men and neurotics, as we have seen, attach a high valuation – in our eyes an over-valuation – to psychical acts. This attitude may plausibly be brought into relation with narcissism and regarded as an essential component of it. It may be said that in primitive men the process of thinking is still to a great extent sexualized. This is the origin of their belief in the omnipotence of thoughts.
>
> (Freud 1912–13: 89)

Wollheim glosses the idea in this passage as follows:

> The infant or primitive man – or, we must add, regressive man – is led by
> the theory he embraces to think of his thoughts as some part of his body or,
> again, of his thinking as a particular piece of bodily functioning, and this concep-
> tualisation provides us with the explanation of such a person's belief in the omnip-
> otence of thoughts. For as he comes to attach, in accordance with developmental
> norms, an exaggerated efficacy to this part of the body or to that particular piece
> of bodily functioning, so he will correspondingly overvalue the psychic phe-
> nomena he has equated with them. So, for instance, in *Totem and Taboo* Freud says
> that primitive man sexualises his thoughts, by which I take him to mean that for
> primitive man not only is thinking an object of sexual attention, it is also a form
> of sexual activity: and if he assigns unreal powers to his thoughts, it is because he
> has already assigned similar powers to his sexual activity.
>
> (Wollheim 1979: 57)

There are difficulties with this exposition, whether as a reconstruction of Freud's
thinking about the omnipotence of thought or as an independent derivation of
the principle of the omnipotence of thought. The two issues can be considered
together. Wollheim's exposition turns on a transition from the idealisation of
bodily, sexual activity, which he says is a developmental given, through to the
equation of this idealised activity with thought, to the resulting idealisation of
thought. Now, Freud certainly recognised that thought can be 'equated' with
physical and sexual processes: that it can become sexualised or idealised, and consequently assigned unreal powers. It is much less certain, however, whether in his
view the sexualisation or overvaluation of thought is always or even typically
effected through its equation with bodily, sexual activity. By the sexualisation of
thought Freud meant that it is hypercathected with libido; alternatively, that it
acquires the significance of bodily, sexual activity. Neither outcome (nor the one
outcome described differently) presupposes that sexualisation is arrived at through
the identification of thought with sexual activity, though such identification is
conceivably *one* path to sexualisation. (For X, 'a' can have the symbolic significance of 'b' without X believing that 'a=b'.) Indeed, it seems a precarious advance
to try to explain the sexualisation and consequent omnipotence of thought in this
way, for if there is a problem with the omnipotence of thought there is a larger
problem with the omnipotence of bodily, sexual activity. Whence the exaggerated efficacy assigned by the infant or primitive man to this activity? This claim
about the exaggeration of bodily powers is the first step in Wollheim's explanation, but left unexplained by him. It is no explanation of this idealisation to baldly
assert that it is in accord with developmental norms, for precisely that development is part of what we wish to understand. Freud is able to explain the idealisation, but only because he seems to have held something like the reverse of
Wollheim's assumption that narcissistic investment in bodily activity precedes

such investment in psychic processes. Expounding magic performance and play as 'motor hallucination', Freud writes:

> If children and primitive men find play and imitative representation enough for them... [it] is the easily understandable result of the paramount virtue they ascribe to their wishes, of the will that is associated with these wishes and of the methods by which these wishes operate. As time goes on, the psychological accent shifts from the *motives* for the magical act on to the *measures* by which it is carried out. ... It thus comes to appear as though it is the magical act itself which, owing to its similarity with the desired result, alone determines the occurrence of that result.
>
> (1912–13: 84)

It is largely because child and primitive man *wish* that their play and magical gestures be powerful that they come to believe that they are, and this explanation spreads to other idealised sexual or bodily activities. In other words, for Freud the omnipotence of bodily or sexual activity supervenes on the omnipotence of thought – of wishes (Freud 1909d: 235, n. 1) – not the other way round. But now the question re-emerges: how does child, primitive and regressed man arrive at the 'immense belief in the power of his wishes' (1912–13: 83)? Contrary to Wollheim's view, Freud provides no detailed answer to this question. But the most natural supposition, that the belief emerges from the *experience of omnipotence*, beginning with that of hallucinatory wish-fulfilment, was articulated by Sandor Ferenczi (1956: 219) in a way which is consistent with the few hints provided earlier by Freud.[16] Ferenczi delineated overlapping developmental stages, each with its own confirming experiences. He describes a period of pre-natal omnipotence when all the organism's needs are met unconditionally; a period of magical hallucinatory omnipotence which is supported by close nursing; a period of magic gestures when the infant controls the nurse, first with uncoordinated and later with intentional gestures; a period of magic thoughts and words to which the nurse responds; and so on. On this account, the experiences from (a conjectural) period of pre-natal plenitude and hallucinatory wish-fulfilment, to the later interactions between infant and responsive care-taking environment, engender and confirm the belief in the omnipotence of wish, gesture, bodily activity and, eventually, language. Almost from the first, however, there is the wish, and each later development in omnipotence – or, rather, the illusion of it – both supervenes on and confirms its power. If this is correct, then the idealisation of thought through its identification with idealised bodily activity, as described by Wollheim, is only a late-coming, subsidiary process. It therefore cannot explain the omnipotence of thought and underpin wish-fulfilment. Omnipotent thinking could not get purchase on a mind which had no consolidated experience of its wishes being fulfilled in reality and by way of FWT.[17]

Wollheim's reconstruction of the principle of the omnipotence of thought as the operation of an 'omnipotent belief' is neither a sustainable exegesis of Freud's thinking nor a viable, independent account of the genesis of wish-fulfilment. Indeed, it is striking that Freud nowhere explicitly states that the omnipotence of thought leads to wish-fulfilment, and it would be remarkable if so potent a connection could have entirely escaped him. For Freud, the omnipotence of thought has, in the main, quite different effects: generating not pacifying wish-fulfilment in the way of the dream or hallucination, but fears and expectations concerning the eventuality of *real* fulfilment, as a glance at the Ratman's anxieties will confirm. When the Ratman thinks, wishes, that someone will die, it is not for him as if that person *has* died; rather, he fears that the person *will* die (1909: 226, 234).[18]

3.8 Wish-fulfilment restricted

In this chapter I have been endeavouring to refute some prominent non-intentionalist accounts of FWT by arguing, in the main, that they are inadequate to the clinical material. But why accept that symptoms (or their kin) *are* wish-fulfilling at all, let alone in the way I have indicated as vehicles of wish-fulfilment – phantasy, dream, symptom – manufactured by the agent, intentionally or not, and functioning – in the maximal cases, intended to function – as (agent's) evidence for wish-fulfilling beliefs? If they, or a large compartment of them, turned out not to be wish-fulfilling, that would hugely simplify matters: it would disburden any account of the relevant compartment of the obligation to explain the refractory feature of pacification, indeed of representation, and obviate the difficulties of second-mind personology. That would of course detach these phenomena from essential Freudian conceptions with which they are theoretically imbricated, but that would scarcely be regretted in many quarters.

Perhaps the net has been cast too far. This is the line Sebastian Gardner takes. When psychoanalysis needs to explain what appear, at least *prima facie*, to be intentional actions then wish-fulfilment is superseded (1993: 140–1, 172) and we must employ phantasy, which 'differs from wish-fulfilment in having the power to manifest itself in intentional action' (1993: 141). Phantasy is defined as 'a non-accidentally inaccessible state, in which the world is represented in conformity with the demands of motivational states and which receives expression in behaviour' (1993: 141).[19] Although there are suggestions in his text that symptoms involving what Gardner refers to as 'acting-out' are wish-fulfilling expressions of desire (1993: 171), and although he states that phantasy 'plays a broadly wish-fulfilling role, as if it were a circuitous form of wish-fulfilment' (1993: 152), his considered view is that 'phantasy cannot be reduced to wish-fulfilment' (1993: 145) and is in fact 'a new theoretical concept' whose introduction is required to obviate the relapse of psychoanalytic explanation into a 'form of belief-desire-and-preference psychology' (1993: 151). To repeat, jettisoning the supposition of wish-fulfilment would disburden any such account of the obligation to explain the refractory feature of pacification and representation. Symptoms largely explicable in terms of phantasy's properties need not be regarded as wish-fulfilling compromises or substitutive satisfactions. So it would seem.

Gardner proposes the following 'non-strategic' analysis of the table-cloth lady's complaint, where 'p' stands for something like 'that her husband not be (or seen to be) impotent' or 'making her husband superior to his past mishap':

desire for p → wish + phantasy that p → acting-out of phantasy that p'.

(1993: 170)

> The analysis... has several components, which are not assembled to form a practical syllogism or strategy. There is, first, a phantastic modification motivated by a wish, of the woman's painful nuptial memory; second, a relation of unconscious seeing-as between the maid and a phantasied witness of her identification with her husband's sexual potency; and, third, an intention directed towards a real person, the woman's present maid, to get her into the room.
>
> (1993: 170)

What is the causal connection between the wishful phantasy and the performance? (Gardner's formula may have been clearer if a causal arrow had been inserted between 'the wish that p' and 'the phantasy that p' – see 1993: 152 – and if he had noted the presumed regression of the initial desire to a wish, but the general picture is plain enough.) If the *whole* performance were the immediate subintentional plastic expression of the phantasy then, as we have maintained, there can be no description under which the performance is intentional. However, this account appears to avoid that pitfall. The performance is divided into two parts, and in the second part the wishful phantasy is conceived to generate an intervening intention to call the maid, on which the lady acts. So two questions arise: (a) What is the relation of the phantasy to the first part of the lady's performance, rushing from one room to another, standing by the table, arranging the stained cloth: does the phantasy motivate that performance or in some sense constitute it? And (b) how does the phantasy generate the intention to ring for the maid?

Take the second part of the performance, the intentional summons to the maid, first. Gardner says that phantasies are 'pre-propositional' and have 'content whose description requires concepts which the subject need not possess, or exercise, in order to have those contents' (1993: 155). He likens them to pictorial representations and 'the relation between phantastic and propositional thought to that between images and discursive descriptions' (1993: 161). This seems plausible: we can perhaps 'read off' beliefs from pictures and pictures may stimulate desires. But the matter seems more complicated with intentions. Pre-propositional items such as wishes and phantasies (on Gardner's account) cannot constitute reasons. *That* negative feature is, so to speak, their *raison d'être*. So the lady has no reason for calling the maid, conscious or unconscious, yet is supposed to act intentionally in doing so. In place of a reason is a phantasy. Can a phantasy cause an intention? Well, perhaps, but only in so far as it approaches a state that can generate belief. In other words, only if the phantasy is belief-like, in some such way as discussed above. There are grades of phantasy. Suppose I hallucinate a crocodile about to bite – I have a very vivid phantasy or image, a lively product of imagination that seems to invade a sensory modality. I may run for it, but if I merely imagine or phantasise a crocodile, as I may in a school-room exercise, no desire or intention to decamp will arise – because no relevant belief is 'attached', as Freud put it. But invocation of belief to explain 'psychoanalytic' action is not open to Gardner: beliefs and desires are just the things his pre-propositional account is supposed to render superfluous. Yet without them it is difficult to see how to cash out the differences between action-engendering and action-stopping phantasies that any adequate account of this material demands.

But Gardner rejects the instrumentalist conception of intentional action flatly (1993: 170, 186). He severs the link between acting intentionally and acting for a reason: amongst an action's sufficient causal conditions, in his view, there may be desire, phantasy and intention; instrumental beliefs are dispensable. It is, he says, the exclusivity of an instrumentalist perspective on action that the concept of acting-out – as instanced by the table-cloth lady – is meant to challenge (1993: 170),[20] and he finds warrant for this claim in the ordinary understanding of *expressive* behaviour. He claims that expressive behaviour such as throwing crockery in anger or raising one's hands in despair is intentional but non-instrumental action. But this seems mistaken. The examples of expressive behaviour adduced by Gardner are either enthymematically intentional (the instrumental beliefs are suppressed or elided) or not intentional at all, but *expressive*. If I clench my fists in anguish, raise them in despair, smile at your joke or smash the crockery, and I do so expressively, then intention is precisely what these actions do *not* manifest. They have an archaeology which precludes a telos. That is not to deny, of course, that the same movements can also be performed intentionally – but then they are not expressive, in the indicated sense. The category of the expressive indicated here consists of those actions which achieve their particular revelatory force and poignancy *precisely because they bypass reason and are contraposed to the intentional.* They expose a nakedness which intention clothes over. So, for example, to describe someone as being convulsed with despair or with laughter, to state that this behaviour is genuinely expressive of states of mind, but to then add that the subjects acted intentionally, is to undermine the distinct expressive force and illumination of the original descriptions.

Even if my characterisation of the expressive is rejected and we concede cases of expressive, non-rational, intentional behaviour, the latter's proponents would have to concede a point also: that the (putative) intentionality manifest in such expressive cases is *radically unlike* the intentionality manifest in the complex performance of the table-cloth lady. That performance is *nothing like* expressing pleasure with a smile or flailing about in rage. What transpires then is that the hiatus which previously existed between unconscious phantasy and intention opens up between these very different forms of allegedly intentional behaviour. That is hardly progress. So the proposal that pre-propositional phantasy can cause an intention and subsequent intentional behaviour faces two serious objections: it denies the links between efficacious reasons and intentional action; and it is deprived of expressive action as a form on which it could model itself. The tension is evident: if psychoanalytic explanation strays too far from common-sense psychology then it cannot claim its protection.

Gardner's explanation of the first part of the acting-out scenario (setting up the table, rushing from one room to another, etc.) is even more fraught, for here intention is not invoked at all. The phantasy does not cause the performance; the performance just *is* the acting-out of phantasy in plastic form, ultimately driven by desire subintentionally: 'the Inner Picture [the phantasy] simply *impresses* itself into the realm of action. Unconscious seeing-as sets up the "props" for acting-out, and thereby provides a channel leading out into the world, through which the force of desire may find wish-fulfilling expression' (1993: 171). This view faces the same difficulty we diagnosed in Hopkins' treatment of the case. The performance surely is intentional, but we established above that an intentional act cannot at the same time also be subintentional. It follows that Gardner's is not a coherent account of the causal structure of the symptom.[21]

It seems then that nothing is gained by dispensing with an analysis of such cases as instances of FWT. The strategy of supplanting FWT with phantasy – somewhat idiosyncratically defined – was intended to circumvent alleged problems associated with rational (belief–desire) explanation. It doesn't. Had it succeeded it would have disrupted the intricate connections Freud delineated between members of the class of wish-fulfilling processes – dream, phantasy, symptom, illusion – and detached phantasy from the orectic or desiderative and wish-fulfilling trends at the centre of Freud's picture of mind – a picture that I believe is largely accurate.

3.9 Wish-fulfilment declined

Most philosophers who have advanced some variation of non-intentionalism have done so because they reject (or fail to consider) intentionalist, strategic accounts of FWT, but recognise that at least some of the relevant domain of phenomena can be explained Intentionally. They attempt explanations using the re-descriptive and causal constructions familiar to common-sense psychology: concepts such as *belief, desire, fear, agency* and the logical and causal relations holding between them. Confronted with the complexities of the psychoanalytic domain, some philosophers are driven to introduce novel hybrid concepts such as *quasi-belief, the wish, propositional reflection* or *neurotic belief,* though these are still conceived as Intentional concepts (Johnston 1988; Gardner 1993; Lear 1998a; Brakel 2009). The understanding that at least a large subclass of the pathological and related phenomena *can* be understood Intentionally is shared doctrine. A further question is whether the phenomena can *only* be understood Intentionally; whether the Intentional idiom is *indispensable* to the explanation of this domain of phenomena. When Freud turned from neuropathology to psychology he believed that the (common-sense) psychological perspective was indispensable, given the limitations of neuroscience in his time. However, he thought of biology as a land of unlimited possibilities and believed, perhaps, that in the future mental illness could be explained in exclusively neurobiological terms. Freud's theoretical tendencies were always reductive but he did not fly in the face of clinical necessity, as he saw it.

The idea that symptoms and their kin (personality disorders, dreams, etc.) are wish-fulfilling is entirely foreign to contemporary biological psychiatry,[22] and has been so at least since the publication of DSM-III, when psychoanalytic concepts began to be systematically purged from psychiatry (Lane 2007). The situation is similar in cognitively oriented clinical psychology (Bentall 2004, 2010), where a kind of amnesia has taken hold about the roots of its key operational concepts. Although the ever-expanding remit of psychiatry, as represented in the DSM and

ICD, comprehends a very full range of pathological affliction (and much else besides), psychiatric research today tends to focus, understandably, on the major psychotic disorders – schizophrenia, bipolar disorder, major depression and a range of disabling anxiety disorders – which tend to resist wholly Intentional characterisation and are not ideal models for the operation of FWT. Even in the psychoanalytic approach to these disorders the, wishful aspects of the disorder are not often remarked (though see the discussion of delusion and borderline symptoms in **5.6, 5.7, 6.4, 6.5**).

Why the neglect of FWT in contemporary biological psychiatry? Well, it is part of the neglect of the Intentional understanding of mental disorder that dominates it. Radical physicalist reduction or eliminativism is solidified into something like an axiom. Many psychiatrists take the view, expressly stated in DSM-IV, that the distinction between mental and physical disorders is 'an anachronism of mind/body dualism' (APA 1994: xxi). They think that some form of mind/body identity theory is unproblematic, or more likely they don't think about the issue at all and adopt the stance Karl Popper once referred to as 'promissory materialism', a term with some bite in this connection. From an identity theory, or from a dual-aspect theory interpreted as not implying property dualism (a tall order), it is concluded – quite erroneously – that a complete account of mental disorder can be given in neurobiological terms, as the result or manifestation of broken brains or sick cells, to use George Graham's metaphors (2010: 25ff). I have already hinted in the Preface, and will discuss in more detail in **Chapter 10**, at why this inference is mistaken. For the present it suffices to notice that even if a complete neurobiological characterisation of all mental disorders could be given in principle, it doesn't follow that an Intentional account is precluded. At most the latter may be superfluous for the purposes of high theory. But if an Intentional account can be given for all or some mental illness (I mean *mental* illness, not those conditions which do obviously have exclusively neurological aetiology – Parkinson's, say)[23] then this leaves space for understanding in terms of Freudian wish-fulfilment. I think it is true that if there were no such space, in an exclusively neurobiological idiom or dispensation, we could find no way to characterise FWT. But I shall argue that the employment of Intentional concepts is not just the best way of characterising mental disorder (Graham 2010: 79) but is indispensable to the task, even if it is not sufficient; that is, even if it must be supplemented by reference to neurobiological concepts.

Of course, accepting the indispensability of the Intentional idiom for the characterisation of mental illness does not thereby entail commitment to an analysis of disorder as instantiation of FWT for all, or indeed any, of the pathological conditions we have been considering. Many philosophers and psychologists still find the concepts of the Freudian unconscious, unconscious agency and divided minds problematic. Such factors, as we shall see in the following two chapters, play an essential role in the psychoanalytic scheme of things in the explanation of at least the manifest *irrationality* of mental illness. They appear to disrupt the rational functioning of mind. But there are plausible alternative explanations of such disruption, at least in some instances. There is in fact a spectrum of perspectives in the literature, ranging from neurobiological exclusivism, or 'neuralism' – as Graham (2010) dubs it – applied to all mental disorder, to approaches which utilise Intentional characterisation but invoke, to different degrees, the intervention of neurophysiological mechanisms, subpersonal or mental but a-rational (primary process) forces.

George Graham, for example, argues that in the major disorders the mind is 'gummed up' by 'non-rational/ a-rational/mechanical/brute neural forces irrupting into the space of a person's reasons or Intentionality' (2010: 126). Graham does not provide much detail about what this 'gumming up' consists in. At one point (2010: 123) he considers the brute causal intervention of Intentional states, of such states being causally disruptive but not by virtue of their Intentional content. But his principal idea is that the gumming up is a result of neurophysiological conditions, susceptibility due to high levels of stress hormones, neurochemical deficiencies, and so on.[24] And such things are certainly possible contributory factors, in at least some conditions. But what if, *as a matter of fact*, the problematic conditions can be explained without them?

As explained in the Introduction, my strategy for establishing the credentials of FWT has several parts. First, the conception of FWT was shown to be coherent. Second, typical, albeit briefly described, cases – of phantasy, dream, symptom – were considered and shown to fit the models of FWT which reciprocally illuminate them. Third, this chapter exposed inadequacies of the subintentionalist and other competing accounts. Fourth, we must provide plausible motivational structures for FWT and an account of mental differentiation or dissociation that can accommodate it, including maximal FWT. To this fourth task we now turn.

Notes

1   Gardner recognises that *preconscious* intentional (strategic) activity, that is to say descriptively unconscious mental activity originating with the ego, does have a place in psychoanalytic explanation. I think that this concession is fatal to his larger project, as discussed in the next chapter.

2   Why, Price (1954) asks, can't assent, which he thinks is a mental act acquiring belief dispositions, be by choice? 'It is not a free choice at all, but a forced one. If you are in a reasonable state of mind. ... you cannot help preferring the proposition which your evidence favours, the evidence you are at the moment attending to, though the evidence which other people have may of course be different. ... It is just not in your power to avoid assenting to the proposition which the evidence, (your evidence) favours' (1954: 209). Why not? If the connection between your (agent's) evidence and the relevant belief disposition or state was contingent then, clearly, there logically could be a situation in which, although all the evidence you have accepted points towards the belief that p, you find yourself believing not-p (Collins 1979). That is not possible *even in irrational states of mind* where what you take to be evidence are phantasies, delusions and other symptoms. The reason, I suggest, is that to believe p essentially involves (and perhaps in primitive cases is identical with) accepting the evidence which in your lights bases p. It is the internality of that relationship which secures the impossibility of believing against the evidence – your agent's evidence. First-person authority or self-knowledge do not constitute objections to this claim because they do not supervene on the relation between empirical evidence and belief. Only in very unusual circumstances might one say 'I believe I am in pain.'

It will be recalled from **(2.5)** that I use 'agent's evidence' to mean the sets of evidence from which we *do* draw conclusions, not only those from which we canonically ought. Thus hallucinations would not ordinarily be accounted sound evidence for conclusions about their objects, but it is a fact that people undergoing hallucinations will draw conclusions from them. I suggested above that the relation between evidence and belief is internal: consequently change in belief can be wrought only through an adjustment to the agent's evidence, the evidence the agent does accept. But even if there is no logical connection between evidence and empirical belief it may *in fact* be the case that in pathology we try to prove things to ourselves by manufacturing evidence that grounds wish-fulfilling, action-terminating beliefs. The rationale for the manufacture of such evidence becomes much clearer in the context of self-solicitude which I expound in **Chapter 5**.

3 On an externalist view of mental content it becomes still harder to see how beliefs can be inserted in the mind by desire – for now we need accommodation in the historical and social conditions which partially confer content.

4 A basic action is performed without performing another (instrumental) action, e.g. moving a limb at will or swallowing.

5 These limitations presumably apply with even greater force to psychosis, but Gardner excludes 'madness' from his considerations (1993: 4, 33) – an unexpected tack given his firm embrace of Kleinian theory.

6 Gardner recognises a role for belief in wish-fulfilment *after* 'the first incursion of the Reality Principle' (1993: 128). It's not clear how he coordinates that event with the advent of language and propositionality. In any case, the supplemented account retains the kernel of the process here described, and it is the inadequacy of that process that I wish to establish.

7 Satisfaction in this context presupposes the obtaining of the actual wished-for state of affairs, a condition unnecessary for FWT.

8 Hopkins 2012: pp. 248, 257, 259. For the Ratman's symptoms, Freud 1909d.

9 The difference between this proposal and the one about the patient with abdominal pain **(3.2)** that we conceded to subintentional explanation is that in the latter case the symptom was *evidence* to ground a belief, whereas in the present case the symptom *is* a belief-like representation.

10 Galen Strawson (2009) maintains that beliefs and thoughts do. Perhaps. But whatever the phenomenology of thinking or believing is like, it is radically different from that of the sensory modalities and imagination.

11 In a personal communication that I have drastically, but I hope not misleadingly, elided, Hopkins writes:

> *phantasies are always forms of (proto) belief or experience*, and these always have a pacifying effect since what desires/drives are pacified by is representations of their satisfaction. ... *I intend (want, hope?) to be using the notion of belief – or better that of the same concepts as take part in belief – as something that is already there in an episode of perceptual experience in which seeing (or touching, etc.) is believing*, so that it also has a deep and pervasive phenomenological aspect... I think something similar applies to stopping (pacifying) desire and action. ...We just take experience to be of how things actually are as it were... With phantasy I think it is partly the same, except that different forms or kinds of imagining that I have not found it possible to describe perspicuously have variable degrees of stopping power, with these related to how far we are taking it as how things are – doing which might be being engrossed, or again imagining so vividly or deeply that one is losing touch. ... I am wanting a concept that does what Hume wants 'vivacity' to do, that is, distinguish different forms of desire-stopping power. Maybe there isn't one, but I am inclined to think that

> desire-stopping and this idea of vividness (*which is also a wrong idea for unconscious phantasy*) are two sides of the same coin. (Italics added)

I am not sure that seeing is always believing and that belief is intrinsic to perceptual experience. So the latter does not seem to me the right phenomenon to elucidate the stopping/pacifying power of phantasy. In any event, *all* phantasy cannot be belief-like, as Hopkins suggests at one point, because most phantasy does not pacify; for instance, most conscious phantasy. The notion that phantasy is intrinsically belief-like obscures the circumstantial conditions, such as engrossment, that enable the passage from one grade of phantasy, say the wishful phantasy, to the wish-fulfilling phantasy. We would lose the distinction between omnipotent phantasy and other sorts. And unconscious phantasy, as Hopkins recognises, presents a special problem. We do know that *some* unconscious phantasy pacifies desire because we know that there is unconscious FWT. But how does it do it? Hopkins suggests that an intrinsic, perception-like characteristic may account for the stopping/pacifying power of phantasy, something like Humean vivacity which will render them belief-like. But then the troubling question arises: to *whom or what* do these efficacious unconscious phantasies appear sufficiently vivacious to stop/pacify desire? The account of unconscious attention that I developed in **2.4** and link to an unconscious executive agency **(4.2)** provides an answer to this question, but it is not one that I think Hopkins would find acceptable.

12 The nature of sublimation and symbol formation is moot. Here I largely follow Hartmann 1964. Contrast Gardner (1993: 132), where plasticity is regarded as an aspect of symbol formation which enables wish-fulfilment to ramify and sublimation is understood, in the Kleinian manner – in my view erroneously – as retaining symbolic significance. For the Kleinian view see Segal (1991: ch. 3); Spillius *et al.* (2011: ch. 10).

13 Her wish, it is clear, was not deeply unconscious. From Freud's description it appears to have been preconscious. But it, in turn, doubtless represented a related infantile wish which was inaccessibly unconscious there.

14 It seems evident that without reason there is no intention. The idea that someone intends to do something but has no reason for doing it is senseless. It has been proposed that there are *actes gratuit*. Even if this conception is not incoherent, the claim that there can be such acts seems empirically false and contrary to a key regulative principle of psychoanalysis: look for the reasons. Whether every intentional action, as well as having reasons, is caused by some proximal executive state such as intention, decision, choice or judgement is an issue that can remain unresolved here. In my view such executive states are neither necessary nor sufficient, though they may play a causal role in most intentional action.

15 Wollheim (1991: 56) exposes Freudian primary process thinking in these terms: 'Viewed as part of [the primary process] the wish is really an embryonic form of desire, marked out by the fact that it seeks satisfaction indifferently in the outer world of reality and the inner world of phantasy. When the individual wishes, or when he wishes sufficiently strongly, he typically cannot distinguish between the representation that he makes to himself of the object of his wish and the object itself'. How is that phenomenon to be explained? In a later paper Wollheim remarks that 'the distinctive feature of this analysis of wish-fulfilment is not the connection between wishing and imagination but the fact that imagination as it occurs in connection with wishing occurs under the regressive or corporeal theory of mind' (1979: 58). The task is then to elucidate this corporeal theory of mind and, as I understand it, Wollheim follows at least two different paths: one that introduces the 'omnipotent belief', and another that takes primary process functioning as basic, not further analysable. Here I consider the first path.

16 '[T]his belief [in the omnipotence of thought and wishes] is a frank acknowledgement of a relic of the old megalomania of infancy' (Freud 1909: 234; 1911b: 219). The belief

in the omnipotence of thought, and the operation of such a belief, should be distinguished from the belief in one's omnipotence, though the latter will often vouchsafe the former. A person under dominance of omnipotent phantasy or the omnipotence of thought may be particularly susceptible to feelings of omnipotence but will not necessarily succumb to them.

17 Winnicott, in many of his writings, emphasised the importance of the caretaker's accommodating and validating the infant's sense of omnipotence.

18 In a remarkable paper (1993b), Wollheim essays to explain the way that introjection, which he understands as supervening on incorporative phantasy, must function if it is to establish internal objects experienced corporeally. At first, his account appears once again to turn on the omnipotent belief: '*The simplest belief of this kind would be that in phantasizing the incorporation of the figure the subject thereby incorporates him*, and this in turn could be accounted for if, not merely did the subject's phantasies include a representation of themselves, but these representations represented them as the very bodily activities that they are of. It is essential to the incorporative phantasy that it represents itself as an actual incorporative process...' (1993b: 72; italics added). But if we ask how the phantasy comes to be misrepresented as corporeal, Wollheim's answer seems to return to Freudian primary process thinking: 'that [thoughts, phantasies] misrepresent themselves in this special way is just a reflection of the mode of mental functioning that currently prevails within the subject. It is the stage of development the subject is at, or the fact that he is still in the grip of the primary process...' (1993a: 70). In other words, the infant mistakes the representation of its wishes fulfilled for corporeal processes or realities for much the same reason that we mistake dream and hallucination for reality. In hallucinatory wish-fulfilment there is 'replacement of external by psychical reality' (Freud 1915e: 187). So I am unclear how, in the end, Wollheim relates the belief in the omnipotence of thought to Freudian primary process thinking.

19 This is not, as we saw **(2.6)**, Freud's view either of phantasy or the scope of wish-fulfilment, and is not (I think) consistent with Kleinian usage either. The stipulation may however have considerable explanatory power.

20 For Freud 'acting out' had a more specific meaning: 'the patient acts outside the transference instead of remembering' (1940a: 177). But the notion of enacting a phantasy is clear enough.

21 The famous episode of the Ratman's cowering before Freud (1909d) seems more amenable to the expressive or 'acting- out' interpretation. Lear's (1998a: 92ff) account of the episode as involving an expression of phantasy, not action, is along the same lines and subject to the same difficulties. He wrongly attributes to Freud a false distinction between acting and acting out. 'Whatever the Ratman is doing he is not doing for a reason. It is not an expression of belief or desire; and thus it is not an action. It is what Freud calls *acting out*' (1998a: 92). But obviously there is at least one reason: the Ratman believes that he is about to be attacked; he desires to shield himself and believes that by cowering or cringing he will make himself a smaller target... or something of that sort. Gardner and Lear both misidentify the Intentional object of the Ratman's fear. It is not Freud that the Ratman fears; he fears his father, whose imago is projected onto Freud.

22 Mainstream contemporary psychiatry is sometimes said to be based on a biomedical model. I think this is a misnomer. Certainly the model is neurobiological but its relative indifference to aetiology-based diagnosis does not consort well with medical diagnosis and nosology in general.

23 An immensely diverse range of conditions are classified as 'mental disorders'; some are best described – and rendered intelligible in – neurobiological terms; and others fairly obviously not so. But if symptoms and related conditions are characterised as *mental* disorders then they must at least partially be characterisable in the Intentional idiom and cannot fully be understood without recourse to that idiom, as I shall argue in **Chapter 10**.

24 Graham does not consider whether symptoms/disorders may be wish-fulfilling, presumably because he disregards altogether the possibility of unconscious deliberation and motivation. Lear (1998a, b) and Brakel (2009) certainly employ unconscious motivation, but in one respect their views are similar to Graham's: they allow for the intrusion of a-rational, albeit mental, elements in the formation of symptoms. In Brakel (2009) the key pathogenic element appears to be the formation of 'neurotic beliefs' under the impression of the primary process. She holds that wishes are satisfied in phantasy, and desires cause a state of 'readiness to act' (presumably proximal intentions). The relation between phantasies and neurotic beliefs is not entirely clear. Neurotic beliefs are 'fuelled by the positive "evidence" supplied by psychic reality' (2009: 118); so perhaps phantasies cause or in some sense constitute 'neurotic beliefs', which then cause symptoms. Perhaps then a discernible form of wish-fulfilment may be extracted: wish → phantasy → grounds for neurotic belief → neurotic belief → symptom.

Chapter 4

Intention and deliberation in Freudian wish-fulfilment

[T]he most complicated and most rational thought processes, which can surely not be denied the name of psychical processes, can occur without exciting the subject's consciousness.

Freud 1900a: 612

4.1 Towards intentionalism

Let's step back a little. In the classical psychoanalytic account neurotic symptoms (and their kin) were conceived as products of conflict, as compromise formations between, at first, libidinal drives and ego-drives, and later between id drives and ego structures. A typical early statement is that 'hysterical symptoms arise as a compromise between two opposite affective and instinctual impulses, of which one is attempting to bring to expression a component instinct or a constituent of the sexual constitution, and the other is attempting to suppress it' (Freud 1908a: 164). Instinctual drives incompatible with the ego are repressed but, given their natural tendency to seek discharge, continue to strive for expression. When the ego's counter-cathectic or defensive forces weaken, a 'return of the repressed' ensues and the repressed material, modified by the defences, achieves expression or discharge in disguised or attenuated form. These expressions are the neurotic symptoms and may be regarded as secondary attempts to bind the anxiety associated with the repressed material. They provide partial release of drive tension or excitations.[1] This *economic* conception of drive discharge is not in principle dependent on the representational content of symptoms. As such it faces an insurmountable problem: it provides an account of what instigates action or originates symptoms, but says nothing plausible about what terminates it.[2]

The view endorsed here enlarges on another strand in Freud's thinking according to which symptoms are acts with meaning, sense or intention. They have representational content that is a compromise between the fulfilments of wishes from opposing elements of personality. They are wish-fulfilling not just in the sense that the drive of which the wish is the representative achieves 'discharge', but in picturing a 'scene' in facilitating circumstances, in which contending wishes are fulfilled or from which it can be unconsciously concluded (after unravelling the primary process and defensive distortions) that they have been fulfilled (Freud 1916–17: chs. XIX–XXIII). In wish-fulfilment theory the stress is on this representational aspect of the account of neuroses Freud developed.[3] We underline that in many cases symptoms do not have representational content contingently; content is manufactured intentionally by agents *to function as evidence* in order to enable the acquisition of wish-fulfilling beliefs. The characterisations are framed entirely in the Intentional or common-sense-psychological idiom.[4]

There are two features of this approach that must be highlighted. For the approach to succeed we must be able to provide a plausible account of the facilitating or enabling conditions under which the representational content is experienced or understood as wish-fulfilling. An account of these conditions in primitive psychic circumstances, such as hallucinatory wish-fulfilment, was provided under the heading of 'engrossment' **(2.4)**, though a broader approach is still wanting[5] and will be pursued in the next chapter. The second feature of this account is its presupposition of complex unconscious mental activity, including unconscious deliberation,[6] the formation of unconscious reasons for acting and of executive states such as intending.

In his recent assessment of classical and contemporary psychoanalysis Morris Eagle insists that 'neurotic symptoms are certainly not understood in the ordinary sense as intended acts' (2011: 70). He acknowledges a difficulty: his own clinical experience appears to gainsay him. He discusses the case of a patient, ST, who, whenever he came close to intimacy and marriage, ruminated on his potential homosexuality and dithered until the liaison was broken. He did this repeatedly, with several girlfriends. Eagle affirms that neurotic symptoms are 'experienced as unintended, ego-alien happenings over which one has no control' (2011: 70) but is forced to conclude that 'the symptom served to protect my patient from the danger that engagement and marriage represented to him' (2011: 71). He goes on, 'I do not begin to adequately understand the mechanism or process that can generate a symptom that is experienced as unbidden, unintended, and involuntary and yet can be purposive' (2011: 71). The aim of this chapter and the next is to show precisely how that might happen.

4.2 Unconscious intention

Stuart Hampshire, a philosopher receptive to psychoanalytic ideas at a time when few philosophers were, wrote that '"Intention" is the one concept that ought to be preserved free from any taint of the less-than-conscious. Its function, across the whole range of its applications, is to mark the kind of knowledge of what one is doing, and of what one is inclined to do, that is fully conscious and explicit' (Hampshire 1974: 125). This intuition seems to be widely shared. The psychologist Daniel Wegner says: '*Intention* is normally understood as an idea of what one is going to do that appears in consciousness just before one does it' (2002: 18). Curiously, partly through the work of Wegner (2002), Benjamin Libet (2004) and others, the view that there are unconscious or non-conscious intentions now prevails. In fact, the shoe is on the other foot, and the contemporary challenge is to demonstrate that there are efficacious proximate *conscious* intentions (Mele 2009). That unconscious intentions (and unconscious efficacious reasons and executive states) are indispensable for psychoanalytic understanding is widely accepted within psychoanalytic thought, and now there is a body of experimental evidence, and a good deal more conceptual clarity, supporting that view.[7]

Though its exact interpretation is moot, one well-confirmed experimental finding is that certain non-conscious neural events, causally efficacious for some prescribed action A, occur a significant period of time before the agent becomes aware of a conscious experience of intending, deciding or willing A. Wegner, who thinks that willing and intention are conscious experiences or feelings, concludes that because the non-conscious neural states are sufficient for action, conscious will, the allegedly subsequent conscious experience, is not part of the causal process in acting, and is therefore an illusion.

But if we abandon the supposition that willing or the other executive states are necessarily *conscious* ideas or experiences, and consider them as functional states initiating, sustaining and guiding intentional actions, then another possibility opens: that the causal antecedents of action detected in the experiments just *are* non-conscious intentions, urges, or decisions, or the neural substrates of them (Mele 2009: 38). After all, non-conscious *standing*, as opposed to occurrent, intentions (my long-standing intention to visit Paris), as well as non-conscious enthymematic intentions in the causal process of skilled action such as playing tennis, have long been recognised. Discounting doubtful semantic intuition, then, there seems to be no principled objection to non-conscious intentions, even to dynamically unconscious intentions,[8] and there is evidence for precisely such states from various sources.

Kaplan-Solms and Solms (2000: 90–115) discuss a patient with a serious language disorder experienced subjectively as 'an inability to think', but more accurately described as an 'inability to *attach words to her thoughts*, resulting in an inability to *bring her thoughts to consciousness* (and to *keep* them there)' (2000: 108). The patient suffered a functional dissociation between her consciousness and executive control, yet 'continued to behave in an essentially reasonable way... to function as an essentially rational and reality oriented agent' (2000: 110–11). The authors conclude that the patient 'retained executive control over her *behaviour*; all that she lost was control over her *consciousness* ... This confirms Freud's revised (1923b) topographical proposals, to the effect that consciousness is not the executive agency of the mind, and that even the ego itself is fundamentally unconscious' (2000: 111).

The idea that the 'executive agency of mind' is unconscious – or more precisely that it need not be conscious, that in pathology at least it recedes into the unconscious – receives support from careful empirically orientated clinical work by the Mt. Zion group (Weiss and Sampson 1986).[9] Their observations support Freud's idea (1940a: 199) that, as they express it, 'a person is able unconsciously to exert some control over his behaviour, that he regulates it unconsciously in accordance with thoughts, beliefs, and assessments of current reality, and that he attempts, by his regulation of behaviour, to avoid putting himself in dangerous situations' (Weiss and Sampson 1986: 5). So they write, for example:

> [T]he belief in castration does not affect behaviour automatically, as, according to the automatic functioning hypothesis, an unconscious impulse is supposed to affect it. A person who is guided unconsciously by a belief in castration is applying a theory to the planning of his behaviour. He anticipates a particular course of action, considers whether it might provoke castration, and decides, on the basis of his expectations, whether to carry it out. A man suffering from unconscious castration anxiety becomes anxious and leaves when a seductive woman approaches him is behaving not automatically but in accordance with a theory which warns him of danger. ... The idea that a person may be guided by beliefs makes it necessary to postulate that a part of the executive agency that guides behaviour on the basis of beliefs may itself be unconscious and indeed deeply repressed.

Weiss and Sampson argue that patients entering therapy do so with unconscious plans to master early conflicts, traumas and anxieties and disconfirm their grim or pathogenic beliefs (1986: 7ff, 84ff). For this, conditions of safety have to be established, and patients unconsciously test the therapist to determine whether the conditions exist in which their plans can be instituted (1984: 101ff). Here is one of those tests (abridged from Eagle 1984):

> The therapist's response to a male patient's gift is to tactfully refuse the gift and to remind the patient of the analytic contract. During the next session the patient begins to talk about homosexual fears and fantasies. The interpretation of this sequence of events is that the patient tests the analyst by offering him a gift, is reassured by the analyst's refusal, which is unconsciously tantamount to a communication that he will not be seduced and therefore constitutes test passing, and then feels that it is safe to bring forth the warded off homosexual contents.
>
> (Eagle 1984: 98)

Many similar examples could be adduced (1986: chs. 4–6). An important feature of the Mt. Zion work is the empirical methodology: the use of relatively large patient populations, direct observation of sessions, the use of controls, making and testing of hypotheses, and groups of experienced analysts to assess the observations. They make a powerful cumulative case for the proposition that there is a deliberative care-taking part of the self **(4.6, 5.5)**, the unconscious ego, which keeps potentially painful emotion, pathogenic beliefs and desires in check or inhibited until it establishes that conditions are safe to consciously become aware of them.

Let's agree, at least provisionally, that actions *can* be caused by efficacious reasons (beliefs and desires) and executive states such as proximal intentions that reside in the unconscious ego, indeed in the deeply repressed unconscious ego.[10] We may then conjecture that in pathology certain executive functions – forming intentions, deciding, choosing – recede, episodically perhaps, into the unconscious, and the appearance of conscious efficacious deliberation in such cases is akin to something like confabulation (**9.5**). But for that conjecture to be placed on a firmer footing a number of difficulties have first to be allayed.

4.3 Unconscious deliberation

I have maintained that in FWT (or more broadly self-solicitude) intention plays a variable and, in the maximal cases such as the anxious scientist and the exhibitionist where self-solicitude is the aim of strategy, a very extensive role. Then it must be possible to construct coherent intentional structures – valid practical syllogisms – for these important cases. But attempts to do so, as anyone who has thought critically about the exhibitionist or the anxious scientist will have quickly realised, run into formidable obstacles. Non-intentionalism has often appeared an attractive option partly because intentionalism appeared impossible.

There is a difficulty that has usually been considered fatal. A first attempt at a practical syllogism on which the anxious scientist may have acted would look something like this:

S wants mother's presence
S believes that by procrastinating mother will be present

S procrastinates

The trouble is that the minor premise, which expresses the agent's instrumental belief, is mad. Who could believe such a thing? Who could act on the basis of such an instrumental belief? Suppose S's mother was known by him to be dead, but he wanted nevertheless – somehow – to experience her presence:

S wants to experience mother's presence
S believes that by procrastinating he can create a hallucinatory sense of her presence

---

S procrastinates

That's still worse, for now the major premise is afflicted as well, and while the instrumental premise can have a certain plausibility – on the principle of getting high to reach a brighter place – it misses its primary aim, for what S really wants is mother's presence, not a hallucination of it.

4.4 Unconscious deliberation and dissociation

But assume now the coherence of a conception of a divided or dissociated mind or self (see **5.6**). Then practical schemas for maximal FWT could be made out as involving a relationship between two person-like dissociated aspects of the scientist's self: a care-taking (= B) and a care-receiving (= A) client self. We would then have forms like the following:

Where A wants or desires that *p*:

B wants most (decides, intends) to satisfy A's desire that *p*
B believes that procrastinating will satisfy A's desire that *p*

B procrastinates

Or where A wants or desires to be consoled or pacified:

B wants most (decides, intends) to console (pacify ...) A
B believes that procrastinating will console (pacify ...) A

B procrastinates

The instrumental beliefs are now odd but they are not mad: they express the sorts of strategies one can acquire as rules of thumb, as skills or practical or procedural beliefs in the caring and concerned management of another – and of oneself *as if* one were another. In fact these are idealisations, for in the typical situation the care-taker is unlikely to be aware of the client self's exact desire or the precise character of its distress; consequently, it is unlikely to have a tailored strategy to satisfy the client self. This is a consequence of the dissociation and therefore mutual opacity between caretaker and client (**4.6, 5.7**). The caretaker is likely to try now one thing, now another. Mother often doesn't know exactly what is wrong with baby, but eventually she will hit on the soothing solution.

4.5 Unconscious deliberation and symbolism

Let's look more closely. In Lecture 17 of the *Introductory Lectures* (1916–17), Freud discusses a compulsive symptom in a 19-year-old girl.

> [T]he most important stipulation related to the bed itself. The pillow at the top end of the bed must not touch the wooden back of the bedstead. The small top pillow must lie on this large pillow in one specific way only – namely, so as to form a diamond shape. Her head had then to lie exactly along the long diam-eter of the diamond. The eiderdown had to be shaken before being laid on the bed so that its bottom end became very thick; afterwards, however she never failed to even out this accumulation of feathers by pressing them apart. ... She found out the central meaning of the bed ceremonial one day when she sud-denly understood the meaning of the rule that the pillow must not touch the back of the bedstead. The pillow, she said, had always been a woman to her and the upright wooden back a man. ... If the pillow was a woman, then the shak-ing of the eiderdown till all the feathers were at the bottom and caused a swelling there had a sense as well. It meant making a woman pregnant; but she

never failed to smooth away the pregnancy again, for she had for years been afraid that her parents' intercourse would result in another child and so present her with a competitor.

(1916–17: 265, 267)

Freud interpreted this ritual as a 'magical' attempt to keep her parents separated, to prevent their sexual intercourse and to ward off anxieties connected with the birth of a competitor. The ritual seems to be a set of intentional actions, but the girl could provide no reasons for performing it and initially found her own actions unintelligible. Presumably she would have rehearsed some such syllogism as: 'I want to sleep; if I want to sleep then I must first perform these acts that I can't really resist, of separating bedstead from pillow; therefore I perform these acts.' Here there is no light, no explanation of why she would think such things. If, however, we follow Freud's principal interpretation, we can construct another practical syllogism for her behaviour.

Girl wants to separate mother and father.

Girl believes that by separating bedstead and pillow she will separate mother and father.

Girl separates bedstead and pillow.

If the girl's action accorded with this unconscious syllogism – if her action was caused in the appropriate way by the desire and belief articulated in the premises – then it was intentional. The major premise, the girl's desire, is not in doubt but the minor premise expresses what appears to be a 'mad belief' and commentators have questioned whether it is possible to hold such bizarre beliefs or to have them engage as motives to action (Hopkins 1982: xxiff). Michael Moore, for example, writes:

[O]ne should question whether the association of one thing with another [her father with the bedstead] is evidence that the girl believes the two things to be the same... In addition, there is evidence to the contrary; unless she is more than neurotic, she would surely declare that she knows the difference between her father and her bedstead. Given the usual assumptions about the consistency of a person's beliefs, there is strong evidence that she does not believe that her father and her bedstead are one.

(1984: 335–6)

Moore assumes that the girl could have held the belief expressed in the minor premise only if she believed that the bedstead was identical with her father (ditto: mother); this, he believes, is unlikely on the basis of an expected denial, had she been asked, and the fact that the belief would be inconsistent with her other, rational conscious beliefs. (He concedes, though, that the girl *might* have had the mad belief if she were more than neurotic.) Now, Moore accepts that the 'ritual is plainly an action of hers', by which he means that the action of separating the bedstead and the pillow is intentional. He follows Jeremy Bentham's inclusive definition of *intentional action* as encompassing all actions done by an actor who knows he is performing them. Since the girl knows 'what she is doing', that is, separating bedstead and pillow, it follows on this criterion that she is acting intentionally. But Bentham's definition cannot be right. Merely knowing that one is performing an action cannot be a sufficient condition for intentionality; there are many actions we know we are performing but which are non-intentional, such as smiling or wearing out one's running shoes. Reasons, expressible in a practical syllogism, are necessary. So what *is* the practical syllogism which explains her action? If she is acting intentionally then there is a reason for her action. To deny that the action was intentional is a position that is defensible – the symptom is, after all, compulsive. But if intentionality is imputed then either a reason for acting – conscious or unconscious – had better be produced or, failing that, a sound argument demonstrating that acting intentionally does not entail the having of efficacious reasons for acting. Bentham's definition is clearly flawed and Moore's use of it here, combined with his rejection of the unconscious syllogism, leads to the untenable position of affirming that the ritual is intentional without an explanation of how it can be.[11]

It is a mark of conscious intention that it is sensitive to circumstance, that it can be withheld or modified in light of relevant rational considerations. These features are lacking in the girl's ritual. So it seems that the act, under the description 'separating bedstead and pillow', is not intentional: there are no conscious efficacious reasons for it and it is not (immediately) vulnerable to rational revision. But the same act-event could be intentional under other descriptions.[12] Several different practical syllogisms concluding with the required action can be constructed. Recall Moore's claim that in order to arrive at the sort of practical syllogism instanced above the girl must have *believed* that the bedstead was her father. In fact, that is not implied in the material and it is not necessary for the girl to have believed it, though it seems possible that she may have believed it. What she appears to believe, unconsciously, is that if she separates the bedstead and the pillow she will have separated her parents. Believing this proposition is not the same as, nor does it presuppose, believing that her parents were identical with the furniture. The sorcerer who sticks pins into an effigy doesn't believe that the effigy *is* his enemy. The distinction underlying the difference here is between one thing operationally *symbolising* another and that thing being *believed to be identical with* the other. And both of these circumstances differ from a third, where one thing is functionally *equated* with another: where there is a Segalian symbolic equation, as I shall call it.

In the case of 'mere' conventional symbolic relations – and there are many different relations of this kind – little or nothing by way of belief or action may ensue: 'm' denotes mass and 'v' velocity, a flag represents a nation, a cane held to his lips by Peter Lorre (in the famous scene in the Maltese Falcon) symbolises homosexuality. An object *A* may symbolise another object, event or conception *B*, but a raft of other beliefs are required to infer that an action upon *A* will have effects on *B* or for *A* to substitute for *B*; the kind of beliefs that the votaries of voodoo may have, for example, or literal believers in the Eucharist. But in certain cases, those involving so-called 'Freudian symbolism', where the thing symbolised is repressed or otherwise unconscious and the symbol is generally open to conscious awareness, the matter may be quite otherwise. The symbol may be mistaken by one part of a person's mind for the object or event or notion it symbolises, sufficiently mistaken at any rate for FWT to ensue. As Petocz (1999) puts it:

> One part of the mind unconsciously takes the symbol to be the symbolised, but for another part of the mind the symbol is simply whatever it is in itself. For the repressed impulse, symbolism is a case of motivated mistaken identity, in which the symbol is mistaken for the symbolised and treated as if it were the symbolised. For the repressing impulse, there is no such mistaken belief; the object or activity in question is acceptable. The combination in one person of these two processes results (for reasons not properly understood) in gratification which is not as complete as would be the gratification obtained from the satisfaction, via primary objects and activities, of the unopposed instinctual impulse.
>
> (1999: 233)

Unconscious symbolism and its effects pervade thought: one person is terrified at the sight of spiders, another weeps for Hecuba, a third discovers the painting's 'hidden' meaning. Just how symbolic relations of this kind are established in the first place and how in certain circumstances the symbol substitutes for the object symbolised is a large question we need not enter into here.[13] Suffice to say that symbolism hugely extends the scope of FWT, as several of our case examples illustrate. It is clear that such symbolism doesn't necessarily entail belief in the identity of symbol and thing symbolised, though there may be such a belief, and it may be operative. If the bedstead girl believes unconsciously that the bedstead is her father (ditto: mother), then from the fact that she separates bedstead from pillow she will be able to *conclude* (unconsciously) that she has separated her parents. In the case I referred to as operational symbolism, what the girl does *seems* to separate her parents when she separates the bedstead and pillow – as she apprehends it unconsciously. It is *as if* she separated them, transiently.

It is now easy to find intention conferring reasons on each scenario, albeit they are unconscious ones. The practical syllogism set out above is an example using the sorcery-like belief ('if she separates the furnishings she will separate her parents.') And the following is an example for the operational symbolic equation:

Girl wants to prevent the conception of a baby-competitor.
Girl believes that by keeping her father/bedstead and her mother/pillow apart she could prevent that conception.

Girl separates bedstead and pillow.

The '/' sign here is meant to indicate that it is not a case of *believing* that father and bedstead (ditto: mother) are numerically identical, but of failing to distinguish between them *qualitatively in certain important respects*. The bedroom furniture, in the girl's case, may symbolise parents, and action upon the furniture may be perceived as affecting the parents. But there is neither numerical nor full qualitative identity here. This is therefore different from the relation I refer to as Segalian symbolic equation (Segal 1957; 1991; Bott Spillius *et al.* 2011: 514–15), where there appears to be almost complete indiscernibility between symbol and thing symbolised, and different processes underlying the equation. Consider Betty:

> Around Easter, Betty came home from the park bringing two twigs which she arranged crosswise and then asked her mother what she thought this was. Her mother answered: 'I guess it is a cross.' Thereupon Betty began to whip her mother furiously, crying all the while that her mother deliberately hurt Jesus' feelings, that she ought to have acknowledged that it was the cross to which He was nailed and which, according to Betty, her mother knew.
>
> (Mahler 1968: 61–2)

Betty's is, of course, a mad belief, and such beliefs tend to ramify and draw around themselves delusional systems and create dissociations which support them more or less well. Betty, for example, must have known that tiny twigs cannot support the body of a man but, presumably, this sort of practical belief and her delusional ones were kept isolated from each other. Some people have literal beliefs about the Eucharist which are not unlike Betty's beliefs about the twigs, though they may have different thoughts about how the material transformations can occur, or not think about them at all. Here is Segal's oft-quoted illustration of symbolic equation in a schizophrenic adult.

> In the first weeks of his analysis, he came into a session blushing and giggling, and throughout the session would not talk to me. Subsequently, we found that before this hour he had been attending an occupational therapy class where be made a canvas stool, which he brought with him. The reason for his silence, blushing and giggling was that he could not bring himself to talk to me about it. For him, the stool on which he had been working, the word 'stool' which he would have to use in connection with it, and the stool he passed in the lavatory were so completely felt as one and the same thing that he was unable to talk to me about it.
>
> (Segal 1986: 50)

In symbolic equation, Segal writes, 'the symbol is so equated with the object symbolized that the two are felt to be identical'. On the other hand, in 'true symbolism or symbolic representation, the symbol represents the object but is not entirely equated with it' (Segal 1991: 35).[14] Incorporating Segalian symbolism, a third practical syllogism can be generated:

Girl wants to prevent the conception of a baby-competitor.
Girl believes that by keeping her father = bedstead and her mother = pillow apart she could prevent that conception.

Girl separates bedstead and pillow.

4.6 Dissociation again

I do not wish to suggest that any one of these syllogisms is *the* correct one: the case is under-described and there is a variety of potential unconscious intentional structures that may account for the girl's action, some not incorporating mad beliefs at all. Mad beliefs and equations, and unconscious pathogenic beliefs of the sort described in Weiss and Sampson (1986) (believing that one is castrated, or that deserting one's parents will kill them, etc.), are common enough, and explicable in terms of early formative experiences and the functioning of the unconscious mind. It is evident that such beliefs may become governing principles of action by entering into unconscious practical schemas determining intentional action. The pathogenic belief that leaving a parent will kill them, and the desire to kill them, for example, are commonly uncovered in psychotherapy as the cause of certain inhibitions. But the sort of behaviour we have been considering may be explained by the other schemas, based on dissociation.

Suppose once again the coherence of a notion of a divided mind (of 'second-mind personology') and of maximal forms of FWT or self-solicitude. Then in the case of the bedstead girl allow that one part of her mind (B) is in caring relation to another, client part (A). We can easily generate valid practical syllogisms that do not incorporate outlandish desires or mad beliefs:

B wants to console (protect, pacify etc.) A
B believes that by separating bedstead and pillow A will be consoled (protected, pacified etc.)

B separates bedstead and pillow

Notice that B's belief is not mad; it is solicitous, the kind of belief a concerned mother may develop for a child. Part A, you will recall, is possessed of the somewhat crazy conscious reasoning 'if only the bedstead and pillow were separated then perhaps I could sleep'. Part B acts to allay the larger desire implicit in this. B acts to satisfy that desire and A unconsciously interprets/sees B's action as a separation of parents.

We find such intrapsychic solicitous roles noted frequently in Freud's work and in many of the pioneer object-relations theorists. Freud writes of the ego's protection of the id, of the ego as a helper[15] and of the internalised superego's solicitude for the ego: 'To the ego... living means the same as being loved – being loved by the superego... The superego fulfils the same function of protecting and saving that was fulfilled in earlier days by the father...' (1923b: 58) and 'if the superego does try to comfort the ego by humour and to protect it from suffering, this does not conflict with its derivation from the parental function' (1928c: 166). Freud came to realise, though only near the end of his life, that some of these self-solicitous relations are 'decisively influenced by the identification with the nursing mother' (Hartmann, Kris and Loewenstein 1964: 39). The internalisation of maternal functions leading potentially to dissociation was recognised by the pioneers (e.g. Spitz

1965: 179; Winnicott 1965: 48). The investigation of such healthy internalisation of caring functions is pursued in e.g. Kumin (1996), Schore (2003), though to my knowledge not to the extent that it warrants **(5.5)**.

Considerably more is known about pathological developments in which the infant, who feels abandoned or despised, identifies with its frustrating or hated objects, or complies with them, turns prematurely upon itself and takes itself as an object. Winnicott's (1965) views on the false self's protection and solicitude for the true self are well known. A number of Kleinian analysts (Bion 1967; Rosenfeld 1987; Steiner 1982), as well as some strongly influenced by Klein (Kernberg 1966, 1975; Ogden 1993) and others (e.g. Bollas 1987; Guntrip 1968), have written about these pathological reflexive attitudes in the context of narcissistic and schizoid object-relations. It is possibly because the self-solicitous relations, including the maximal forms of FWT, are so frequently dominated by pathological developments that they often take the form of self-deceit, symptom, delusion and pernicious illusion **(Chapters 6 and 7)**.

At this point we can discern some closure. We can begin to see the capacity for self-solicitude and maximal FWT as consequences primarily of the internalisation of caretakers and their functions – though, of course, such functions may be augmented from elsewhere. There is a relationship that the self has to itself which is not one of repudiation and hostility but one of solicitude, caring, consolation and, at its best, cherishing; though perhaps, more often, it degenerates into pandering, appeasement and deceit. Much caretaking is conscious, but much may be unconscious. Maximal FWT, as I have described it, involves strategies in which the self sets out unconsciously but intentionally to provide for itself the fulfilment of wishes, usually for the self-solicitous purposes of gratification, consolation or protection. It does this by telling itself stories (as in dreams and daydreams), manufacturing phantasies and symptoms or delusional scenes which, so to speak, alter the evidential field for the client self. It creates a congenial imaginary world in which mere wishing *seems* to have made it so. As we saw with the café-avoiding girl, it can succeed in this enterprise because of the very conditions generated by its reflexive attitude: by splitting itself it creates opacities: the self to which it ministers lacks the discrimination to expose the wish-fulfilling project. And now we see at once how the last practical syllogism for FWT articulates the practical expression of an important structural condition of mind. Of course, many difficulties with the notion of a dissociated mind remain, but the very possibility of maximal FWT constitutes a new argument for just such dissociation.

4.7 Sartre's censor argument resolved

Moreover, it now becomes apparent how the Sartrean censor argument **(1.5)** can be expeditiously disarmed. David Pears (1984) had already proposed a successful means of dealing with it. He suggested in effect that the duality in the protective sub-system – the censor – of knowing what is not supposed to be known, an inevitable and lethal implication of Freudian views according to Sartre, didn't matter because the protective system has as its environment and concern the wellbeing of the defended system. Its problems are not those of the main system, and because one can be aware of a belief without sharing it, the protective system can tolerate the duality without embarrassment. This, I think, is essentially correct. Gardner (1993) has advanced two supposedly conclusive objections to Pear's manoeuvre: no adequate explanation, he claims, has been provided for either (a) the causal origin of the protective sub-system (1993: 76–7) or (b) the irrational contents of the sub-systems (1993: 114). I think that these curiously unpsychoanalytic objections are ones from which psychoanalytic theory could have rescued Gardner. Psychoanalytic theory can answer these objections as a matter of course. As regards (a), the internalisation of maternal caring functions, and other internalisations leading to dissociation, may be organised into self-like structures of the unconscious protective ego **(5.6–5.7)**. And for (b), psychoanalysis gives us insight into the many ways in which irrational, bizarre and pathogenic beliefs are retained in unconscious and, indeed, conscious mental life.

It remains now to explore in more detail the developmental conditions of the dissociation of mind and the relations between the dissociated aspects of mind that make FWT – or more broadly, self-solicitude – possible.

Notes

1 Freud often emphasises that this formula fits hysteria best and requires modifications for the other transference neuroses, for example the modification required for obsessional neurosis (Freud 1909d: 192ff). It does not apply to what Freud referred to as the actual neuroses.

2 It is possible to develop more sophisticated accounts of drives incorporating cognitive components, as in the work of Maze, Petocz, Boag, Newberry and others (Mackay and Petocz (eds.) 2011). But as I read it these accounts pass beyond anything in classical psychoanalysis and also face insuperable difficulties, though I cannot enter into that here.

3 In Otto Fenichel's (1945) great compendium of classical psychoanalysis, the economic account is the basic model of symptom formation. In that work the idea that symptoms are wish-fulfilling and have representational content – sense, intention, meaning – is scarcely mentioned directly, though present implicitly. It is common to distinguish two trends in Freud's thinking: between a drive-discharge, hydraulic or causal account and a non-causal semantic or hermeneutic one. The drive-discharge model is inadequate, though I do not believe that the semantic or hermeneutic approaches preclude causation. The latter idea seems to rest on the view that reasons can't be causes. They can – providing causation is not tendentiously tied to a strict nomological account of it.

4 The symptom, the dream say: things are not as you fear; they are really thus and, so, as you wish they were. It is in this sense that every symptom can be said to be an attempt at self-cure (McDougall 1986). One represents oneself as cured.

5 The approach in Hopkins (2012) combining psychoanalytic and neuroscientific insights may well throw light on the enabling conditions of FWT.

6 I have chosen to use 'deliberation' though it carries connotations of careful, prolonged reasoning that I do not want. Alternatives such as 'thought' are too vague and 'reason' in philosophy carries too much freight. I want to capture the notion of unconscious reasoning or ratiocination that involves weighing desires and beliefs and arriving at decisions and forming intentions, without the aspect of hesitancy.

7 Freud (1901b). There are important differences between what is referred to in some circles as the cognitive unconscious (and important differences within that class), the Freudian preconscious or (roughly) unconscious ego and the dynamic unconscious or id. For the purpose of this chapter these differences are not critical.

8 For some conceptual difficulties with this view see Bennett and Hacker (2003: 77ff). They worry that no conventions are laid down for the transposed use of the concepts from conscious to unconscious contexts, but the relevant parts of psychoanalytic theory may be viewed as laying down precisely such conventions.

9 How are we to conceive of this notion of an 'executive agency of mind'? Well, we can say that it is the locus of deliberation, judgement, decision, choice and agency. It is not implied that there is some one place either in mind or the brain where such functions play out, or that they cannot be resolved into simpler component units; but such functions there certainly are and theory must find a place for them. In his later work Freud conceived of the ego as an executive agency, a mental structure arbitrating between the demands of reality, the id and the superego. How the ego does this Freud did not, for understandable reasons, satisfactorily explain.

10 The view that the executive agency may be deeply unconscious and not just preconscious is, of course, Freud's (1923b, 1940a: 162).

11 Perhaps an executive state such as proximate intention arises without there being a reason for it; perhaps it is caused by a phantasy **(3.8)**. But if this is possible – it is certainly questionable – it can occur only in so far as the phantasy functions as a reason.

12 Here, as elsewhere, I follow Davidson's (1963) way of individuating actions.

13 These matters are discussed in Petocz (1999), the most authoritative treatment of Freudian symbolism in the literature. I want to thank Agnes Petocz for helping me clarify some of the issues in this section. As noted in the text, I cannot follow her view that Freudian symbolism entails an (unconscious) belief in the identity of symbol and symbolised (1999: 234). Nor do I see symbolic wish-fulfilment as merely a matter of drives changing their objects because drives, in my view, do not possess the complex cognitive and consummatory machinery necessary to make this conception work. The effects of unconscious symbolism may perhaps best be understood as branching from the 'seeing-as' relation explored by Wittgenstein (1958 [53]: II, xi). He provides many examples of *seeing as*, *seeing an aspect* and *the dawning of an aspect*. A triangle may be seen as a mountain, a chest as a house (as in children's games), and so on. Sometimes this requires interpretation – a tale has to be told, the object must be re-located to a new context. Wittgenstein's thought seems to be that not all changes of aspect turn on interpretation. 'To interpret is to think, to do something; seeing is a state' (1958 [53]: 212). It is unintelligible to say (he says) that I see a fork as a fork; no interpretation. But in other cases interpretation is possible, as when I come to see the fork as a weapon. The possibility of interpretation and symbolic understanding (moving on from Wittgenstein) evidently rests on a base of beliefs, desires, capacities etc. that we may call a person's s-state. When one attends to a thing one attends to it under a concept (as an actor) or aspect (as Hecuba). So attending to the actor on the stage, depending on my s-state, including my unconscious s-state, I may see her as Hecuba or, perhaps, (unconsciously) as my mother or as my self, and I may weep. I may be seeing through the eyes of a child. I see her as Hecuba (or mother or self) in the same way as I see the triangle as a mountain but with much deeper and complex resonance. I am seeing one thing as something else in terms of an interpretation which arises from my s-state. This seems to ground the basic effect of unconscious symbolism. A man may see his wife as his mother and from this all sorts of well-known difficulties may follow. It may be that the wife symbolises mother as a result of projection, or something of the kind. That may well be the case and the projective tendency is part of the man's s-state – the sum of tendencies to see this one thing as

another. This view has certain affinities with Joseph Sandler's conception of actualisation. He writes:

> the symptom is not only a disguised 'surface expression' of the unconscious fantasy, but also a source of the perceptual information providing a concealed and symbolic identity of perception in relation to the unconscious wish it satisfies. ... the perceived manifest actualization is unconsciously understood and unconsciously translated back into its latent meaning. In terms of the topographical model this 'decoding' and understanding would take place in the Pcs. system, while in the structural model it can be attributed to the unconscious ego. Essential to the process is the need for consciousness to be protected from the knowledge of what is going on.
>
> (Sandler 1976: 40)

This notion of unconscious understanding work is, I think, consilient with the above account of unconscious symbolism and could easily be united with our earlier account of engrossment.

14 Building on Klein's (1930) formulations, Segal provides an account of how symbolism emerges from the more primitive symbolic equation. The earliest symbols (symbolic equations) are parts of the external world identified with aspects of the self through projective identification. These early symbols 'are not felt by the ego to be symbols or substitutes but to be the original object itself' (Segal 1986: 53). Initially differentiation between self and object is obscured. 'Then, since a part of the ego is confused with the object, the symbol – which is a creation and a function of the ego – becomes, in turn, confused with the object which is symbolized' (1986: 53). The evolution of the symbol from the symbolic equation is coordinated with development from the paranoid–schizoid to the depressive position. Projective identification is used to deny separation and loss, but once they can be tolerated in the depressive position, the symbol can be used 'not to deny but to overcome loss' (Segal 1991: 42). This account of symbol development is, I think, problematic, but we do not require here an epigenetic account, only a distinction between operational symbolism and Segalian symbolic equation.

15 'It is not only a helper to the id; it is also a submissive slave who courts his master's love. Whenever possible it tries to remain on good terms with the id; it clothes the id's Ucs. commands with its Pcs. rationalisations; it pretends that the id is showing obedience to the admonitions of reality, even when in fact it is remaining obstinate and unyielding; it disguises the id's conflicts with reality...' (1923b: 56). In his last work, Freud writes:

> The core of our being... is formed by the obscure id, which has no direct communication with the external world and is accessible even to our own knowledge only through the medium of another agency.... The id knows no solicitude about surviving and no anxiety; or it would perhaps be more correct to say that, though it can generate the sensory elements of anxiety, it cannot make use of them.... The other agency of the mind which we believe we know best and in which we recognize ourselves most easily – what is known as the ego – has been developed out of the id's cortical layer, which, through being adapted to the reception and exclusion of stimuli, is in direct contact with the external world (reality). ... Just as the id is directed exclusively to obtaining pleasure, so the ego is governed by considerations of safety. The ego has set itself the task of self-preservation, which the id appears to neglect.
>
> (1940a: 197–9)

Chapter 5

The self in self-solicitude

> [T]he will, when its servant, the intellect, is unable to produce the thing desired, compels the servant at any rate to picture this thing to it, and generally to undertake the role of comforter, to pacify its lord and master, as a nurse does a child, with fairy tales, and to deck these out so they obtain an appearance of verisimilitude. Here the intellect is bound to do violence to its own nature, which is aimed at truth, since it is compelled, contrary to its own laws, to regard as true things that are neither true nor probable, and often scarcely possible, merely in order to pacify, soothe, and send to sleep for a while the restless and unmanageable will. We clearly see here who is master and who is servant.
>
> Schopenhauer 1966, II: 216–17

5.1 Reprise

We began by observing that persons are subjects of ineluctable wishes or desires. Some of these can be satisfied by appropriate action but others, which are impossible or very difficult to satisfy in the ordinary sense, may be satisfied substitutively, in the manner of FWT, or be relinquished altogether, or be sublimated. FWT involves various techniques and processes involving the tendentious selection or manufacture of 'agent's evidence' in phantasy, illusion, symptom formation and the manipulation of other people. The simplest forms of FWT, infantile hallucinatory wish-fulfilment and most dreams, involve desire operating subintentionally or expressively in the primitive mental conditions Freud described as primary process functioning. At the other extreme there are complex, reflexive processes in which imaginal representations and enactments are used intentionally for the purpose of fulfilling wishes. Some types of daydream are examples of this, as are, less obviously, many forms of wish-fulfilling symptom and enactment. The reflexive, intentional forms of wish-fulfilment may be viewed as members of a class of self-caring or self-solicitous activities that includes self-gratification, self-consolation, self-abasement and, in some of its forms, self-deception **(6.1)**. (Since most of these processes supervene on FWT, we focus on the latter.) Self-solicitude may also involve the regulation of painful affect and anxiety; this may be achieved automatically, perhaps preconsciously, where early maternal soothing functions have been adequately internalised, or they may require deliberative agency. Contemporary psychoanalytic investigations into affect-regulation (Schore 1994, 2003; Fonagy *et al*. 2004) may be seen as directed at one compartment of self-solicitude. The modes of self-solicitude may enter into various auxiliary or superordinate relations with each other. Self-abasement can be an instrument of self-appeasement, and self-deception is often in the strategic service of some superordinate mode of self-solicitude, like self-consolation or self-justification **(6.3)**. In self-solicitude the self takes itself as an object to be cared for; importantly, caring for the self involves a concern to satisfy its desires or wishes, including its unconscious desires or wishes, especially those which attach to the self's significant objects.

Several hurdles have been cleared. Objections to the conception of unconscious intention (and other unconscious propositional attitudes) have been answered **(4.2)** and two worrying objections arising from Sartre's 'censor argument' allayed **(4.7)**. Because a radical intentionalism is at the core of our thesis, it was necessary to identify a range of plausible unconscious practical syllogisms accounting for unconscious intentional agency. Unconscious intentional agency entails the division or dissociation of mind into independent centres of agency (at least on the assumption that the conscious executive function remains uninterruptedly an independent centre of deliberation, choice and action) and we examined some reasons for thinking that the mind is indeed subject to such radical partition **(4.6)**. But such disunity – 'second-mind personology' – has been held up as a decisive objection to the intentionalist (or unconsciously strategic) functioning of mind. **Chapter 3** argued, however, that there are no satisfactory alternatives to intentionalism and, therefore, partition; none that can meet the touchstone of clinical adequacy. This chapter will endeavour to make a virtue of partition and identify the final links between dissociation and maximal FWT, and so close the circle.

5.2 A very brief history of the divided self

The belief that people have two or more souls, or that their souls can undergo division or be torn in conflict, was a feature, in varying forms, of the Siberian shamanism that entered Greek thought in the seventh century BCE, home-grown Greek Orphism and the later Manichaean conceptions found in Persian and some early Christian thought (Burkert 2004; Dodds 1951). It is probable that such widespread beliefs are engendered by experiences of inner conflict, multiplicity or fragmentation that are, of course, common in humankind. Plato, however, was the first to formulate such issues in recognisably philosophical ways and provided the earliest arguments for mental partition. Since then philosophers have considered various partitive conceptions of mind, largely because the idea of partition or dissociation of mental contents and activities appears to offer a way of understanding problematic forms of ambivalence, mental conflict and incoherence of belief, especially those which characterise the so-called paradoxes of irrationality, weakness of the will (*akrasia*) and self-deception. Plato himself was exercised by the phenomena of ambivalence and *akrasia* and the doctrine that goes under his teacher's name: the Socratic paradox.

Socrates proclaimed that nobody willingly errs. In *Protagoras* Plato has him say: 'It is not in human nature to be prepared to go for what you think is bad in preference to what you think is good' (2009: 358d). Everybody acts in what they perceive to be their own interests; if they fail to act in what is their *true* interest the cause is defective knowledge, not defect in desire or motive. It is a pity that this doctrine seems manifestly false. People often do knowingly act against their best interests; they take the inferior course knowing that there is a better course. They smoke cigarettes knowing it will kill them, enter into destructive relationships knowing it will hurt them. How is that possible? The solution advanced in Plato's *Republic* is to partition the mind into three conflicting elements: the first, reason; the second, appetite or desire; and the third – *thumos* – rendered variously as spirit, anger, pride or indignation. Reason seeks the Good but may be overwhelmed by the other elements: reason is not master in its own house.

But why partition and not just acknowledgement of the obvious fact that people are often riven by conflicting desires and fail to integrate their beliefs and harmonise dispositions? Plato has several arguments (1966: 434ff), none of them strong, but combined with the religious conceptions, the striking phenomenology of conflict and multiplicity and the tendency of Greek thought to group similar mental functions into faculties, Plato's conceptual innovation offers reasonable explanation of at least some inner conflict, the phenomenology of mental dissociation and *akrasia*.

In Euripides' *Medea*, performed several decades before Plato wrote, Medea says, just before she is about to vengefully murder her children: 'I know what wickedness I am about to do: but the *thumos* is stronger than my purposes, *thumos*, the root of man's worst acts.' Medea recognises being horribly powerless against *herself*. She doesn't say: I know what wickedness my *thumos* (my rage, my indignation) is about to do. Yet it appears as if she feels overpowered by an alien force. Plato's conception of mind partitioned into mutually exclusive and, as it were, opposing vectors, offers an explanation of her conflicted action, if not of the hovering paradox that Medea's *thumos* is *not* an alien force: she 'owns' it, and seems to know it. Behind multiplicity there lurks a unity that threatens to undermine Platonic – and substantially related – applications of strong partition.[1] This theme will resurface below.

As noted in **(1.3)**, the rich harvest of philosophical investigations into self and multiplicity in the Ancient world was squandered in the thousand years of Christian totalitarianism that followed (Martin and Barresi 2006). In the seventeenth century Descartes asks, in the first of his *Meditations*, what manner of thing he is; he answers that he is a conscious being, a mind or soul. In the sixth *Meditation* he adds: 'I am unable to distinguish any parts within myself. I understand myself to be something quite single and complete' (Descartes 1972).[2] This conception of the mind or self has, of course, been extraordinarily influential and is compelling not least because of the pre-philosophical intuition that in each of us something inner, single, an essential 'me', is the unitary locus of perception, deliberation, decision and agency; this aspect of personal identity, of some unitary thing remaining constant over time, seems on the face of it to be a condition of our understanding others, of our moral and reactive attitudes to them and our judicial institutions.

Nevertheless, by the middle of the nineteenth century the idea that the mind can fall apart into something like separate selves or subpersonalities had considerable currency. We saw that during its course, demonic possession as a clinical entity was gradually replaced by hysteria and multiple personality (Ellenberger 1970), and many researchers concluded that 'the human mind was rather like a matrix from which whole sets of sub-personalities could emerge and differentiate themselves' (1970: 139).[3] At the same time various conceptions of an unconscious mind were also in the air, and not only over the Continent. J. S. Mill discusses conceptions of the unconscious in his *An Examination of Sir William Hamilton's Philosophy* (1865) and William James provides detailed discussion of the splitting of consciousness in *The Principles of Psychology* (1890). Psychoanalysis evolved against this backdrop, and we noted **(1.5)** that Freud's special achievement in this connection was not only to develop an illuminating and comprehensive conception of the (topographical) Unconscious, but to develop and link a particular polypsychic or partitive conception incorporating the features of that Unconscious – the structural theory of the agencies id, ego and superego – to the developmental and object-relational perspectives: to indicate some of the ways in which the intense need for objects in the course of development fundamentally modifies the structure of the mind.

5.3 Freud and the structure of mind

Before examining Freud's views in detail it will help to sharpen the conception of an *independent agency* of mind **(1.5)**. Gardner (1993), distilling some work of Pears (1984), has identified the following criteria for what he calls 'subsystems', which are much the same sort of thing Freud called 'agencies' or 'structures': (a) subsystems have their own points of view or subjectivity; in particular they can have the representation 'other sub-system' in a way that the agent as a whole cannot; (b) they are autonomous 'rational centres of agency', that is, they exercise strategic, intentional agency in pursuit of their own goals; and (c) they are subjects of mental ascriptions which exclude such ascriptions to the whole person. Implied in these conditions is a fourth worth expressing separately: (d) the agencies possess a degree of coherence sufficient to support the attributes noted in (a)–(c). And to approach closer to the conditions assumed in psychoanalytic discussion of these matters it is necessary to add a fifth, not implied in the first four: (e) there is a degree of continuity in the agencies; they persist as – in some sense – *parts* of the self, can undergo change, and are not merely summoned into existence at critical moments.[4]

Freud's topographical account of mind is not radically partitive. The Ucs. is separated from the Pcs. by censorship, but is not conceived as a person-like agency. The innovations that concern us here appear definitively as the structural theory of *The Ego and the Id* (1923b). Here the developmental and object-relational perspectives are linked to the internalisation of objects which gradually structure the mind into the agencies id, ego and superego.[5] Moreover, the agencies are now understood to enter into relations with each other, much as people do. These ideas were entirely new, a break from all earlier conceptions of divided minds. Earlier psychological accounts generally attributed dissociation or splitting to constitutional degenerative factors, and later philosophical motives for partitioning turned on the exigencies of irrationality and conflict. Such matters were not of course unnoticed by Freud. But the idea that the *preconditions* for dissociation (and irrationality and conflict) were set largely by developmental factors, principally the structuring of mind resulting from identification, was his alone. Although it is now recognised that other factors besides identification are involved in structural differentiation and dissociation, the vicissitudes of identification retain a preeminent place in psychoanalytic thought.

Freud and later theorists saw the explanation of multiple personality in the ego's inability to integrate identifications:

> If they [the ego's identifications] obtain the upper hand and become too numer-
> ous, unduly powerful and incompatible with one another, a pathological out-
> come will not be far off. It may come to a disruption of the ego in consequence
> of the different identifications being cut off from one another by resistances;
> perhaps the secret of the cases of what is described as "multiple personality" is
> that the different identifications seize hold of consciousness in turn.
>
> (Freud 1923b: 30–1)

It seems to me that the role of identification in structural differentiation and dissociation is overestimated, and that in contemporary psychoanalysis we cannot find a consensus on the ways in which the mind may be divided. The relations between, for
example, structural differentiation into agencies in the Freudian sense, splitting of the
ego, of the self, multiple personality (dissociative identity disorder), dissociative phenomena as a response to trauma or loss, false-self development, pathological organisations of the self (Rosenfeld 1987; Steiner 1993) and some other contingencies is quite
obscure. Evidently there are different causes for and forms of each, not all of them
corresponding to differentiation into agencies in the Freudian sense. Freud himself
realised that he was onto something new when he began to investigate splitting of the
ego (1927e). Trauma, false-self compliance and the need to sustain attachment to
objects can be important causes of dissociation or splitting, and may perhaps constitute
the most salient features of personality structure. Bowlby (1998) discusses a little girl in
which a split-off or segregated part of her ego retaining a relationship to her (deceased)
mother was largely de-activated but episodically manifested in fugue-like states, whilst
another part governed her everyday life. His description is most interesting:

> the system that is segregated and unconscious is an organised one and no less
> self-consistent than is the system with free access to action and consciousness.
> Furthermore, the segregated system is characterised by all the cognitive and
> affective elements that qualify it to be regarded as mental, namely, desire,
> thought, feeling and memory. From time to time, also, when it takes control of
> behaviour, the segregated system shows itself to be so organised with reference

to persons and objects in the environment that it is capable of forming plans and executing them, albeit in rather clumsy and ineffective ways.

(1998: 345ff)

It seems in a case such as this that the Freudian structural model recedes into the background and can find little application. The situation today is not unlike that described in the nineteenth century, when it was proposed that 'the human mind was rather like a matrix from which whole sets of sub-personalities could emerge and differentiate themselves' (see Ellenberger 1970: 139). I return to this theme below.

Why did Freud introduce the structural division of the psychical apparatus? There were several reasons, all of them of great clinical and philosophical interest. Freud tells in several places how forcibly he had been struck by the clinical picture of melancholia. In it,

the ego [is] divided, fallen apart into two pieces, one of which rages against the second. This second piece is the one which has been altered by introjection and which contains the lost object... [a critical] agency develops in our ego which may cut itself off from the rest of the ego and come into conflict with it.

(1921c: 109)

and

during a melancholic attack [the] superego becomes over severe, abuses the poor ego, humiliates it and ill-treats it, threatens it with the direst punishments, reproaches it for actions in the remotest past... as though it had spent the whole interval collecting accusations...

(1933a: 61)

Delusions of self-observation in some patients also suggested partition (1933a: 59) and Freud was even more forcefully impressed by the negative therapeutic reaction encountered in clinical work, which he linked to an unconscious sense of guilt or need for punishment. In many cases he found that after therapeutic progress the patient, instead of showing improvement, declines: 'there is something in these people that sets itself against their recovery, and its approach is dreaded as though it were... a danger' (1921c: 390). In linking the unconscious sense of guilt to the need for punishment, and both to resistance and to moral masochism, Freud presciently recognised that resistance emanated not only from the superego but also from the ego, which had developed a masochistic attachment to the superego.

The sense of guilt, the harshness of the superego, is... the same thing as the severity of the conscience... The fear of this critical agency (a fear which is at the bottom of the whole relationship), the need for punishment, is an instinctual manifestation on the part of the ego, which has become masochistic under the influence of a sadistic superego; it is a portion, that is to say, of the instinct towards internal destruction present in the ego, employed for forming an erotic attachment to the superego.

(1930a: 136)

Many similar passages could be reproduced describing erotic, aversive and malevolent relations between the id, ego and superego. Notice that the conflicts are not merely conflicts of desires or beliefs; they are more like a conflict of arms. They involve aggression, triumph, humiliation and suffering. There are more transparently libidinal relations also.

> The fear of death in melancholia only admits of one explanation: that the ego gives itself up because it feels itself hated and persecuted by the superego, instead of loved. To the ego, therefore, living means the same as being loved – being loved by the superego, which here again appears as the representative of the id. The superego fulfils the same function of protecting and saving that was fulfilled in earlier days by the father and later by Providence or Destiny. But, when the ego finds itself in an excessive real danger which it believes itself unable to overcome with its own strength, it ... sees itself deserted by all protecting forces and lets itself die.
>
> (1923b: 58; also 56)

Further, the ego could take a component of the superego, the ego-ideal (or, as it might be better put, the ideal self) as an erotic object: the ego-ideal becomes 'the target of the self-love which was enjoyed in childhood by the actual ego' (1914c: 94). Loving the ego-ideal *recovers* the lost narcissism of childhood, which must imply at least a transient identification with the ego-ideal. Here we can in fact discern three distinct processes that Freud does not always clearly distinguish: the narcissistic rewards of living up to the ego-ideal or the ideals implicit in the superego; the reward of being loved by the superego; and loving the ego-ideal (ideal self) with which one is identified and thus recovering the lost narcissism of childhood.

On the Freudian account, the agencies ego and superego differentiate from the id largely as a result of identification with objects. Objects are first phantasised as being incorporated through a body orifice; then in some circumstances there may supervene a further vicissitude, introjection, in which they acquire a kind of permanence in the mind; beyond that, under favourable conditions, some introjects may be identified with and their features appropriated.[6] Identification is motivated by a variety of factors, but most significantly for Freud it is a consequence of the inability to relinquish libidinised objects. 'It may be', Freud says, 'that ... identification is the sole condition under which the id can give up its objects' (1923b: 29). To retain a relationship to objects we modify our own characteristics to accord with a model and thereby achieve a kind of internalised, reflexive relationship between self and self-modeled-on-object. Freud puts this point colourfully: 'When the ego assumes the features of the object, it is forcing itself, so to speak, upon the id as a love object and is trying to make good the id's loss by saying: "Look, you can love me too – I am so like the object"' (1923b: 30). In becoming like the object we adopt some of the repertoire, perspectives, perhaps physical characteristics (such as gait) and, critically, attitudes which the object was perceived as having towards us. *We internalise and adopt roles or personae, though not necessarily public ones.* As well as new perspectives and attitudes, new aspects of the self are acquired, and aspects are what one perceives from particular perspectives. An example may make these matters clearer.

In his earliest discussion of identification, in *Leonardo da Vinci* (1910c), Freud speculates on the sources of Leonardo's homosexuality. He suggests that for a while the young Leonardo had an intense and exclusive relationship with his mother that was suddenly terminated. The boy then represses his love for her and 'puts himself in her place, identifies himself with her and takes his own person as a model in whose likeness he chooses the new objects of his love...' (1910c: 191). That seems to account for an aspect of Leonardo's narcissistic object choice, Freud's main theoretical concern in the paper. But he then continues:

> A man who has become a homosexual in this way remains fixated to the mnemic image of his mother. By repressing his love for his mother he preserves it in his unconscious and from now on remains faithful to her. While he seems to pursue boys he is in reality running away from other women, who might cause him to be unfaithful.

Here Freud has an insight not elaborated till much later. In remaining faithful to his (deceased) mother Leonardo is perpetuating a relationship, but not just with a mnemic image or the memory of his mother. These things are possible – remaining faithful to memories as to ideals and vows is not unknown – but they would not account adequately for the features of Leonardo's narcissism: his apparent self-love, self-sufficiency, love of boys of certain types, etc. The underlying structure of that narcissism, which at this stage Freud cannot fully articulate, is that Leonardo is maintaining a relationship with himself-identified-with-mother; so his mother lives on in him and retains a relationship with him, though for her love to be expressed through him, *his* (probably ideal) self has to be projected on to other boys.

There is one more thread I want to tease out from this Freudian tapestry. The structural differentiation brought about by identification, which creates the macro-agencies ego and superego and defines the scope of the id, does *not*, in Freud's view, entail disunity or conflict in the self. It creates the preconditions for dissociation and conflict between agencies. Although the agencies are 'realms, regions, provinces, into which we divide the individual's mental apparatus...' (1933a: 79) the apparatus is – paradoxically perhaps – conceived as a unity, at least in health. Freud's insistence on this point is frequently overlooked. 'One must not take the difference between ego and id in too hard-and-fast a sense' (1923b: 38), he says:

> We were justified, I think, in dividing the ego from the id, for there are certain considerations which necessitate the step. On the other hand the ego is identical with the id, and is merely a specially differentiated part of it. If we think of this part by itself in contradistinction to the whole, *or if a real split has occurred between the two*, the weakness of the ego becomes evident. But if the ego

remains bound up with the id and indistinguishable from it, then it displays its strength. The same is true of the relation between ego and superego. In many situations the two are merged; and as a rule we can only distinguish the one from the other when there is a tension or conflict between them. In repression the decisive fact is that the ego is an organization and the id is not. The ego is, indeed, the organized portion of the id. We should be quite wrong if we pictured the ego and the id as two opposing camps...

(1926d: 97; my italics)

Freud distinguishes here between structural differentiation and 'a real split' between the agencies. As already noted, there are many different notions of splitting and dissociation in the literature, so it will be apt to give this kind of splitting a special name to distinguish it from the others: the slightly archaic 'diremption' will serve. And now this distinction invites questions about the circumstances in which structural differentiation (brought about largely by identification) turns to diremption. (It also casts in deep relief our uncertainty about the precise way in which the agencies should be understood.) Freud mentions 'tension or conflict' between the agencies, but we have seen reason not to interpret these conditions too narrowly. If we review the examples of intrapsychic relations above it appears one common circumstance is that in each case one agency or part of the self is treating another as if it were an external object, as something other than itself. Freud is explicit that the self can treat itself as it can external objects:

> ... the ego now enters into the relation of an object to the ego ideal which has been developed out of it, and... all the interplay between an external object and the ego as a whole, with which our study of the neuroses has made us acquainted, may possibly be repeated upon this new scene of action within the ego.
>
> (1921c: 62)

> ... the ego is in its very essence a subject; how can it be made into an object? Well, there is no doubt that it can be. The ego can take itself as object, can treat itself like other objects, can observe itself, criticize itself, and do Heaven knows what with itself. In this, one part of the ego is setting itself over against the rest. So the ego can be split; it splits itself during a number of its functions – temporarily at least. Its parts can come together again afterwards.
>
> (1933a: 58)

We do not have a firm grasp of this vicissitude of splitting. (Notice that in this late passage Freud is using 'ego' in the pre-structural sense, as denoting the whole self.) Does treating oneself as an object always induce diremption? It would seem not. It may be that this kind of splitting is *sometimes* a consequence of the self treating itself as an object, and that whether it occurs depends on the nature of the particular relations between parts of the self, the perspectives and aspects assumed by the self: perhaps those relations which determine the attitudes involved in treating (parts of) oneself as an *external* object. Or it may be that diremption is a *precondition* for the self to take itself – a part of itself – as an external object. These relations will be considered further in a moment, but first it seems in order to summarise the findings of this section and disarm some objections to them.

I think that the protracted citation and discussion supports the following propositions:

(1) Freud conceived of the structures or agencies as capable of entering into a broad range of mutual 'personal' relations which can only be partially characterised as involving conflict of motives and beliefs; for example, sado-masochistic relationships.

(2) They are conceived as autonomous centres of agency with their own perspectives, motives, capacity for intentional action and for representing the other agencies, and a degree of mutual opacity.

(3) The self's taking (part of) itself as an object (sometimes) involves its diremption into the kind of entities specified in (1) and (2).

(4) Despite conditions (1) to (3), Freud enjoined some kind of underlying unity in the self.

5.4 Indulging in metaphor, hypostatising phantasy?

There are two objections that threaten to undermine entirely the constructions I have placed on the cited passages. First, that in these passages Freud was merely indulging in metaphor; second, that he was hypostatising phantasy.

Heinz Hartmann and his colleagues long ago endeavoured to cleanse psychoanalytic metapsychology of metaphorical and anthropomorphic formulations and set its theory on a foundation of mechanical causes operating on and between subpersonal, functionally defined mental structures. Thus in their influential paper 'The formation of psychic structure' (Hartmann, Kris and Loewenstein 1964) they chide one of Franz Alexander's early books in which 'the id, ego, and superego have indeed become exalted actors on the psychic stage'. Their reaction to Freud's treatment of the phenomena which elicited the structural theory is revealing.

> ... a more generalized penetration of the phenomena... becomes possible only at some distance from immediate experience. This was the function of Freud's structural concepts. If we use these concepts in a strict sense, the distance from experience grows. Freud's metaphorical usage of his own terms clearly intended to bridge this gap. It might thus be said that Freud's usage bears the imprint of the clinical source from which the concepts were originally derived, the imprint of the communication with patients. Requirements of communication may ever and again suggest richness of metaphor, but metaphors should not obscure the nature of the concepts and their function in psychoanalysis as a science.
>
> (1964: 33–4)

Although they allege taint by metaphor, the authors recognise that the Freudian agencies were intended to capture certain kinds of clinical manifestation, the 'exalted actors on the psychic stage'. The cited passages from Freud fill out the sense of the phenomena at issue. But the authors think that these clinical entities, the 'actors' or the self in certain registers are not basic to Freud's thought and have no place in scientific explanation. They argue that Freudian agencies are best considered as underlying, subpersonal organisations of functions and associated contents interacting causally under determinable laws to yield the surface behaviour and experience of whole persons. In a more recent treatment of the same issue, Hopkins (1995) also argues that the Freudian agencies, although distinct and autonomous, are meant to be understood not as agents bearing propositional attitudes, but as subpersonal neural systems functionally defined. These systems can be described teleologically; that is, in terms of goals and information which are in turn related to motives of actual persons (the parents) that are embedded as neural prototypes in the systems. Such descriptions of the agencies are said to be useful and 'serve to generalise over clinical data' because, as Freud importantly observed, the way people 'actually function depends upon the prototypes by which they represent themselves and their relations to others' (1995: 475). But when we do so describe them we speak only metaphorically.

> We may describe such systems as if they had motives, in describing their goals and information on which we take them to operate; but we do not take these descriptions to have the same consequences as in the case of the desires and beliefs of persons. ... Freud's distinct systems constitute one person, and the way these are ascribed motives, although metaphorical, is nonetheless genuinely explanatory, so far as it goes.

It should be plain that neither of these accounts corresponds to Freud's mature thought about mental structure. Freud did provide (incomplete and problematic) functional descriptions of the agencies (1923b; 1940a), but the passages cited above show that he was prepared to use a *vocabulary of relationship* to describe their mutual relations far richer than anything that can be cobbled together out of properties plausibly attributable to subpersonal systems, such as goals and information; indeed, richer than anything that can be cobbled together from the propositional attitudes *belief* and *desire*. He did so, I think, because he recognised that the complexity of the relations between the agencies as he characterised them required descriptive materials that outran anything available in an idiom apposite to subpersonal systems – the language of his metapsychology, for example. The later attempts by theoreticians of ego-psychology to flesh out a subpersonal account of the structures highlights this limitation. Consider Hartmann's (1964) recommendation that 'tension' be used instead of such words as 'disapproval' to describe a relation between superego and ego. Suppose that *tension* was indeed the kind of relation that could intelligibly subsist between subpersonal systems. That is primitive but the principle at issue would seem to remain unaltered even if more sophisticated neurobiological substitutes were available. Then it seems evident that the number of relations subsisting intrapsychically between agencies (and between agencies and introjects) must outrun those available for reference in any subpersonal or neuroscientific idiom. In the present case, we could not even begin to variegate *tension* to cover for disdain, contempt, hatred, reproach – the list is very long – each of which carry nuances essential to a clinical language adequate to the accurate description of intrapsychic relations. Freud's rich Intentional descriptions were born of fidelity to clinical reality. He may have considered them provisional, but they were not intended to be metaphorical.

Even if they were not *intended* by Freud to be metaphorical, in the sense that Hartmann wished to eschew, could Freud's descriptions be construed as metaphorical in the sense that Hopkins enjoins and so save the subpersonal characterisation of the agencies? I think not, for reasons already foreshadowed. The personal idiom necessary to an adequate description of the complexity of intrapsychic relations is in principle not reducible to, or eliminable in favour of, any conceivable neuroscientific replacement. That is because the content of mental states is often determined by circumstances external to the brain, so that no matter how detailed the neuroscientific description may be, it will often fall short of specifying the content of mental states (supposing this was neurobiologically possible in some future time) and the relations between them; *a fortiori* the relations between agencies **(10)**. My contention is that Freud's descriptions of the agencies in terms appropriate to selves or persons were not intended to be metaphorical, and are not metaphorical, because the agencies were not conceived in his later thought as subpersonal entities, and are not such. They are, I think, better conceived as protean expressions of the self or person; or, as I shall say, *personations*, in a sense to be explained **(5.6)**. If that is correct, then it yields several satisfactory corollaries. The agencies being self-like or personal are therefore not in competition with cognitive modules, 'stupid' homunculi, functional organisations or other products of decomposition. And we seem to have the right kind of entity to answer to the clinical phenomenology. However, it must be admitted that the character of the agencies has become still more obscure and it becomes more pressing to ask whether what we have taken for substantial protean entities are not just the shadows of phantasies, as the second objection urges.

Consider this vignette. A patient

> would rave against girl children and in fantasy would describe how she would crush a girl child if she had one, and would then fall to punching herself (which perpetuated the beatings her mother gave her). One day I said to her, 'You must be terrified being hit like that.' She stopped and stared and said, 'I'm not being hit. I'm the one that's doing the hitting.'
>
> (Guntrip 1968: 191)

This abbreviated case is underdescribed, of course, and some interpretation is assumed without discussion. This person certainly *seems* to be radically dissociated, much in the way denoted by 'diremption' above. It may be urged, however, that the appearances can be explained as the consequence of a unified agent acting out a complex phantasy or pantomime in which the characters are phantastic misrepresentations of the self.[7] In this account of the structures, the vignette which could plausibly be construed as a dramatic engagement between ego and superego (or related figures) is really the enactment, the acting out, of a complex phantasy. I believe that approaches along these lines fail to accommodate essential details of this kind of case. First, such phantasies must have causes and reflect, in Gardner's phrase, 'a stretch of causally efficacious psychological reality' (1993: 180). Second, for a phantasy to be efficacious – to be wish-fulfilling – it must operate in conditions which enable it to be so. What are the psychological conditions which give rise to such a phantasy and enable it to be efficacious? Well, it would seem that this patient identifies with her mother (Guntrip elaborates on this feature later on), who was experienced as hating her and, consequently, she now hates herself, or some childish aspects of herself. Her hatred is so overwhelming that she phantasises destroying other children and acts out by punching herself. Recalling the discussion of Leonardo we may conjecture that in these performances she is maintaining a wished-for dual relationship with her mother: on the one hand, by identifying with her and on the other, by masochistically yielding to her. These, or some such, psychological configurations causally articulate her phantasy. But now, for this putative phantastic scenario to express her various wishes and to be efficacious in pacifying some of them, *must there not already be in place* the kind of diremptions and mutual opacities between parts of the self which we entertained above? For it would seem to be precisely a dirempted psychological reality which gives rise to this particular phantasy. How else could she phantasise that she is mother, or that she is strong like mother, when that phantasy is her own creature and the assumption of strength is defensively predicated on awareness of her weakness? How can she triumph over herself when she is her own victim?[8] How could she be so unsympathetic and careless of her own pain and needs if it were not that she was profoundly dissociated? In sum, it would seem that diremption, whose assumption phantasising of the proposed kind is supposed to render superfluous, would have to be partly the cause of the phantasy and a condition of its efficaciousness. Phantasy can reflect and exploit psychological reality but cannot go counterfeit for it.

So the objections to the strongly partitive interpretation placed on the cited passages from Freud founder. It does seem to be Freud's mature view, and it seems to be the correct view, that the (mental) self can split – dirempt – into parts or personations of the self which satisfy the conditions for independent agency outlined earlier. In some of these cases diremption may lead to internal conflict of motive and incoherence of belief of the sort that philosophers have traditionally considered, but it is not, or not only, *engendered* by that sort of conflict. In the cases discussed the vicissitude is intimately linked to the identification with external objects in the formation of the agencies. It should, however, be noted that identification itself is sometimes precipitated by conflict, and that there may be other determinants producing results similar to diremption.

However, from the fact that the self can divide in the respects considered here it may not follow, as Freud indicated, that there are *no* threads that bind its parts together. It may be that further consideration of the relations between the agencies or personations will yield principles of self-unity which transcend division, and that these principles are themselves prerequisites for clinical understanding. This theme can be pursued through the work of an outstanding psychoanalytic pioneer.

5.5 Fairbairn

Whereas Freud saw structuralisation largely as an inevitable developmental process proceeding even without conflict – the id growing up, as it were, and the ego being socialised – Fairbairn's view is that structuralisation occurs because the caretaking (usually maternal) environment is (inevitably) inadequate and therefore a product of conflict.[9] The neonate's ego is unitary and is confronted with an object that is in some measure unsatisfactory. Attempting to improve its external circumstances, the infant internalises the unsatisfactory object. (Fairbairn modified his views about the internalisation of the earliest objects, but that is not germane here.) However, the price of purchasing outer security is inner insecurity. The internalised object retains the characteristics reflecting maternal failures: specifically, an exciting, tantalising aspect and a rejecting aspect. So the internal situation now confronting the child is similar to the earlier external one and a second defensive process is set in train. The ego splits off these bad aspects, leaving it with three internal objects: the exciting object, the rejecting object, and a satisfying nucleus that becomes attached to the conscious central ego as an ideal object. The two remaining bad objects are then repressed but, since parts of the ego remain 'attached' or 'devoted' to them, these parts of the ego are also repressed. 'We thus appear to be driven', Fairbairn concludes, 'to the necessity of assuming a certain multiplicity of egos' (1952: 89–90).

The endopsychic situation now consists of a central ego (CE) attached to the relatively satisfying ideal object (IO), an anti-libidinal ego (AE) attached to the rejective object (RO) and a libidinal ego (LE) attached the exciting object (EO). At a later stage good objects are internalised as defence against internal bad objects. The Freudian superego now appears as a conglomeration of characteristics of the AE, EO and the augmented IO. Fairbairn claims, rightly I believe, that the permutations of internal relationships afforded by this endopsychic model allow for greater explanatory resource than Freud's tripartite model. The permutations underlie many recognised clinical conditions and can be seen perspicuously to perpetuate earlier unsatisfactory interpersonal relationships. For example, the AE displays an 'uncompromisingly aggressive attitude... towards the libidinal ego... based on the latter's cathexis of the exciting object and its own cathexis of the rejecting object; and it is thus a reflection of the original ambivalence of the individual towards his libidinal objects' (1952: 171). The AE's attack on the EO represents persistence of the child's original resentment against the temptress, the tantalising mother who fails to satisfy the very need she excites (1952: 115). But it does not appear to be Fairbairn's view that the subsidiary egos are *identified* with their objects, only that they cathect or are 'devoted' to them. Then why, it may be asked, should they take on their object's attitudes? Why, for example, should the AE embody the child's hatred of his libidinal needs unless it acquired these from the RO by identification, the RO's attitudes in turn reflecting perceived parental hatred? For modification of this kind in the character of the ego(s) seems to require, as we noted above, the assimilation of a role – of the *modus operandi* of hatred, say. It would seem necessary to recognise that the roles of the subsidiary egos *are* effected through their identification with, and not just their cathexis of, internal objects. And this is a step which some theorists have taken (Ogden 1993; Grotstein 2009).

A further factor has to be considered at this point. Fairbairn observed that Melanie Klein had failed to explain how incorporative phantasy could give rise to internal objects as endopsychic structures (1952: 154). They could not be 'figments of phantasy' and must therefore be recognised as structures. Since they are endopsychic structures, Fairbairn reasoned, 'they must be themselves in some measure dynamic; and it should be added that they must derive their dynamic quality from their cathexis by ego structures' (1952: 177).

Again, Fairbairn appears not to go so far as to identify internal objects with ego-structures; he says that they acquire their dynamism from being cathected by ego-structures. But how they do so is unclear. Ogden (1993) and others have taken the further step of attempting to explain the dynamism of internal objects as a consequence of their identification with parts of the ego. 'In brief', says Ogden, 'internal objects are subdivisions of the ego that are heavily identified with an object representation while maintaining the capacities of the whole ego for thought, perception, and feeling... The fact that this structure (the internal object) is experienced as non-self is accounted for by means of its profound identification with the object' (1993: 150).

If we, too, take this step, we really are landed with a multiplicity of egos – and a multiplicity of problems. An original unitary ego is fragmented into at least six subsidiary egos and potentially a further budget of internal objects which are sub-divisions of the ego(s). The fundamental condition of personal unity that underlies our ascriptions of agency and responsibility, that enables us to understand others and ourselves as persons, seems utterly lost. Who is in charge? If different subsidiary egos or constellations of them assume 'control' at different times, on what principles are these shifts in agential dominance determined?

In the *Controversial Discussions* Fairbairn stated that 'internal objects should be regarded as having an organised structure, an identity of their own, an endopsychic existence and an activity as real within the inner world as those of any objects in the outer world' (Clarke 2006: 56). If internal objects are to be regarded as organised, person-like agents then Fairbairn is certainly right: they must be provided with identity conditions and specification of mental content. But what *is* known of their identity conditions, motives and character in general? It seems to me that sometimes there is something, but never much. In the course of therapy some re-identifiable figures with, let's say, attitudinal consistency, will regularly emerge (or be inferred) in phantasy or action. It is important also that these figures seem to know a great deal about the person's inner life, including her unconscious motivations – a feature Freud noted of the superego. But we do not attribute to the subsidiary egos the features of full personhood, most importantly first-person perspective, in which (in Locke's phrase) they are selves to themselves; nor do we wonder much about their moral and intellectual virtues and vices. These facts suggest that the 'personal' character, if that's what it is, of the subsidiary egos is considerably circumscribed.

How are we to understand the kind of radical partition apparently entailed by Fairbairn's account of dynamic subsidiary egos and internal objects? One possible response is to interpret the endopsychic situation in the manner of Plato's division of mind. The divisions differ in their preferences and the actions of the whole are determined by 'economic' considerations, or a kind of vectorial addition or social choice as in Glymour's (1991) interpretation of Freud. One of several difficulties with this account is that it is silent on the complex motivational and affective intrapsychic relations which are striking features in Freud's and Fairbairn's later work.

Another response is to insist that partition is only apparent, an epiphenomenon generated by the colourful metaphorical language occasionally used by Freud and perpetuated by Klein, Fairbairn and others. Such divisions as there are, it is claimed, are to be found in the neurological substratum, in the opposition of drive structures or other more complex sets of motivational structures. The attributions to these structures of complex Intentional properties are merely metaphorical – clinically useful perhaps, but without ontological significance. A range of otherwise quite different views are consistent with this approach (Boag 2005; Hartmann 1964; Hopkins 1995, 2012; Maze 2009) but appear inadequate to the clinical appearances, as argued above.

A final response, broadly Kleinian in inspiration, denies partition by rendering passive the entities which Fairbairn asserted were active or dynamic. Internal objects and subsidiary egos do not *actually* hate or attack the self; they are phantasised or experienced as hating and attacking the self. The ego is not split in reality, it is experienced *as if* it were split, a consequence perhaps of dissociative phantasies such as those underlying projective identification. The difficulty with this proposal, already outlined in **5.4**, is how to understand the form the phantasies take without predicating them on some stretch of pre-existing psychical reality. Presumably the phantasies take shape on the basis of *dispositions* to phantasise in scripted ways that represent conflict between supposed agencies or splits in the ego (Wollheim 1984, 1993; Sandler and Sandler 1998). But these dispositions would seem to be grounded in the very agencies, in the dirempted structures, that the phantasying is supposed to render superfluous. What else could reflect the dispositions to so phantasise? So it seems after all that we are returned to something close to the Freudian and Fairbairnian picture of psychic structures or agencies in personal relations dramatised in part in phantasy.

5.6 Egos, selves and personations

To this point I have been using the terms 'mind', 'self' and 'person' without much distinction or care, and introduced my own term, 'personation' **(5.4)**, in an attempt to capture the idea of a person in a certain register or role. Now more care is required. 'Person' is a term with juridical roots, but it carries a lot of baggage in philosophy. (Human) persons are usually distinguished as those human beings who possess the concept of *person* and have certain standing recognised in law, conditions that exclude infants and the brain-dead, though they are assuredly human beings. However, I will use the concepts of *person*, of being *person-like* and, especially, of *personation* without these conditions. That may be a little misleading, but it's impossible to extract the term I need from 'self' or 'human being' without clumsy neologising. *Personation*, on the other hand, is already with us. According to Webster's Dictionary, it means to play a part; to assume a character. I will stipulate that *a personation is a human being or person engrossed in a role*. 'Personation' is preferable to 'persona', since the latter suggests the notion of a mask or pretence, whereas the reference here is to something like a transformation, perhaps transitory, or an assumption of another self.

In his early work Freud used 'das Ich' ambiguously to signify sometimes the whole person, sometimes a subpersonal, neural structure and sometimes the conscious mind. After *The Ego and the Id* he reserved the term translated as 'ego' for one structure within the mind, constituting together with the id and the superego the whole mind, psychical apparatus or 'psychical personality' (1933a). Neither Freud nor Fairbairn tell us in any detail what structures are, but it is notable that Freud considered the id as a structure. He writes of 'the structures we have assumed to exist – the ego, the super-ego and the id' (1923b: 42); the ego, however, is organised, while the id is not.[10] But the fact that both consider structures to be 'person-like' has the happy consequence that the language of personal relations, including of course the Intentional or common-sense-psychological idiom, can be enlisted in the description of intrapsychic relations.

Rejecting Freud's tripartite structure, 'ego', for Fairbairn, denotes the whole mind. Freud's identification of the ego, 'the I', as a component of mind was already problematic and Fairbairn's use highlights the problems. Although the matter is very controversial, I accept the line of reasoning which rejects identification of the self, 'the I', the ego, with the mind (or soul) or some inner agentive thing. The ego, the 'I', cannot be my mind because I am not my mind. My mind is not balding and cannot drink a cup of coffee. 'I' does not refer to some inner thing, and is not referentially ambiguous either, referring now to my mind, now to my body: in my mouth it refers to this psycho-physical person, me.[11] Fairbairn, to my knowledge, always used the language of subsidiary egos, the language of mind. Most who have followed him have slipped into referring to these egos as part-selves, subselves or subsidiary selves (Pereira and Scharff 2002; Clarke 2006). They implicitly conceive of selves as things that are 'in' persons or human beings, that persons 'have' but at the same time essentially are. On these views, selves are inner agents that can enter into relationships with other selves, threaten, sabotage, suffer, and so on. But this conception of *self* as an inner agentive entity leads to confusions similar to those about mind. My inner self is not balding and if I *have* a self then it is a mystery who is the 'I' who has it. I agree with those who argue that *self* understood as inner thing is philosophical illusion exploiting a grammatical peculiarity: the fact that we can separate such terms as 'myself', 'yourself', and suppose that my self is something I have and your self is something you have (Bennett and Hacker 2003: ch. 12).

There are, however, less problematic uses of 'self'. It may be used synonymously with 'person', as when I say 'Why don't you just take your self out of here!' And it is often used (though more confusingly) as a stand-in for 'sense of self', 'self-image', 'self-conception' or 'self-representation'. We see ourselves in mirrors, are reflected in other people's attitudes towards us, sense our bodies and mental states and form conceptions of what we are like. But selves in *that* sense are not independent agents, not subsidiary egos, though they may hugely affect how persons behave.

My use of 'self', as in 'self-solicitude', is intended to refer to the whole (psycho-physical) person or human being – but to avoid some misunderstandings, even at the risk of inviting others, let us turn to *person* and begin with a part of Locke's famous definition: 'a thinking intelligent Being, that has reason and reflection, and can consider itself as itself, the same thinking thing in different times and places...' (Locke 1968: Bk. 2, ch. 27, sec. 9).

I want to consider only one of the conditions Locke regards as necessary for personhood. (I have already dropped the idea of a person 'considering itself as itself', i.e. as exercising the concept of self.) *Persons have reason and reflection*, are rational: not, of course, in that they always use the best evidence and make the right inferences, but in being creatures that deliberate, decide and *act for reasons*. Fully explicating that notion is difficult but it will be sufficiently clear intuitively for our purposes. I think it will be granted that if subsidiary egos and internal objects do not act for reasons, they are not independent centres of agency as these were defined above.

Consider again Guntrip's patient, the punching girl. From an external perspective we see a person, wracked by internal conflict, punching herself. When she speaks she does not seem to speak for the whole of her. There appear to be at least two perspectives in this person: one from the part doing the punching and one from the part being punched. They appear to be mutually alienated: the speaker says she's not being punched, she's doing the punching. This situation is obscure, but examining the patient's development and the way in which internalisation has come to structure her person sheds some light on it. We know from Guntrip's observations that she has identified with and taken on (or in) the perspective of a punitive mother whilst retaining the aspect of the detested child she may at bottom feel herself to be, a 'child within' who maintains a relationship with the internalised mother.[12] One natural way of describing the situation in Fairbairn's terms is that a part of the ego (or personation of the self), the LE, is being maltreated by another punitive part, the AE. The LE is unconsciously perceived by the salient part under the aspect of a wretched, dependent being, whilst from the LE's perspective the AE part appears under the aspect of the punitive mother. The AE doesn't see her object as herself, she sees only a child she hates, and something similar applies from the other perspective. Perceiving each other as alien, these parts treat each other as if they were external objects. The patient thus appears to be divided in perspective, subjectivity and agency, in all the terms of strong partition noted above.

This is a striking enactment of an internal relationship. We can observe a relationship of even greater complexity played out largely intrapsychically in a patient whose 'destructive narcissistic organisation' (DNO) pretends to be a friend but is bent on destroying her.

> Only very gradually did she understand that the idealisation of her destructive-ness did not give her freedom, and that this was a trap into which she had fallen through the hypnotic power of the destructive self which posed as a saviour and friend who pretended to take care of her and give her whatever warmth and food she wanted so that she would not have to feel lonely. ... In fact, how-ever, this so-called friend attempted to spoil any contact she was trying to make in relation to work and to people. During analysis she gradually became aware that this exceedingly tyrannical and possessive friend was an omnipotent very destructive part of her self, posing as a friend, that became very threatening if she attempted to continue cooperation in analysis or any progress in her life. For a long time she felt too frightened to challenge this aggressive force and whenever she came up against this barrier she identified herself with the aggres-sive narcissistic self and became aggressive and abusive towards me.
>
> (Rosenfeld 1987: 117)

Notice the evident inadequacy of describing these cases as instances of *akrasia*, self-deception or wishful thinking, or as mere conflicts of drive. An adequate description must employ vocabulary apposite to the affective and conative faculties as well as the cognitive and orectic ones. Let's consider these cases from a high altitude and recall that 'personation', as used here, refers to a person engrossed in a role. The role may largely be determined by salient parental identifications but the influence of maturational factors, experience and phantastic distortions need not be excluded; nor, indeed, the possibility of personation as a sustained role in which identification plays no part. We can think of the four figures in the vignettes as personations. Personations may be activated simultaneously, as an actor may simul-taneously play several roles – for example, when A plays B pretending to be C – or near simultaneously, as when a child impersonates in play: now I am mummy, now I am daddy, now I am me.[13]

In both vignettes each personation has reasons or *motives* for acting as they do. In Guntrip's patient the AE part despises the LE part and abuses it. The LE has perhaps become masochistically attached to the AE. In Rosenfeld's false-friend case the DNO wishes to keep its subject in submission and sabotages attempts to escape its thrall. Each personation has a motivational set or script. But there are also reasons for the animation or activation of each personation, which are not reasons *for* the personations. For example, in the punching girl's case there appear to be reasons for activating the AE, representing the rejective aspect of her mother. Guntrip men-tions several: identifying with and revivifying the parent sustains a kind of relation-ship with her; it represents the struggle to preserve an ego; it confers a sense of power on the girl, even if only over her self. We shall say that these are reasons for *activating* a personation. So at any one time the personations have their motives, their own reasons for acting in particular ways, but there may also be a reason why *that* personation is activated at that time. Whose reason? Well, there appear to be several abstract possibilities.

It could be a reason for any other of the personations. There are two people in the front seat and the driver, exhausted, hands the wheel over to the other. The first driver has, say, reasons for heading in a certain direction and also for activating the second driver – he wants to rest, etc. The second driver may have different motives from the first and turn the car around. Wanting to turn around was a reason for the second driver but not the first. The question of *who* is in charge at time *t* resolves into the question, who has the wheel? Perhaps there are backseat drivers who dictate who should have the wheel. A person, in this model, is a congeries of personations; actors fully absorbed in their roles when activated, without private lives. Venn-like imagery would depict a person as a set of partially overlapping circles, coalescing in health and separating in illness, rather as Freud imagined the relations between agencies. But a kind of unity is preserved because rationality reigns: there are reasons for *which* personation is activated and motives for what the personation does. There is the possibility that the behaviour of a person thus constituted may be understood, because we understand persons acting for reasons.

Other possibilities exist. There may be reasons for activation of personations which are reasons for an elusive actor, a major star, who is never entirely engrossed in a role but animates them all. Such an actor will have his reasons for playing Hamlet. Hamlet has his reasons for killing Claudius. Hamlet's reasons are not the actor's reasons; the actor has no reason to kill Claudius. The actor activates the Hamlet personation and enacts Hamlet's motives; and, if the cast is short, he may enact Claudius' role too; this actor has a private life but, rarely out of a role, is difficult to discover.

This last abstraction corresponds perhaps to what Guntrip (1961: 138) had in mind when he wrote that the human psyche is 'the kind of entity that carries on its own internal development by differentiating itself into a number of *dramatis personae* ... The one person functions actually as a group of persons and that is the psychologically objective fact that theory has to represent'. It is reminiscent (once again) of that nineteenth-century perception that a person is a matrix from which a range of different personalities emerge.

We might like to think of this person as a central ego (person) activating *as need be* the subsidiary egos but, being engrossed in the roles that constitute them, losing herself to her own interiority. One ego, then, and many roles or personations, sustained as long as they are required. *Personal unity, qualified, is preserved, but so too is a concept of the subsidiary egos as independent centres of agency. For each personation this central ego enacts satisfies the conditions for independent agency by virtue of their exclusive engrossment in, their exclusion of everything incompossible with, the roles enacted* (2.4).

Whether or not the abstract construction adumbrated here can answer to the complexity of psychic life, it is clear that there are in general rational connections between subsidiary egos (and internal objects), and reasons that motivate them. Rosenfeld's patient – that part of the patient perhaps with which Rosenfeld has contact – has reasons for activating the DNO and clinging to it: it provides the illusion of strength, and company. But when activated, the patient *is* the DNO, though not exclusively. The DNO has reasons (motives) for clinging to the patient whilst torturing her. If there were not such rational webs then much psychotherapy, which may be seen partly as exploration of the reasons a person has for activating personations and partly as moderating the pathological aims which may be written into the motivations of the personations, would be a forlorn task. It is because there are discernible rational connections in persons between subsidiary egos and internal objects – between personations – that it is unnecessary to appeal to Freudian economic or energic principles or other quasi-mechanical or non-Intentional expedients setting out where, as it were, the psychic accent falls.

But another possibility cannot be excluded, if we may remain for one last moment on this abstract plane, in which all rational connections simply break down: the second driver just wrenches the wheel from the first driver's hands for no intelligible reason. These cases present the greatest difficulty for understanding and psychotherapy.

5.7 Personation, self-solicitude and Freudian wish-fulfilment

Now what has this discussion of diremption – of that form of dissociation in which the macro-structures (agencies) and internal objects stand in stark opposition – and personation to do with self-solicitude, and FWT in particular? This: it should now be apparent that some personations are precisely the kind of entities that fit the bill for being both the autonomous, self-solicitous, though not necessarily benign agencies, and their client agencies introduced in **4.4** and **4.6**. And the self-reflexive configurations I have abstractly delineated – the relations between personations – can, when in self-solicitous mode, answer to the requirements of maximal FWT. But I have described only a matrix of abstract possibilities without explicit appeal to empirical considerations that would specify the genesis, number or nature of the agencies or personations. Earlier, it is true, we followed Freud and Fairbairn in their different accounts of mental partitioning and the role of identification as the principal agent of structuralisation. However, we are not committed to those structural accounts as representing, in Fairbairn's phrase, a basic endopsychic situation. They may represent particular pathological formations, 'psychic retreats' perhaps (Steiner 1993), or common but not universal configurations. This possibility is implicit in Freud's discussion of the diremption and reconsolidation of the psychic personality cited above. In certain conditions it may be more accurate to describe the personality in terms of different oppositions: between true and false self, a dominant self against an alien self, a central self against libidinal and anti-libidinal selves, and so on (see comments in **5.3**). The determination of which particular configuration is dominant in a person at a particular time is an empirical question. I have tried to show the *possibility* of such configurations meeting the requirements for self-solicitude.

In the genesis of self-reflexive relations, of which self-solicitude is a species, the internalisation of one particular relationship stands out. The relationship between first carers and child provides the foundation, or a very important part of the foundation, for many later self-reflexive relations. At the root of self-solicitude, including maximal FWT, is internalisation of the maternal caring function. Caring – care-taking – may be benign but also malign. As a consequence, the relationship that the self (person) has to itself may be loving, considerate, consoling, respectful, but may degenerate into pandering, appeasement, deceit and hatred.

Freud, as we saw above **(4.6)**, eventually realised the formative influence of the internalisation of maternal functions. One of the pioneer 'baby watchers', Rene Spitz, writes: 'The acquisition of action patterns, the mastery of imitation, and the function of identification are the devices which permit the child to achieve increasing autonomy from the mother. Imitating mother's actions enables the child to provide himself with all that his mother provided before' (Spitz 1965: 179). And according to Winnicott: 'The infant develops means for doing without actual care. This is accomplished through the accumulation of memories of care, the projection of personal needs and the introjection of care details, with the development of confidence in the environment' (Winnicott 1965: 48). He notes an important pathological development: 'In one extreme case an intellectual overgrowth that is successful in accounting for adaptation to need becomes of itself so important in the child's economy that it (the mind) becomes the nursemaid that acts as a mother substitute and cares for the baby in the child self' (Winnicott 1988: 139–40).[14]

In a passage I encountered recently, Christopher Bollas writes:

> Every infant... internalizes into the ego those processes in which he is the other's object, and he continues to do so for a long time. Our handling of ourselves as an object partly inherits and expresses the history of our experience as the parental object, so that in each adult it is appropriate to say that certain forms of self-perception, self-facilitation, self-handling and self-refusal express the internalized parental process still engaged in the activity of handling the self as an object... Through the experience of being the other's object, which we internalize, we establish a sense of two-ness in our being, and this subject-object paradigm further allows us to address our inherited disposition, or true self, as other. We use the structure of the mother's imagining and handling of our self to objectify and manage the true self.
>
> (Bollas 1987: 51)

This is right, I think, so far as it goes, but the passage raises several immediate questions. Many self-reflexive activities, in which one takes oneself as an object, do not involve diremption. Activities such as looking after one's interests or talking to oneself as a Dutch uncle need neither be unconscious nor supervene on a deep division of the self. Self-concern, self-regulation of this kind is so conspicuous and natural that it is noticed only when missing, as in some infantile psychosis (Mahler 1968: 32) and alexithymia. Moreover, not all self-solicitude involves *benign* self-regulation. Indeed it would appear that in most pathological cases there is malign self-solicitude, diremption and withdrawal of executive function into the unconscious.

Much caretaking occurs consciously and deliberately, but much of it is unconscious. In simple cases, perhaps, subsequent to subintentional hallucinatory wish-fulfilment, we can conceive of the self-solicitous function as written into the unconscious ego – at first as procedural knowledge and later as technical beliefs – creating evidence for the child-like id which, engrossed in its inner world, interprets the evidence as wish-fulfilling. The evidence may be a phantasy, symptom or enactment. Maximal FWT has been explained as involving strategies in which a dissociated aspect of the self – a personation – sets out unconsciously but intentionally to provide for its client gratification, consolation or appeasement by fulfilment of its wishes. It does this by manufacturing phantasies, symptoms, delusional schemes to alter the evidential field for the client self, which then arrives at wish-fulfilling conclusions **(Chapter 6)**. It creates an imaginary world more congenial for that self; a world in which mere wishing makes it so. It can succeed in this enterprise because of the very conditions generated by the reflexive attitudes consequent on the diremptions created by precarious internalisation. We can now see that the capacity to take oneself as an object in the manner that can support maximal FWT is a consequence of dissociation, not the cause of it. Being dissociated, there are internal opacities: the self to which the self-solicitous part ministers lacks the discrimination to be aware of the wish-fulfilling project. The practical syllogisms for FWT set out in **4.4** and **4.6** articulate the practical expression of this structural condition of mind.

We can now also see whence the loss of interiority that follows on diremption and the self taking itself as object. There are two points, each dominating the scene according to the way the psychical accent falls. First, the personation in solicitous identification becomes engrossed in its role, and the more it does so the more it will tend to see its client personation (the self as object) from the perspective of the role model, the object with which it is principally identified, and adopt attitudes towards the client (itself as another personation) which that object was perceived as adopting towards it. The personation comes to see the client as the object with which it is identified once saw it: from the outside and as something apart from itself. There is, in other words, a loss of access to the client personation because the subject personation has a perspective that becomes all the more imposing as it is engrossed, consumed by its role. Recall that engrossment excludes all that is incompossible with the attentional project **(2.4)** which, in this instance, is the assumption of an identity. Second, the subject personation sees the client personation from the outside, constrained by the salient features of that object which is partly determined by the objects with which the client personation is identified. That such loss of interiority or opacity in the whole self is necessary to the accomplishment of FWT was demonstrated in the cases of the café-avoiding girl and the anxious scientist **(1.5)**.

But why should the internalised maternal functions come to constitute separate centres of agency? Why diremption? In general, in health, they don't constitute separate centres of agency; there occurs no significant diremption – as Freud emphasised **(5.3)** and Fairbairn entertained as a theoretical possibility. However, given the long period of dependency and helplessness of the human infant, few escape the unavoidable deficiencies, and sometimes deliberate cruelty, of their carers. Wholly felicitous outcomes where there is no malign internalisation and no diremption are likely to be scarce; in pathology, especially most serious pathology in which environmental failures are prominent, diremption can be expected to be common. The precise determinants for malign internalisation and structuralisation are, as noted previously, a matter for empirical investigation. It is notable, however, that Fairbairn's predication of the internalisation of bad objects on a traumatic, or cumulatively traumatic, maternal environment is fully consistent with recent studies of early trauma which highlight dissociation and a withdrawal into the inner world as its most notable psychopathological consequence (Schore 2003: 124ff, 128ff). In general terms, whilst the internalisation of benign maternal functions is necessary to achieve a capacity for self-regulation and self-solicitude of a quite ordinary kind, of quotidian self-concern, there is also the jeopardy of internalising malign maternal functions and attitudes which lead to diremption and the formation of malign personations and pernicious forms of self-solicitude.

How do the various examples we have considered look from this perspective? The self-consoling phantasy created for ourselves is a benign example of the self-soothing function derived at least in part from parental internalisation (or imitation), from the parent knowing how 'to make it better', knowing what stories to tell, knowing how to restore our self-esteem with love. Of course, the capacity is elaborated and honed with experience. It's easy to overlook that its success is predicated on a degree of dissociation between the observer of the phantasy and the maker of it, and that it belongs, as Freud once said of the dream, in a pathological series, in the realm of unrealism, harmless though it generally is.

The symptomatic enactment is a more complex affair. We can imagine the man who becomes an exhibitionist (**3.2**) regressing, becoming increasingly more needy and anxious. Then a personation is activated: *the* exhibitionist who acts out a script provides the evidence whose unconscious meaning consoles the man who activates the personation of the exhibitionist, who *is* (at the same time) the personation of the exhibitionist. The wish-fulfilling strategy is predicated on a deep diremption between the man and the man who is the exhibitionist. The man activates the personation of the exhibitionist (whose full dramatic script he may not know) and becomes engrossed in the role; at the same time, or perhaps shortly after, the man unconsciously interprets the ludicrous performance as proof of his masculinity, his capacity to impress or terrorise women or allay castration anxiety, or whatever may be the gravamen of his discontent. So not only the personation but the circumstances in which he may be taken in by the performance require diremption.

The case of the bedstead girl may be similar. An enactment by a personation experienced as an obsessional part is unconsciously interpreted by her child-self personation as the wish-fulfilling achievement of separating her parents. Rosenfeld's patient may be understood along the same lines, but with a malign twist. Here – let's say – the child-self personation summons up the friend who turns out to be a monster that will destroy her. In activating the DNO the child-self is acting self-solicitously, summoning a needed companion; however, she does not know, or seems not to know, the malevolent script that motivates the companion.[15] The DNO takes on a life of its own. And, of course, for the DNO to be a companion she cannot know that it is her invocation. The personations are mutually opaque, and neither her role in activating the DNO personation, the DNO's personation's motivational script nor the unconscious significance of her relationship to the DNO experienced in phantasy are known to the patient consciously. But notice that, nevertheless, the child-self appears to have reasons, motives, for activating the DNO, and the DNO has its motives too.

It is tempting to suppose that in Guntrip's patient we have, as it were, a clear anatomical picture of the anti-libidinal ego as the embodiment of maternal hatred, or of what was experienced as hatred, mistreating the child-self; a harsh superego or AE punishing the poor ego or LE. But where then is the wish-fulfilling aspect of the enactment? Deeper analysis may show that the anti-libidinal element of the self, the AE personation, is activated by the libidinal ego, the child-self personation, for the reasons already listed: for companionship, for evidence of identity with or relationship to a powerful mother, or perhaps for the rewards of masochistic suffering.

Psychoanalytic vignettes are always underdescribed, but if our understanding of these vignettes as cases of self-solicitude is not too far off the mark it must follow that the agencies or personations are capable of unconscious interpretation or seeing-as. That must follow because the wish-fulfilling beliefs attributed to the personations (that one is powerful, not alone, etc.) are unconscious and supervene on such unconscious interpretations of symbolic or disguised phantasy and enactments. Moreover, we are once again driven to the view that in some pathology – and with respect to *that* pathology – the executive function of mind retreats into the unconscious (4.2). At the least, the activation of personations – or, phrased in the more usual idiom, the maintenance of relations with parts of the self and with internal objects – in the pursuit of FWT, or of self-solicitude more generally, is an unconscious process. Once again we have arrived in a roundabout way at a Freudian tenet – with a qualification. Kaplan-Solms and Solms write of 'Freud's revised (1923b) topographical proposals, to the effect that consciousness is not the executive agency of the mind... that even the ego itself is fundamentally unconscious' (Kaplan-Solms and Solms 2000: 110–11). We may be more cautious: executive agency is sometimes unconscious, and certainly appears to be so in psychopathology supervening on Freudian wish-fulfilment.

Notes

1 For cogent consideration of the Freudian agencies understood in the Platonic fashion see Glymour (1991). In 'Paradoxes of irrationality' Davidson enunciates the 'Medea principle': 'a person can act against his own better judgement, but only when an alien force overwhelms his or her will' (1982a: 294) It seems to me not so clear that Medea does experience her *thumos* as an alien force. Rather, as we say, 'she can't help herself': unity underlies the dissension within her soul. This paradox haunts Glymour's account as it does Plato's. It may be noted that in the Classical period, conceptions of self were in disarray. The notions of *psyche*, *pneuma*, *phren*, *thumos*, *nous* floated around much as our ideas about mind, soul, spirit, self do today.

2 In consonance with Christian doctrine: if I am indivisible, and destruction is understood as decomposition, then what I am essentially is indestructible and will survive bodily death.

3 Thus Freud and Breuer: 'we have become convinced that the splitting of consciousness which is so striking in the well known classical cases under the form of "double conscience" is present to a rudimentary degree in every hysteria, and that a tendency to such a dissociation, and with it the abnormal states of consciousness (which we shall bring together under the term "hypnoid") is the basic phenomenon of this neurosis. In these views we concur with Binet and the two Janets...' (1893: 12).

4 Amongst philosophers only Pears (1984) and, perhaps, Rorty (1988) have, to my knowledge, argued explicitly for a conception of mind whose parts satisfy the conditions for independent agency, but the parts are transient. Pears' views are extensively criticised by Gardner (1993), amongst others. According to Gardner, Pears affirms that 'the mind is divided into parts, which are numerically distinct centres of rational agency, each of which has its own reasons for action, in which respect they are related to one another in the way that different persons, considered as rational agents, are' (1993: 67). Gardner argues that this (kind of) view falls victim to the well-known Sartrean paradoxes. We saw reason in **4.7** to doubt this.

5 The structural theory (1923b; 1926d; 1940a) is equivocal. Freud seems sometimes to have conceived of the agencies as subpersonal systems functionally defined and mereologically constituting the mind. This characterisation has been elaborated by the ego-psychologists (e.g. Hartmann 1964; Hartmann, Kris and Loewenstein 1964). Sometimes Freud figured the agencies as quasi-independent, self-like entities bearing personal relations to each other, but still mereologically constitutive of the mental self. This is the view explored below and developed by Fairbairn (1976), who conceives of the central ego, libidinal ego and anti-libidinal ego as having ego character but as being distinct compositional structures. A conception of the agencies – or at least of the ego and superego – often attributed to Melanie Klein, as phantasy parts or as the Intentional objects of phantasy, is not, I think, a structural conception in the way Freud understood this notion: that is, as involving more or less coherent, enduring *organisations* of mental processes of which agency is a feature.

6 Freud (1923b: 48): 'we have said repeatedly that the ego is formed to a great extent out of identifications which take the place of abandoned cathexis by the id; that the first of these identifications always behave as a special agency in the ego and stand apart from the ego in the form of a superego, while later on, as it grows stronger, the ego may become more resistant to the influences of such identifications.' It is unlikely that the processes Freud gathers under the heads of introjection and identification can be considered to supervene entirely on incorporative phantasy, and perceptual-cognitive processes play a dominant part in many kinds of internalisation.

7 Gardner, for example, insists that the 'genuine' (Kleinian) concepts of ego and superego reduce to 'phantastic misrepresentation of the person' (1993: 179). He recognises that there are other (ego-psychological) concepts of ego and superego which stress their agentive character, but ignores them. So he is able to maintain (1993: 40ff, 175ff), astonishingly in light of the textual evidence, that (Freud's) 'structural theory breaks definitively with Second Mind conceptualisation of the unconscious', and the agencies are 'far from being agents' and 'decidedly not sub-systemic' (1993: 176). On Freud's account the ego and superego are not merely phantasised as agents, phantasy parts or the phantastic misrepresentations of the person; they *are* agents. The ego's agential character is evident in almost everything Freud says about it in his later period. And as regards the superego, it 'enjoys a certain degree of autonomy, follows its own intentions and is independent of the ego for its supply of energy...' (Freud 1933a: 92).

8 Consider the implications of the (Kleinian concept of) the envious superego, of self-envy. You can only envy the possession of what you believe you don't possess. Yet

self-envy, of one's gifts, successes, creativity, is very common. There must be a profound diremption and opacity between the self that envies and the envied self.

9 An optimistic corollary, emphasised by Clarke (2006), is that pathological structuralisation is, in principle, avoidable and may be undone, through therapy or other means.

10 Fairbairn overlooks this point, and that causes considerable mischief in his critique of Freud's view of drives and object relations.

11 This line of argument, in relation to the self rather than mind, is vigorously rejected by Galen Strawson (2009). He contends that there are selves, inner mental things, distinct from the human being or person. Even if he is right about that, the kind of self (SES-MET) that he urges on us cannot be the kind that enter into the complex reflexive relations of concern in psychodynamic thought.

12 Stephen Mitchell has stated that the key transition to post-classical psychoanalysis occurred when the id began to be conceived as self-like, as a child (1993: 103ff). Agnes Petocz has noted that Freud's own choice of *das Es* already points to the child-like nature of the id – the German word for child (*das Kind*) being neuter, so that a child would be accustomed to being referred to by the pronoun 'it'.

13 It is instructive that in Klein (1929) and Fairbairn (1931) *personifications* are regarded as expressions of structural entities.

14 Alan Schore's (1994, 2003) investigations into the neuroscience of affect regulation have emphasised the internalisation of maternal regulatory functions which allow for the development of a 'self-comforting capacity' (2003: 21). Kaplan-Solms and Solms write that Schore (1994) has demonstrated 'that the physical maturation [of the sub-cortical limbic and brain-stem structures] is significantly guided by certain aspects of early mother-infant interaction. *The ventromesial frontal cortex is thereby shown to almost literally embody an internalized, containing mother*' (2000: 234). See also Kumin (1996).

15 The structure of the DNO is very much more complex than that suggested here but that is not, I think, germane to the point I wish to make.

Part II

Applications

Chapter 6

Self-deception and delusion

For man prefers most of all to believe what he would like to. Passion influences and infects the intellect in innumerable ways that are sometimes imperceptible.

Bacon 1854: I, 49

6.1 Self-deception

The essential problem of FWT is how it is that one can, if indeed one can, fulfil one's wishes in the absence of their true objects. The problem of self-deception (SD) is how it is that one can, if indeed one can, deceive oneself. If self-deception, or at least much of what has been said to be self-deception, can be shown to be in the service of FWT, then the second problem, or at least much of it, would collapse into the first. This is a reasonable expectation. It is reasonable to begin with the expectation that much of what passes for self-deception, like interpersonal deception, is motivated, and indeed intentionally motivated, in circumstances similar to those which provoke FWT – in situations of inner conflict, painful loss, humiliation, and so on.

The vast literature on self-deception does not in the main fulfil the expectation, for several different reasons. Many philosophers deny that self-deception must be modelled on deception.[1] This is puzzling on the face of it because it is unclear how to identify the conceptions they investigate *as self-deception*, and not some related thing. There are many ways other than deception in which we acquire false beliefs and induce false beliefs in others: by confusing, befuddling, coercing, cozening, and so on. Most reflexive attitudes and actions – self-appraisal, self-loathing, self-aggrandisement – retain the essentials of their other-directed proto-types, and there seems no reason to regard self-deception as an exception. Some philosophers distinguish between *strong* forms of self-deception in which (roughly) an agent's self-deceptive intention leads to her holding incompatible beliefs, and weaker forms in which (roughly) an agent finds herself deceived or misled through some form of unintentional self-misleading. The strong forms attract considerable scepticism. But since they are modelled on the paradigm of interpersonal deception, they should be, it seems to me, considered the *conceptually central* forms of self-deception, even if they are not the most common forms and even in the circumstance that they are not instantiated.[2] It will transpire, however, that the exploration of maximal FWT enables us to find a secure place for them in the life of the mind.

The conceptually central cases, we say, are modelled on interpersonal deception. In the simplest cases of interpersonal deception (a more elaborate treatment will follow), when A deceives B, A intentionally gets B to believe a proposition that A does not believe. Deception involves lying with the intention to deceive (inadvertent misleading is not generally regarded as deceiving), and lying generally involves passing off as true something the liar believes to be false. A can lie without deceiving B because B may not believe him, and A can lie without intending to deceive if, for example, A knows that B isn't going to believe him anyway. Putting aside the complications, when I deceive myself I am, on this model, both A and B, so in successfully deceiving myself I both believe some proposition and also not believe it. Such doxastic inconsistency is problematic but does not stretch common-sense psychology to breaking point because it merely exposes what we well know – that our doxastic and conative fields are not fully integrated and can be dis-integrated. It becomes acute, however, when belief engages with action. (Suppose I believe that it is raining but also that it is not raining; will I carry an umbrella?) That problem is defused if we suppose that the relevant motivational structures (of beliefs, desires, affects) are segregated, and that one or the other is deactivated. (Repression, splitting of the ego or dissociation are intended to answer to such phenomena – see **5.3**). But there is worse. In self-deception I am the *agent* of my deception. How do I manage to get myself to believe what I don't? Moreover, it is (at least in strong cases of self-deception) my *not* believing some proposition that is usually implicated in the motivation of my getting to believe it.

Some plausible minimal conditions for strong self-deception can be set out as follows:[3] to be self-deceived about a proposition p in a strong sense, an agent must:

(1)   believe that p;
(2)   intentionally deceive herself into believing that p (though p may be true);
(3)   hold the belief that p is epistemically unwarranted;
(4)   hold the belief that p is causally sustained by a contemporaneous desire;
(5)   also believe, contemporaneously, not p.

To sharpen these requirements, consider a case of self-induced deception (SID). Brian McLaughlin (1988) introduces Mary:

> In order to miss an unpleasant meeting three months ahead, Mary deliberately writes the wrong date for the meeting in her appointment book, a date later than the actual date of the meeting. She does this so that three months later when she consults this book, she will come mistakenly to believe the meeting is on that date and, as a result, miss the meeting. Mary knows that she has a poor memory and a very busy schedule. And she justifiably counts on the fact that when she consults the book around the date in question, she will have

forgotten the actual date of the meeting and that she wrote the wrong date. Sure enough, three months later, having forgotten the actual date of the meeting and the deceitful deed, she innocently acquires the intended mistaken belief by consulting the appointment book. Her deceitful strategy succeeds.

(1988: 31–2)

Mary has intentionally misled herself. It is correct to say that at the culmination of her stratagem she is deceived about the date and has practiced a kind of deception upon herself. However, this is not sufficient for SD in any strong sense because it doesn't have to satisfy conditions (3) to (5). Thus Mary's acquired false belief is properly based on sufficient evidence, notwithstanding that it was she herself who manufactured it. The evidence, the entry in her appointment book, is certainly adequate for her inference: she regularly draws such inferences about her daily agendas. In SD, on the other hand, there is always some distortion of the evidential relation. Further, Mary's false belief is not causally sustained by any contemporaneous desire. She did not and does not desire that the appointment be on the date inscribed in her appointment book. Finally, Mary does not, if the strategy succeeds and she cannot recall her original intent, believe, at this time, at any level, that the appointment is not on the date inscribed. It is true that if the act of deception occurred at the moment that she inscribed the wrong date in her book, as we should have to say on some accounts of the identity conditions for action, then at that moment she did believe the appointment was not on that date. Still, we are not troubled by the co-existence of contradictory beliefs because, of course, at that time she did not believe that the appointment was on the date inscribed.

Now, according to some philosophers' conditions, (1) to (5) cannot be satisfied. According to others, although they may be met in rare instances of self-deception, SD along these lines is by no means typical. In his careful consideration Brian McLaughlin (1988) states that although there are 'paradigmatic' acts of SD involving intentional deceiving which satisfy the conditions, *unintentional self-misleading* can also lead to self-deception. There are, he argues, weaker candidates for SD that do not satisfy condition (2).

> [I]ntentional misleading is *uncharacteristic* of self-deception: to think otherwise is to overintellectualize what typically goes on in self-deception. It might be insisted that a self-deceiver must have deceived himself. But one might claim in response that unintentional misleading *ipso facto* counts as unintentional deceiving and so as deceiving. Thus, when a self-deceiver unintentionally misleads himself, he deceives himself. ... I claim, a self-deceiver characteristically misleads himself by means of rationalization, over-compensation, and evasion in a context in which he thereby counts as deceiving himself, even though he lacks a deceitful intention.
>
> (1988: 53–4)

With one marginal qualification (see below), this seems to be mistaken. I do not deceive myself, because I do not lie to myself, if I just unintentionally mislead myself, since it is evident that SD must at least retain the feature of *lying* – reflexively. In the interpersonal case, although one can be deceived into believing what is true (if, say, the deceiver thinks the proposition he gets you to believe is false, but in fact it is true) and one can be deceived into believing what is believed true by the deceiver (if the deceiver gets you to believe some instrumental falsehood from which you infer the proposition which he holds to be true and wants you to believe),[4] for there to be an act of deception there must, it seems evident, be an intentional passing off of *some* falsehood*, where 'falsehood*' refers to some proposition believed false by the deceiver (though of course it may in fact be true). There must, that is, be a lie. To lie is to pass off – to utter, to indite – a falsehood*, to misrepresent the facts as they are believed to be, *with the intention of so doing.*[5] But I can lie to you without deceiving you (you may not believe me) or without even trying to deceive you. I may know that you won't accept the lie or I may be indifferent as to whether you do or you don't, in which case although I am still lying I can hardly be said to be trying to deceive you. It was said facetiously of a desert tribe whose directions to travellers were notoriously untrustworthy that their love of truth was so great that they could seldom be persuaded to part with it. The tribesmen may have been liars in so far as they misrepresented the facts as they believed them to be, but not necessarily deceivers; for, given knowledge of their own reputation, they may have had no expectation that anyone would believe them and no intention of misleading. We rarely tell lies without intending to deceive, but it is plain that such an intention is not a necessary condition of lying. Of course, had someone believed the tribesmen, they would have been deceived, but that would still not make intentional deceivers of the tribesmen.

If there has been no lie then there has been no deception. I do *not* deceive you if I merely unintentionally mislead you. To think otherwise is to gloss a distinction of real importance. For example, it is because of the distinction that we are able to defend ourselves, as we often do, by expostulating: 'I'm sorry if I misled you. I didn't mean to... you must have misinterpreted my intentions...' and so on, and easily defeat the charge of deception. Government ministers mislead parliament if they unwittingly provide it with false information. This is not regarded as lying or deception even if anyone believed them. It is a much more serious matter if the minister intentionally misrepresented the facts – that is to say, told a lie. That attracts a penalty that mere misleading does not. It follows that if SD is to reflect interpersonal deception in its main features, it must retain the feature of lying – to oneself – and unintentional misleading is insufficient to capture this feature. I do not deceive myself, because I do not lie to myself, if I just unintentionally mislead myself.

The point can be reinforced by contesting something Mark Johnston says: 'To be deceived is sometimes to be misled without being intentionally misled or being lied to. The self-deceiver is a self-misleader' (1988: 65). I do not know whether Johnston intended these sentences as an argument, though it rather looks like it. In any case, although there is an awkward sense in which the first proposition is true, the second does not follow from it. What would support the second proposition is another of the form: *to deceive* is sometimes just *to mislead*. But this proposition, I have argued, is false. What obscures matters is that there are circumstances (this is the qualification to which I alluded two paragraphs up) in which although I may not deceive you, although there may not be an act of deception, you may still be deceived *in* me: we do on rare occasions say that we have been deceived when we have only been misled. One example is when, having systematically misinterpreted my behaviour for some time, you are subjected to a rude awakening and feel suddenly deceived. You may then wish to express your disappointment by saying that you have been deceived all along, although you may recognise that there was no deception on anyone's part.

Even if there are such circumstances in which we unintentionally mislead ourselves, and we are misled – so that we are, in this peripheral sense, self-deceived – it is surely mistaken to present the features of these cases as if they represented a significant species of SD, let alone a conceptually central type. Indeed, it would be better not to describe them as cases of SD at all. It seems best to designate as SD only those instances in which the *self deceives*, in at least this sense: that there is an intentional act of passing off a proposition believed false by the deceiver, in circumstances in which it has the effect of deceiving. For one can lie without deceiving, and one can deceive without intentionally deceiving and hence be self-deceived without intending to deceive oneself. Consider the relationships between you and me as regards lying, deception and consolation:

(1) You unintentionally misrepresent the facts.
(2) You intentionally misrepresent the facts.
(3) I accept the unintentionally misrepresented facts.
(4) I accept the misrepresented facts you intentionally misrepresented.
(5) You intend me to accept the unintentionally misrepresented facts.
(6) You intend me to accept the facts you intentionally misrepresented.
(7) You intend to deceive me.
(8) You intend to satisfy my wish(es).
(9) You intend to console me.
(10) You intend to please me.

Although at (3) I may be misled, it is not until (4) that I have been deceived, that a lie is told which I accept. At (5) you may think that you are enlightening me, for you may believe that your version of the facts is correct. You are obviously not trying to deceive me, and if I accept your version of the facts I will have been misled but not deceived. At (6) you are trying to mislead me (or whatever your understanding of the intentional passing off of a lie is), and if you have brought your action under the concept of deception, as at (7), and I accept your lie then you will have intentionally deceived me. But (6) doesn't necessarily involve *intentional* deception: you may be merely trying to console or to please me; you may not know what deception is; you may be an ingénue or a saint. One way in which you may try to satisfy my wishes or console me or please me is by intentionally deceiving me. But, of course, you can console or please me without doing that. You can intentionally console me by deceiving me, but not intentionally so, if you do not see your action as deception.

6.2 Subintentionalism again

Based on the interpersonal model, then, one can be self-deceived if one tells oneself a lie which one accepts. But lying to oneself, even if it doesn't involve an intention to deceive (but some other intention such as consolation), involves an intention to misrepresent the facts as they are believed to be, an intention that cannot enter the focus of consciousness if the lie and potential deception are to succeed. Lying to oneself threatens diremptions in the self, and to avoid them makes the invocation of subintentional mechanisms once again an inviting option **(3.2)**. To avoid the need for intentional deceitful belief-fixing strategies, simpler psychological mechanisms are alleged as typical causes of unintentional self-misleading. They are supposed to underlie wishful thinking (WT) and are typically variations on the theme of desire biasing the selection, acknowledgement or avoidance of evidence; that is to say, they are typically subintentional or expressive processes. WT is motivated, but not intentionally: emotions and desires 'skew the belief-forming process' (Graham 2010: 203). The wishful thinker need not be engaged in a deceitful strategy, but in the typical case of WT (and SD) a desire will bias the wishful thinker in such a way that he misleads himself, albeit unintentionally, into believing or continuing to believe that p. A wishful thinker, on this view, is typically an unintentional self-misleader. How is desire supposed to do it?

> What might happen in a typical case of wishful thinking is this. One's desire that p affects one's interests and attention in such a way as to bolster one's belief that p in the absence of adequate evidence, or even in the face of disconfirming evidence. This might happen as follows. The desire affects one's interest so as to make what one perceives as evidence for p psychologically salient: such evidence 'captures' and 'absorbs' one's attention. In this way, the desire works to accentuate the positive and eliminate the negative from consideration. ... Consider a case of charitable wishful thinking: one likes a person and wants the person to succeed in a certain endeavour. The evidence one possesses indicates that it is more likely than not that the person will fail. But one does not realize this. For, as a result of one's charitable attitude, what one perceives as evidence in favour of the person's eventual success captures and absorbs one's attention, while what one perceives as evidence against this deflects it...
>
> ... our charitable wishful thinker might not have had, at any level, the slightest suspicion that his friend would not succeed.
>
> (McLaughlin 1988: 43, 45)

This is neat but unpersuasive. Granted, desire can attract and deflect attention, highlight evidence and induce engrossment. It may be true, as McLaughlin also suggests, that habits of mind and dispositions like optimism play an important role in determining salience: moods and interests tend to determine the things that interest and stand out for us. It may be that desire can push unfavourable evidence into the background by pulling favourable evidence into the foreground (1988: 43). Perhaps desire is able to do all this sometimes.[6] But it is difficult to see how this appeal to subintentional mental mechanics can explain the appraisal and selection of evidence involved in the example of the charitable thinker. The conception of the 'charitable attitude' conceals a complexity that has to be unravelled. It cannot be, as McLaughlin tendentiously expresses it, that the unfavourable evidence merely 'deflects' attention, as a bright surface might deflect one's gaze. The evidence must first be *appraised* and recognised as *unfavourable*, for it is in its character as *unfavourable evidence* that it is discarded. That appraisal implicates the aims of the charitable thinker, for when evidence is judged adverse, it is so because it is adverse to those aims. The selection of evidence is therefore based on evaluation and judgement that in the final analysis involves intention, albeit unconscious intention. Indeed, the charitable thinker has a strong *reason* for judging in the way that he does and for discarding the unfavourable evidence. He wants to believe that the person he likes will not fail but fears (believes) that he will. And that, at bottom (his wishes and beliefs giving rise to specific avoidant strategies), seems to be the efficacious reason, the reason *why* he intentionally resists the unfavourable evidence and fixes his attention on the favourable.

The failings of these subintentional strategies are familiar and they become even more acute in the case of SD. Even if subintentional or other non-intentional mechanisms can account for some wishful thinking (and FWT) they cannot suffice for SD, even weak SD, for with the appeal to mental mechanics it seems inappropriate to speak of the agent as misleading herself, let alone deceiving herself. It is not clear that *she* has done anything at all. If anything, it would be more apt to say that she has been misled by her orectic and cognitive apparatus.

I have been arguing that in all SD there is, at the least, an act of lying, an intentional passing off of a falsehood*. Is the charitable thinker passing off a falsehood*? Well, he is warping (tendentiously selecting) the evidence, a part of which will provide epistemic warrant for the wish-fulfilling belief that his favourite will succeed. There is good reason to think that he is doing so with the intention of getting himself to believe something which he believes ('at some level') to be false. So he seems to be manufacturing a kind of lie, intentionally misrepresenting or distorting the facts as he believes or fears that they are, and if he accepts the misrepresentation he deceives himself. And this process, we have seen strong reason for believing, is largely unconscious. Does it follow that he is (unconsciously) intending to deceive himself? It depends on the circumstances. If he is intentionally warping the evidence then he has a reason for doing so. That reason may involve a desire to deceive himself, but equally he may see his activity as self-consolation or protection, and so on. He may desire, he may intend, to get himself to believe something favourable, but he may not see that as involving deception. The charitable thinker may not have brought what he is doing under the concept of deception (and, *a fortiori*, self-deception), in which case he cannot be intending to deceive himself, though what he does is, in the circumstances, deceiving himself. In my view the charitable thinker *is* deceiving himself, but not for the representative reasons advanced by McLaughlin. Intention is at work in the manufacture of his 'lie', but we have no way of knowing from the material at hand whether he is intentionally deceiving himself.

6.3 Self-deception and Freudian wish-fulfilment

Once it is accepted that intention is at work in the strong cases of SD, a question rarely asked in this neck of philosophical psychology arises: why should anyone go to the trouble of trying to deceive themselves? The question is rarely raised because most of the received non-intentional accounts of SD obviate or, at the least, impoverish the motivational variety and complexity manifest in SD. But in light of our discussion, and the preceding discussion of FWT, it should be clear that there are different forms of SD distinguished by (amongst other things) different motivational structures, as there are different forms of FWT, and we can see how these two sets of conceptions are related. Self-deceptive processes and strategies are frequently in the service of self-solicitude and of FWT in particular. We may deceive ourselves to satisfy ineluctable wishes in the manner of FWT, to console ourselves, to regulate painful thoughts and emotions, to sustain self-esteem, and so on. It seems possible, if only in a rough and tentative way, to match the modes of self-solicitude described in earlier chapters with some of the phenomena advanced as candidates for self-deception. The kinds of unintentional misleading which have been advanced as underlying typical forms of self-deception, as on McLaughlin's account of the charitable thinker (if that account were successful, which I have doubted), would correspond with FWT by way of subintentional mechanisms, as in hallucinatory gratification where desire directly generates phenomenal content that in primitive psychic conditions constitutes agent's evidence for wish-fulfilling belief. The lie to oneself can be brought into relation with the creation of counterfactual wishful phantasies which, if accepted as agent's evidence, may result in wish-fulfilling self-deception: the daydreams used to undo humiliating *faux pas* and some mild forms of delusion may be typical examples. Intended self-deception is a form of self-solicitude (mostly maximal FWT) in which the self treats itself as an object to be cared for or consoled or, perhaps paradoxically, appeased, abased or persecuted, where deception is the apt instrument. Such self-deception supervenes on the structural models explored earlier (**4.4, 4.6, 5.5–5.7**) and the beauty of it, if I may so express it, is that those models preserve an important feature of *self*-deception: the deceiving agent and the client agent cannot be divorced too far – the mental distance or rupture between them cannot constitute 'second-mind personology' – for then we have *other*-deception, but our model preserves their identity.

The model also answers several common objections perennially directed against the conception of strong SD. Why should the deceiving agency be interested in self-deception? Does it like lying for its own sake? Does it suppose that it knows what is best for the deceived agency? If the self-deception is consoling or palliative, is that because the deceiving agency is altruistic? On the other hand, self-deception is often disastrous for the person as a whole: 'he never should have taken that last drink but convinced himself it wouldn't affect his driving'. Why should the deceiving agency seek its own destruction (see e.g. Johnston 1988: 64–5)?

The immediate appeal of these sorts of objections is engendered by the restricted focus of the usual sorts of examples provided in the philosophical literature, and the shallowness of their analyses. Almost invariably ignored, because the Freudian unconscious is ignored, is the total conative set, the field of evidence or set of considerations, *including unconscious considerations*, which have a bearing on the determination of the will. Why does one succumb to the lure of that final drink and not another? Why sometimes and not at other times? Well, what is the unconscious significance of that drink for this man now? Having won a lottery? Having lost his wife? Yearning, like the Sybil at Cumae, to die? If the total conative set of the self as subject is examined we would generally find rational action in the sense of acting appropriately to that set, conserving, as Marshall (2000) says, what is important to it.

It is another strength of the models of self-solicitude developed in earlier chapters that they felicitously accommodate these common objections. The benign self-solicitous agency, largely the product of the internalisation of benign maternal caring and the development of self-concern, is not 'altruistic' but does have its client agency's interests at heart. It may indeed deceive the client, but this is no more mysterious than that a mother may tell a child soothing stories or consoling lies. Of course, it is done, as explained, in an unconscious register. It is unlikely that the deceiving agent brings its activity under the concept of deception and so sets about intentionally deceiving its client self, but there is no doubt that we frequently minister to ourselves, try to provide consolation, satisfaction, appeasement as best we can, unconsciously. Under what descriptions the consoling self (or personation) sees its own actions will vary from case to case. In the most likely circumstance the deceiving or consoling self believes that by performing some function or procedure it can console the object self, without knowing clearly the content of the object self's unsatisfied desire or the reasons for its distress. Mother often doesn't know exactly what is wrong with baby, but she will eventually hit on it. Mothers accumulate a set of routines that work, and these are eventually internalised by the infant and become reflexive. A person with depressive or paranoid propensity can be overwhelmingly distressed but eventually stumble on the right wishful phantasy, strategy or delusion that offers *some* measure of relief. Projective and introjective phantasies may be such processes. The paranoid person will still feel persecuted and the depressed one depressed, but it may be better to be persecuted by an external object than an internal one, and better to maintain a relationship with a bad, soul-destroying, hyper-critical object than to have no object at all. Such wishful solutions may be happenstance but others, it has been argued, are strategic, the intentional activity of personations.

How is such caretaking knowledge acquired? Through internalisation of caretaking, usually maternal, functions and procedures, and through the process of growing up with, and understanding, ourselves. Skills in the management of our internal world are acquired in much the same ways as those acquired for the management of external circumstances. It is notable that psychotic children who are unable to internalise maternal functions and skills usually lack the capacity to attend to fundamental needs such as eating, dressing or playing. Dreaming, too, seems to be impaired (Mahler 1968).

On the other side, the reflexive attitudes of self-hatred and self-envy are very common, if not universal, afflictions, and may be acute in pathological conditions such as borderline personality disorder, psychotic depression and schizophrenia. Here the motivation of the deceiving self may be quite perspicuous, as in the case of Rosenfeld's patient where the DNO or mad self sought to deceive, cozen or tear away its client self into a delusional phantasy world in the unfolding of its hatred and envy (Rosenfeld 1987; Steiner 1982, 1993). (The *activation* of the DNO, you will recall, is a more complex affair.) Furthermore, the actions of even the benign caretaking self may have unfortunate consequences for the person as a whole. In the pathological circumstances in which the broad types of FWT are brought into play, the caretaking self is bent on ministering to the object self and may be governed by an excessive compliance to the demands of the object self, a profligate need to gratify the self as object. As Freud puts it, the ego heeds the id (or the superego) rather than reality (Freud 1924b, 1924e). In some pathological cases there is a deformation of the caretaking self and the problems and demands of the self as object – typically the infantile self, the child within – dominate it. That is a common configuration: the person remains in bondage to the satisfaction of imperative, infantile needs, to a tyranny of desire.

It might be asked why the client self is so biddable, so easily taken in? How can the protective or consoling agency just 'slip' false beliefs into the client self and the latter embrace them passively (Johnston 1988: 84)? The objection is easily allayed. Recall earlier discussions (2.4, 5.7). The consoling agency does not just *slip* beliefs into the client self. It manufactures evidence in phantasy, symptom or enactment, or tendentiously selects from the total evidence to constitute a restricted conative field as agent's evidence. The client self accepts this evidence because of the particular disposition of attention – engrossment – that prevails in it. To put one possible configuration of this circumstance in Freudian terms, what the id perceives is either its own internal states or what comes to it filtered through the ego: 'no external vicissitudes can be experienced or undergone by the id except by way of the ego' (Freud 1923b: 38). Moreover, the client self is typically distressed, in urgent need and receptive to consolation, constrained by the available evidence and the play of its desires upon that evidence.

6.4 Delusion

In 2.1 I quoted a passage written by Wilhelm Griesinger, a psychiatrist with claims to being the father of biological psychiatry, observing (amongst other things) that 'in mental disease... we see clearly how supposed possession and imaginary realizations of good things and wishes, the denial and destruction of which furnished a moral cause of the disease, constitute commonly the chief subjects of the delirium of insanity' (Griesinger 1867: 108–9). It seems obvious even to the untrained, and was so even to an arch-*Somatiker* like Griesinger, that many delusions are wishful, reactions to loss or intolerable frustration, patches over rents in the ego's relation to the external world (Freud 1924b: 151).

Freud early on noted two characteristics of delusion: first, it is one of a group of pathological states which do not produce direct effects on the body but only mental indications; second, it is characterised by the fact that in it, 'phantasies have gained the upper hand – that is have obtained belief and have acquired an influence on action' (1907a: 44–5). Since every phantasy is 'the fulfilment of a wish, the correction of unsatisfying reality' (1908e: 146), it follows in his view that every delusion is wish-fulfilling. In psychosis the subject turns away from reality, dragged away by the id, and constructs a delusional alternative reality along wishful lines (1924e: 186–7). But delusional constructions were not exclusively psychotic, in Freud's view. Milder constructions appear in neurosis, and religion he regarded, as we shall see in the next chapter, as a mass delusion (1930a: 84–5).

This view of delusions as having wishful aetiology is certainly consilient with many psychiatric conditions. Delusions are frequently of an obviously grandiose or compensatory character, or defensive or self-referential in ways designed to maintain some semblance of self-esteem or to deny, often manically, unbearable realities. Even where these conditions are not conspicuous, it often does not require much psychological acumen to spot them beneath the surface. And it has been observed that cultural and circumstantial factors which set norms of aspiration, of what constitutes loss and success and so on – of what is desirable – substantially shape delusions. For instance, during the Great Depression delusions of wealth were unusually common, and grandiose religious delusions appear more common in Abrahamic religious cultures, with their adoration of omnipotent beings, than in others. Yet wishful aetiology, though still dominant in psychoanalytic thinking about delusions, does not seem to enjoy the favour of most corners of contemporary psychiatry or clinical psychology.

The reasons for this are thin and dismaying, and turn on superficial examinations of the relevant phenomena. Many delusions certainly do not appear wish-fulfilling. Paranoid persecutory delusions or delusions of being observed or gossiped about may be very distressing. So, too, the delusions often found in psychotic depression, about being an irredeemable sinner, a murderer, someone unworthy of life. These facts have seemed to many theorists to be fatal to the wishful aetiology hypothesis. Further, and not without connection to this conviction, Karl Jaspers (1997) influentially maintained that 'primary' or true delusions are incomprehensible and meaningless. They are scrambled products of a disordered brain. Being meaningless to both observer and subject, delusions can scarcely be wish-fulfilling. Jaspers allowed that there were 'secondary' delusions that could be meaningful, though these were of subsidiary import to the illness. (It should be kept in mind that a delusion may be meaningful to its subject but unintelligible to *us* – see Radden 2011: 58.) In line with Jasper's conception, many thinkers have assumed that if delusion is the product of a disordered or broken brain then it *cannot* be wishful because it cannot be meaningful. Finally, presumably impressed by these considerations, even researchers who are prepared to entertain the meaningfulness of at least some delusions, recognise that they may contain kernels of circumstantial truth and reject the disordered brain hypothesis have embarked on unpromising lines of research – any line indeed but the Freudian one – and have, so to speak, crowded it out.[7]

6.5 Delusion as Freudian wish-fulfilment

A detailed consideration of the many superficial proposals in the literature intending the explanation of delusions would make the wishful aetiology hypothesis look brilliant, but for reasons of space, that task cannot be attempted here. I will endeavour only to show how plausible and well-grounded that hypothesis is.

In the psychiatric literature, delusion is usually regarded as a species of belief or judgement. Thus DSM-IV defines a delusion as:

> A false personal belief based on incorrect inference about external reality and firmly sustained in spite of what everyone else believes and in spite of what usually constitutes incontrovertible and obvious proof or evidence to the contrary. The belief is not one ordinarily accepted by other members of the person's culture or sub-culture (e.g., it is not an article of religious faith).
>
> (APA 1994: 765)[8]

As many commentators (Bentall 2004: ch. 12; Graham 2010: 195ff; Radden 2011: *passim*) have noted, this definition is not altogether helpful. Delusions can be true; there are delusional states of mind which are not patently cognitive, delusional moods or imaginings, for example; there are mass delusions (Freud and many others thought religion one such); therefore non-acceptance by the many cannot be an adequate epistemic criterion of delusion, since acceptance isn't a criterion of non-delusion. However, many delusions clearly are beliefs, and false ones at that, and for simplicity I will restrict attention to those.

It must be granted at once that not all the items typically regarded as delusions are likely to be wish-fulfilling. A sharp blow to the head or pickling the brain in alcohol may induce delusions, and although it does not follow that these delusions *cannot* be wish-fulfilling merely because they originate in brain damage, it seems likely that a damaged brain can render mental processes so mangled and unintelligible, to both the brain's owner and observers, to exclude the possibility of wish-fulfilment. Indeed, it may be wondered whether the sort of item that Jaspers had in mind, that is completely incomprehensible to the observer and to the subject – even unconsciously – can be considered delusional *belief* at all. *What* is believed, and *who* is deluded? A meaningless proposition cannot be believed and there is nothing for the subject to be deluded about.[9]

Delusions, then, are of different types – in content of course, but very probably also in the sense that they may be presumed to have categorically different causes.

They may, for example, arise from different kinds of neurological damage, but it doesn't follow that any one kind or all kinds of such damage is a necessary condition for delusion: delusion may arise in circumstances where there is no neurological damage.

If delusions are considered, as they are by most psychoanalysts and some clinical psychologists (Bentall 2004), to belong on a continuum of beliefs (or phantasies construed as belief-like) – normal, false, irrational, superstitious, self-deceptive – then since we know that wishes can play a causal role in the origin and sustainment of these other beliefs (even if, as we have seen at length, there is disagreement about just how they do so), a wishful provenance for delusions appears a tenable proposition.[10] Our task then is to disable the objections listed at the end of **6.4** – objections that arise in the main from a refusal to countenance the possibility that a delusion may have unconscious meaning for its subject, and a neglect (or perhaps ignorance) of the complexity of intrapsychic relations and agency.

Here is a simple case. Freud's patient is a non-psychotic, middle-aged woman suffering a delusion of jealousy (1916–17: 250ff). She had confided to a malicious maid that nothing would hurt her more than to discover that her husband was unfaithful. Sure enough, the next day she receives an anonymous letter declaring her husband's infidelity. Thereafter, in the teeth of ascertainable facts, she is gripped by a distressing and unshakeable delusion. At this point in his description Freud digresses to ask what psychiatry would say about the case, and answers: next to nothing. The psychiatrists of his time would search for hereditary connections and propose a precarious prognosis, and that is all.

But Freud was interested in the *content* of the delusion and a little probing soon uncovered the following facts. The middle-aged woman was deeply, though largely unconsciously, in love with her young son-in-law. This was of course an intolerable pass for the older woman and her delusion was constructed as a complex attempt to defend herself from guilt, and perhaps to provide an excuse, presumably along these lines (Freud does not spell this out): 'It is not I who wants to have an affair, my husband does; and suppose I did, he is already doing it...' Freud remarks that 'the phantasy of her husband's unfaithfulness thus acted as a cooling compress on her burning wound' (1916–17: 252). It is now evident that 'the delusion has ceased to be absurd or unintelligible; it had a sense, it had good motives and it fitted into the context of an emotional experience of the patient's. ... [the delusion] itself was something desired, a kind of consolation' (1916–17: 253). Thus, with some exploration of the subject's circumstances, with a little insight, with interpretation that would not strain the common-sense understanding of erotic relations possessed by most adults, the delusion is seen to be meaningful and wish-fulfilling, consoling and self-justifying in the manner of FWT.

Often delusions of being observed or persecuted yield to similar analysis. Such delusions can of course create intolerable anxiety and anguish. Psychoanalytic interpretation often reveals the observers or persecutors to be projected aspects of one's self or of internalised objects, and so to have, as Freud said, a 'real foundation' (1914c: 95–6). He held, for example, that the delusion of being observed arises from a projection of the ego-ideal or superego experienced regressively; that is, as an archaic object or person. Distressing as such a condition may be, analysis often reveals that something of overriding import is preserved: the delusion sustains the relation to the parental object that constitutes the unconscious core of the figure of the observer or persecutor. A belief that one is being observed or even persecuted affirms that one is alive and related, that one matters, perhaps indeed that one is *very* important: the quarry of the CIA, the cynosure of the religious world, and so on. Returning to Rosenfeld's patient **(5.6)**, we can now see her persecution by the DNO as a kind of wish-fulfilling delusion in which she retains a relationship to a needed grandiose figure, with which at times she identifies and becomes the chief personation.

In their remarkable study, Kaplan-Solms and Solms (2000: 207ff) discuss several patients with brain damage in the ventromesial frontal area of the brain who display florid psychotic behaviour. The authors are able to relate their patients' psychotic delusions to the features identified by Freud as definitive of unconscious (id) processes: exemption from mutual contradiction, primary process functioning (mobility of cathexis), timelessness, replacement of external with internal reality. In particular, most of their patients' delusions are transparently wishful: thus one patient disavows being in a hospital and delusionally phantasises being on a river barge with which he had previous pleasurable associations. He misrepresents strangers as familiar friends and family. Another patient's 'sense of time always seemed to follow a wishful model': it was always 5 p.m., the time his wife visited. Regularly, a wishful internal reality replaces external reality – a patch, as Freud said, placed over the rent with the world. On the basis of their analyses of these and other clearly neurologically damaged patients, the authors hypothesise that 'the ventromesial frontal cortex performs the fundamental economic transformation that inhibits the primary process of the mind' (Kaplan-Solms and Solms 2000: 230). In other words, it is a function of the higher mental (cortical) functions to inhibit the desiderative or wishful aspects of mind.

As already noted, even if in specific cases gross neurological damage causes psychotic delusions, it doesn't follow that *all* delusions are caused by such damage, that they are caused by a broken brain. Interestingly, what the above evidence does suggest is that even where there *is* a broken brain, in these cases neurological damage to the cortical inhibitive functions, the delusions that are consequences of damage will still mostly be wish-fulfilling. It would follow that even if striking, primary delusions such as those found in Capgrass or Cotard's syndromes result from disease of the brain or defective cognitive modules, wishful explanation is not precluded. We might, however, expect the wishful activity of mind to cease if there was damage to the neural structures that subserve them, primarily the SEEKING system, in Panksepp's scheme (Panksepp and Biven 2012).

Despite its a priori attractiveness and favourable empirical evidence, many researchers go to extraordinary lengths to evade the wishful motivation hypothesis, even when their own data strongly suggests it. Bentall (2004: 323ff), for example – after rejecting a number of widely received views on the aetiology of delusion – notes that selective attention seems to play some part in them; that deluded people have

difficulty adjusting their beliefs in the light of evidence; that they avoid disconfirming information; that they have an inability to think clearly; that they may have
deficient 'theory of mind', that is, the capacity to understand other people's
thoughts and moods; that they tend to suffer from something with unknown cause
which he calls 'epistemological impulsivity', a tendency to form hasty and extreme
judgements; that possibly deluded people do not know how to go about testing
hypotheses; that 'emotional and motivational factors provide a third possible explanation for the deluded patient's tendency to jump to conclusions' (2004: 326); that
they may have a high need for closure; and others.

All of this would suggest to anyone who does not have a bias against psychoanalytic understanding that the motive forces behind delusions are desires or wishes:
that it is *desire* (as we have amply demonstrated) that can effectively direct attention,
lead to epistemological impulsivity, make people jump to conclusions, avoid uncon-
genial evidence, hold wish-fulfilling beliefs tenaciously in place and indeed manufacture evidence in phantasy and enactment. It would seem that Bentall and other
psychologists and psychiatrists almost exclusively fixated on the cognitive and cog-
itative functions will consider just about any expedient to explain delusion rather
than recognise the desiderative, wishful and indeed erotic and destructive aspects of
mind. The poverty of much recent discussion of delusion is precisely because so
many researchers ignore the ineluctable wishes that instigate and sustain delusion,
and the unconscious meaning of the wish-fulfilment (FWT) that renders its subject
so unwilling to part with it. Bentall says that the recent psychological work he cites
prodigiously – using the usual tools of cognitive psychologists, viz. questionnaires
and laboratory methods – has made huge strides in the investigation of delusion,
compared to previous decades 'when there was hardly any evidence to discuss'
(2004: 328). On the contrary, this work has held back understanding and, at its best,
has re-invented the spokes of the wheel. His view is partly the product of the superficial conceptions of science widespread amongst cognitive psychologists, in particular of the methods appropriate to the proper study of humankind.[11]

George Graham (2010) recognises that delusion cannot be adequately defined or
characterised in purely descriptive or phenomenological terms. He does not discuss
the wish-fulfilling hypothesis but rejects other aetiological or motivational accounts,
according to which delusional beliefs are acquired either wilfully or by some cognitive processing error. Instead he turns, to throw light on the matter, to delusions'
consequences.

> Belief-acquisition conditions may and often do lead people into error, but, I am
> claiming, it's what a person does with or because of the attitude, or fails to do,
> that makes for a delusion. Acquisition is one thing; upshot or consequence is
> another. ... I contend that it is not falsity, bizarreness or irrational origin of an
> attitude that makes delusion. Delusions constitute, I propose, a failure of prudent
> self-comprehension and responsible epistemic self-management and it is *that* sort
> of failure and its impact on a person that makes for a delusion...
>
> (2010: 206)

One might ask why there is failure in self-management, an issue Graham leaves unaddressed. But a better question to ask is: why does the deluded person cling to the delusion and endure its negative consequences? Well, according to Graham, there comes a point when the rational, person-level or Intentional understanding of behaviour must be supplemented by reference to a-rational brute causal neural forces describable only in a non-Intentional idiom. If the persistence of delusions cannot be explained Intentionally, then the invocation of neurobiology becomes a necessity: 'Look for a brute causal mechanism as responsible for such behaviour. True, it is not as if Intentionalistic explanation is *a priori* excluded from such cases. Though straining credulity, we may continue to cite palliation in explaining the persistence of a Capgrass delusion. But nevertheless such an explanation may just not fully or plausibly explain the behaviour' (2010: 207). The mind, as he says, gets 'gummed up'. Graham doesn't have much to go on but proposes that a 'dopamine induced sense of salience' may 'help to explain why a conviction of a delusional sort is not abandoned' (2010: 208). The brain-reward system, he says, 'a-rationally irrupts into the space of reasons' (2010: 218). Graham believes that similar irruptions occur in all psychotic disorders and they explain the disorder's irrational, involuntary, uncontrollable character (2010: 117ff).

Perhaps, though the vagueness of his proposals for the neural irruptive forces is striking. Still, there is nothing to exclude such explanations in principle, and it is quite certain that in some mental disorders neurobiological intrusions into the space of reasons play a part. But equally, as Graham acknowledges, Intentional explanations are not excluded a priori. Graham thinks that exclusively Intentional explanations strain credulity, at least for some of the grosser delusions. But by ignoring the possibility of unconscious motivation and other psychoanalytic conceptions it can scarcely be said that he has looked for them assiduously. Earlier chapters have indicated how symptoms, including delusions, may be brought about through a variety of processes of Freudian wish-fulfilment, and the exclusion of these processes can only be determined case by case, where they are demonstratively absent. In previous chapters we observed the complexity of motivational processes and strategies, ranging from the subintentional and expressive operation of motives to complex maximally intentional strategies of self-solicitude deployed to manufacture evidence for grounding wish-fulfilling beliefs. We also considered some of the conditions, most carefully the vicissitude of attention designated *engrossment*, that enables such agent's evidence to grip the mind. In the present context we would trace the way in which ineluctable wishes give rise to delusional thoughts and how these thoughts are converted into delusional beliefs. It is unnecessary to repeat that discussion. Instead we will move into other territory, where Freudian wish-fulfilment dominates the life of the mind.

Notes

1 For an overview see Mele (1987), McLaughlin and Rorty (1988). A strong current of work in the phenomenology tradition points in the same direction; cf. Sartre (1969); Wilshire (1982). For a recent view from biology see Trivers (2011).

2 It may be, as Whisner (1992) and others suggest, that kinds of self-deception not closely modelled on other-directed deception are 'the most frequent type' (though it is quite unclear how they measure frequency), but even if that were so it would not establish these types' *conceptual* centrality.

3 Garnered from McLaughlin (1988: pp. 30, 40, 45).

4 It is sometimes alleged against police that they falsify or fabricate evidence against suspects whom they believe to be guilty, and who may very well be guilty, but against whom there is insufficient genuine evidence for a conviction. If the jury accepts the fabricated evidence, they will have been deceived into believing what the police believe to be true.

5 *Possibly*, A can lie by passing off a proposition he believes true – if, for example, A tells the truth believing that B will believe the opposite of what A tells; my intuition is against this, but intuition on this point varies. You can, however, deceive a person in certain circumstances by depriving him of evidence, if you believe that this will mislead him. This is still a kind of lie because it is an intentional misrepresentation of the facts as you believe them to be.

6 Cf. Gardner (1993: 21): 'In wishful thinking, a desire either produces the congenial belief directly, or it reshapes evidence immediately related to it; no intention is involved. ... The supposition that belief is directly vulnerable to desire in this way, and that there are simple mental dispositions (such as the brute magnetism of entertaining beliefs that represent the world in pleasing terms), are perfectly legitimate, and no doubt account for much weak self-deception. But no combination of them can account for strong self-deception, for the reason that strong self-deception manifests, we have seen, *practical rationality*, and exercising practical rationality requires an intention'. Gardner is right, I think, about practical rationality being a necessary condition of strong SD, but I find the idea of direct causation of belief by desire, unmediated by agent's evidence, problematic, as indicated above **(3.2)**.

7 See the approach in Bentall (2004) and the research he cites in ch. 12, and also Graham (2010) ch. 8.

8 Cf. Jaspers: 'The term delusion is vaguely applied to all false judgements that share the following characteristics... (i) they are held with an extraordinary conviction, with an incomparable, subjective certainty; (ii) there is an imperviousness to other experiences and to compelling counter-arguments; (iii) their content is impossible' (cited in Ghaemi 2007: 204).

9 I have observed schizophrenic patients talk 'word salad' and was assured by the psychiatrists present that the speech was completely meaningless. It certainly appeared so semantically, but one could not but sense the powerful illocutionary and perlocutionary forces at work – attempts to achieve *something* by their words and to affect the listener.

10 Bentall (2004) doesn't use the language of 'phantasy' or directly acknowledge unconscious processes, though he does refer to 'implicit beliefs' and goes at least part of the way towards wishful aetiology when he argues that 'self-protection' is (often?) the motivation for delusion.

11 Although it is obvious to any casual observer of animal life or the human scene, and although it follows from evolutionary theory that sex and aggressive rivalry and destructiveness are immensely significant, these obvious facts pass unnoticed by many researchers in the human sciences. One would gather, for example, from Bentall's (2004, 2010) and Graham's (2010) books that sex, aggression and the vicissitudes of object relations play no part whatever in the aetiology of psychosis, or in the lives of the mentally ill. In neither book is there the briefest mention of desire, sex, aggression or indeed of most of the other passions that govern human life – an extraordinary triumph of Puritanism and narrow vision in the human sciences.

Chapter 7

Religion

> Never, neither indirectly nor directly, neither as a dogma nor as an allegory, has religion yet held any truth.
>
> Nietzsche 1994 [1878]: 79

7.1 Freud on religion

You will recall from **1.1** Freud's astonishing claim that

> The whole course of the history of civilization is no more than an account of the various methods adopted by mankind for 'binding' their unsatisfied wishes. Myths, religion and morality find their place in this scheme as attempts to seek a compensation for the lack of satisfaction of human wishes.
>
> (1913j: 186–7)

Freud had much to say about religion (1907b; 1912–13; 1921c; 1927c; 1930a; 1939a), some of it speculative and demonstrably mistaken, all of it of great interest. His view of religion as wish-fulfilling is, I think, essentially correct but requires modification and elaboration, a task I will undertake here.

In their 'psychical origin', Freud says, 'religious ideas... are illusions, fulfilments of the oldest and most urgent wishes of mankind' (1927c: 30). These wishes, he thought, related principally to being cared for and protected by father, and he never quite coordinated this view with his growing appreciation of the significance of the maternal relation and the maternal aspects of divine figures.

> When the growing individual finds that he is destined to remain a child forever, that he can never do without protection against strange superior powers, he lends those powers the features belonging to the figure of his father; *he creates for himself the gods whom he dreads, whom he seeks to propitiate, to whom he nevertheless entrusts his own protection...* The defence against childish helplessness is what lends its characteristic features to the adult's reaction to the helplessness which *he* has to acknowledge – a reaction which is precisely the formation of religion.

An illusion, as Freud employs the concept, is a wish-fulfilling belief that is engendered by a wish. It may be true despite its provenance. But, Freud's settled view was that religion is delusional, or delusion-like, not merely illusional. Delusions, in his framework, are not only engendered by wishes; they also (a) contradict or (what is not the same) disavow reality and (b) are immune to change through rational considerations. So, he says, religion 'comprises a system of wishful illusions together with disavowal of reality, such as we in an isolated form find nowhere else but in amentia, in a state of blissful hallucinatory confusion'. However, he quickly adds: 'these are only analogies, by the help of which we endeavour to understand a social phenomenon; the pathology of the individual does not supply us with a fully valid counterpart' (1927c: 39).

Although in his early work Freud frequently depicts religion as neurosis, especially obsessional neurosis (1907b), he concedes later that it may function to obviate neurosis – but only because of its delusional character. Religion has the effect of 'depressing the value of life and distorting the picture of the real world in a delusional manner – which presupposes an intimidation of the intelligence. At this price, by forcibly fixing them into a state of psychical infantilism and by drawing them into a mass delusion, religion succeeds in sparing many people an individual neurosis' (1930a: 84–5). Religion, then, is *delusion-like*: it involves something approaching a psychotic divorce from reality.[1]

Three features of the views exposed so far require elaboration. First, although there are excellent (I believe unanswerable) metaphysical and epistemological objections to most foundational religious beliefs, and although there is good reason to think that many religious people do function at a somewhat monothematic delusional level (as we shall soon see), Freud was well aware that psychology could not determine whether religious ideas were true. He thought that religion was delusion-like not because of any intrinsic characteristics of its representations visible to psychology, but because religious ideas grossly affronted reality and, combined with their outlandishness and weak evidentiary and philosophical support, would considerably be undermined by their wishful provenance. The religious apologetical literature is so crammed with charges that Freud committed the genetic fallacy that it is apt to quote this passage in full:

> To assess the truth-value of religious doctrines does not lie within the scope of the present inquiry. It is enough for us that we have recognised them as being, in their psychological nature, illusions. But we do not have to conceal the fact that this discovery also strongly influences our attitude to the question which must appear to many to be the most important of all. We know approximately at what periods and by what kind of men religious doctrines were created. If in addition we discover the motives which led to this, our attitude to the problem of religion will undergo a marked displacement. We shall tell ourselves that it would be very nice if there were a God who created the world and was a benevolent Providence, and if there were a moral order in the universe and an after-life; but it is a very striking fact that all this is exactly as we are bound to wish it to be. And it would be more remarkable still if our wretched, ignorant

and down-trodden ancestors had succeeded in solving all these difficult riddles of the universe.

(1927c: 33)

Second, there is some ambiguity in his view quoted above (1927c: 20) as regards the extent to which unconscious infantile wishes, whose object is parental solicitude, are being satisfied in the life devoted to gods, *as well as* the adult's quite realistic dependent needs and anxieties, unrealistically directed at powerful, protective, albeit illusional beings. The extent to which gods are unconsciously identified with parental objects is a little muddy in this text, for the difference between infantile wishes preserved in the unconscious and conscious adult wishes which are genetically infantile, though entirely realistic, is not explicitly recognised. Freud's statement that 'the recognition that this helplessness lasts throughout life made it necessary to cling to the existence of a father, but this time a more powerful one' (1927c: 26) suggests that the emphasis is on allaying adult dependent needs – real needs for security and love in a world of hostile contingency, for living in the sight of caring beings – though these happen to have the same character as the child's. However, the general drift of Freud's and subsequent psychoanalytic thought is clear. As a rule, supernatural figures unconsciously *represent* parental objects and relating to them symbolically or substitutively satisfy unconscious infantile wishes for consolation, protection and love, at the same time as adult dependent needs and desires. Freudian wish-fulfilment, as has been shown, is generally over-determined.

Third, Freud refers to individuals 'creating' gods for themselves (1927c: 20). This is surely mistaken and scarcely compatible with his notion of religion being a mass delusion, though of course the simultaneous formation of similar individual delusions in a mass is conceivable on the model of hysterical contagion. By and large, though, religious ideology, practices and institutions are not individual creations like phantasies; they are cultural constructions to which children are exposed, usually at a very early age, much as they are to wish-fulfilling fairy tales and the ethnocentric values of their culture. They have, however, a more potent role than other prejudices in structuring mind, one that will be examined in considerable detail presently. Of course, there are people who *have* 'created' gods for themselves: the founders of religions such as Zoroaster, Jesus, Muhammad. And there are mentally ill people who create novel ideologies and put on the garb of religion. Shoko Asahara, the megalomaniacal founder of Aum Supreme Truth, who was responsible for the sarin gas attack on the Tokyo subway in 1995, initially drew inspiration from Buddhism but found that religion not wholly congenial to the universal destruction he intended to visit upon his enemies (Post 2007: 213ff). Later, encountering the Bible, he was inspired by Revelations, saw at once the remarkable parallels between Christ and himself, declared himself to *be* the Christ, and promulgated a new religious teaching that attracted many followers. We can incidentally see very clearly in this formation a religio-cultural eclecticism, and in this respect, in not creating gods *de novo*, even the great religious reformers were not so very different. Freud was aware of the distinction between the wishful motives for religion in the individual and the fact that religions as cultural organisms pre-exist individuals and enlist them to their purposes, but he was, I think, insufficiently attentive to the distinction and provided an incomplete account of the operation of FWT in the formation of religious ideology, practices and institutions.

7.2 Distinctions

Although it is difficult to avoid formulations in general terms, it must be borne in mind that religions are complex congeries of ideology, practices, rituals, attitudes and institutions, and that the kind of explanation apt for one aspect of religion may be inappropriate for another. The explanation of how particular religious beliefs evolved, for example, may be of an entirely different order from the explanation of rituals. Some religious beliefs may have their source in the need to feel protected (say); ritual may have its source in something quite different – in basic emotional systems such as PLAY (Panksepp and Biven 2012) perhaps, or in the harnessing of rewarding neurochemicals by means of group dancing or induced trance (Thompson Jr. 2011: 82ff). And finer distinctions *within* religious ideology, kinds of rituals, and so on would be required for anything like an adequate accounting. For reasons of economy I am going to focus on religious ideology and its relation to certain types of character; that is to say, on only one element of religious phenomenology.

There is great diversity amongst religions and no single thread binds them together. The worship of gods is at the centre of many religions (theism), but by no means all. Some religions invoke powerful beings who are not worshipped but figure prominently in ritual; others appear (to us) like systems of metaphysics or magic. Some people assimilate religion to science and ideologies such as communism, environmentalism and atheism; indeed, any reasonably systematic body of thought. This assimilation is confused. Apart from obvious epistemological differences, it deprives the concept of religion of any distinctive content. It detaches religion from its history, ritual, worship, prayer, revelation and, most importantly, the transcendent or supernatural. Some people think that the essence of religion is not ideology or dogma but certain feelings or attitudes towards deity or cosmos. William James famously defined religion as 'the feelings, acts and experiences of individual men in their solitude, so far as they apprehend themselves to stand in relation to whatever they may consider the divine' (James 1971: 31). The main thing, he says, is 'the experience of deliverance' from loss of meaning, melancholy and the sense of pervasive evil. Its fruits are the 'loss of all worry, the sense that all is ultimately well with one, the peace, the harmony, *the willingness to be*' (1971: 185). Many people will recognise such experiences and consider them quintessentially religious. That, however, is an error. Why, detached from embedding religious doctrine, should such experiences be considered *religious*, and not, say, as stages in recovery from melancholia or the birth of wisdom? The capacity for reverence, spiritual sensibility and inwardness, are neither conditions over which religion has proprietary rights nor definitive of it. There is no sense in the idea of religion without specific ideology or institutional or social expression (McTaggart 2012 [1906]).

There is also great diversity *within* religions. There are significant denominational differences in all the major religions, but religious identity is especially complex in our time because the longing for group identity drives people who divest religion of almost all defining doctrinal content to profess religious affiliation. As various surveys show, denial of the Resurrection or even deity does not bar people from identifying themselves as Christians, and people who accept neither Torah nor worship will identify themselves as Jews. Religious, ethnic and national identities have become blurred in many dispensations. Recognising this variety and contingency (or superficiality) of religious profession, and for other reasons soon to emerge, I will concentrate discussion on groups I refer to as *religiose*, and mostly those in the Abrahamic religions. They include most of the groups currently identified as fundamentalist, though not only them. Their characteristics are considered below.

It is in fact difficult to define religion satisfactorily, but it is best to have at least a rough characterisation as backdrop. John Haldane's pithy definition is useful: religion, he says, is 'a system of beliefs and practices directed towards a transcendent reality in relation to which persons seek solutions to the observed facts of moral and physical evil, limitation and vulnerability, particularly and especially death' (Haldane 2005: 17).

I make no attempt to refute religious conceptions here, but what I say about the character of the people who take them most seriously contributes to undermining those conceptions. Moreover, the supposition of deity and supernatural beings shared by the Abrahamic religions is extraordinarily extravagant. If persuasive socio-psychological explanations for religious beliefs and practices can be uncovered then that weakens, though it does not of course refute, the usual legitimising claims made for them. It weakens the case for religion because the socio-psychological explanations are metaphysically much less extravagant and outlandish and more consistent with the best picture of the world we have, the scientific–naturalistic one.

Let us suppose, then, that the worship of gods is central to religions, and let us focus on the Abrahamic monotheisms. Now, even if gods exist, it does not follow that anyone has good reasons for believing that they do, and therefore good reasons for engaging in religious commitments. Even if there *are* good reasons or arguments, it does not follow that they are what motivate people to religion. In fact, most religious people are 'simple believers', as Aquinas called them: there may be rational grounds for religion but they are not the reasons why these people turn to it. Our interest here is in the reasons or underlying motives for which the vast majority of religious people do *in fact* embrace religion, and those reasons may be very different from the avowed ones. I do not mean only that most religious people have failed to justify their religious beliefs in a rational manner, or that they have swallowed these beliefs uncritically, or on the basis of unreliable testimony, faith in revelation or authority – though they mostly have done those things. I will argue that their beliefs are, as a rule, non-rationally motivated by unconscious desires and dispositions. For the majority, the overt motives derived from natural theology, religious reflection or faith are really idle wheels, or wheels turned by forces unknown to them – though, of course, it does not *seem* like that to them.

7.3 The religious and the religiose

I make a rough distinction between the religious and the religiose: between those for whom religious ideology can be conceived, approximately, as a matter of opinion or belief, and those for whom it is a powerful expression of conviction and character. Belonging to a religion, having a religious identity, can obviously satisfy a broad range of conscious and unconscious needs and dispositions. Many of the religious people I know personally derive much social satisfaction from engaging in their religious communities: they enjoy the festivals and value the sense of belonging. The finer questions of theology, or of a personal relation to God, rarely engage them. These are matters on which they would be prepared to change their minds, should they be interested in doing so, which they rarely are. Religious profession in such cases may be orthodox and sincere, yet fail to deeply engage the passions. These 'simple believers' may also derive unconscious satisfactions of needs and dispositions universally deposed in humankind, in some people more liberally than others. For example, various obsessional needs can be satisfied in the 'magical' placating gestures of daily ritual (regular prayer, beads, donning phylacteries, making the cross, touching venerable objects, etc.). Hysterical needs to separate the lower (sexual, profane) aspects of the personality from the higher (moral, spiritual, sacred) ones both fashion, and are accommodated in, the architecture of most religions. These same needs can find expression in prejudices such as racism or classism,[2] or in exclusionary social and political ideology, but also in more harmless participations.

But the passional, dispositional quality of faith may be radically different. The religiose are people for whom the relationship with God (or other supernatural beings), and with their religious group, is an intense and deep engagement born of immense unconscious investment. Their belief is tenacious, radicates deeply in the personality, is driven by intense need – though not of the sort they consciously imagine – and influences remote aspects of their lives. I will presently show how in such cases religion fulfils (in the manner of FWT) unconscious wishes and dispositions relating to unconscious aspects of the self and imagos of parents and others. That explains why religiose attitudes are often mirrored in other attitudes – to politics, morality and, particularly, gender issues. Character, to be sure, is partly shaped by religious upbringing. But conversely, particular features of religions are attractive to people with specific psychological needs and dispositions. A person who accepts the Biblical injunctions against homosexuality is likely to have adverse attitudes towards it. But character is attracted to, and selects, doctrine: only people with certain dispositions are likely to find the Biblical injunctions congenial or acceptable. The religious beliefs and attitudes of the religiose are held in place by the unconscious wishes that their religion satisfies. The shoe fits and they wear it.

I will be most concerned here with examining narcissistic elements of personality since these are, I think, most salient in the religiose and driving much of the religious extremism and violence in the world today. Primary expressions of religiose confession will be exposed as more or less unconscious wishful attempts at sustaining self-esteem and identity, suppressing guilt and shame, covertly expressing envy and hatred and fulfilling wishes for specialness, superiority and belonging.

These attempts are conducted both at an individual level through the exploitation of religious doctrine and through powerful group or tribal identifications.

7.4 Fundamentalism and the religiose

The term 'fundamentalism' has well-defined meaning within the historical context of conservative American Protestantism. The fundamentalist movement emerged from roots in nineteenth century millenarianism and grew in the early twentieth century, largely in reaction to upheavals threatening traditional social arrangements and values, especially the liberal Biblical scholarship challenging the literal truth and inerrancy of the Bible. A group of millenarians and like-minded evangelicals published a series of tracts, 'The Fundamentals: A Testimony of Truth', intended to set out the fundamental beliefs of Protestantism. These were, in Malise Ruthven's words:

> the inerrancy of the Bible; the direct creation of the world, and humanity, *ex nihilo* by God (in contrast to Darwinian evolution); the authenticity of miracles; the virgin birth of Jesus, his Crucifixion and bodily resurrection: the substitutionary atonement (the doctrine that Christ died to redeem the sins of humanity); and (for some but not all believers) his imminent return to judge and rule over the world.
>
> (Ruthven 2004: 11)

The tracts achieved wide circulation and influence. In 1920 a conservative Baptist editor, Curtis Lee Laws, declared that 'Fundamentalists were those who were ready to do battle royal for The Fundamentals' (quoted in Ruthven 2004: 7). Since then the term has acquired promiscuous associations and is now used to designate an agglomeration of religious ideologies and attitudes, and even non-religious ones ('economic fundamentalism', 'environmental fundamentalism' etc.). In the media the term is applied to Islamic groups such as the Taliban, the Muslim Brotherhood, the Wahhabis, al-Qaeda and others. Within Christianity, there is now included much of the conservative Christian right: many evangelical, Pentecostalist and other charismatic churches, Jehovah's Witnesses, Exclusive Brethren, in addition to the (historically) fundamentalist churches in the United States. Catholic integralism in certain respects also belongs here, as do a considerable number of Hindu, Sikh and Buddhist groups. Judaic fundamentalism includes the ultra-Orthodox Haredi groups and the Gush Emunim in Israel ('Bloc of the Faithful'), the backbone of the settler movement.

Clearly there is no single dogmatic or practical feature that unites these diverse expressions of religious identity, and there are numerous features that distinguish them. Nevertheless, there are criss-crossing similarities – family resemblances – in certain basic beliefs, values and attitudes. It will be useful to summarise the main commonalities here.

(1) Most fundamentalist manifestations are reactions by beleaguered believers to preserve their distinctive identity in the face of a rapidly changing world and

secularisation. Most groups therefore have unifying myths about a Golden Age before their tradition was contaminated by the new ways. In Islam, the era of the Prophet and his immediate successors, the 'rightly guided' Caliphs, is deemed to be such an age; American fundamentalists tend to idealise the time of the founding fathers, or 1950s small-town America; some Jewish fundamentalists look back to the time of David and Solomon. The preservation of identity is equated with restoration of this earlier state, which then becomes one of the group's objectives.

(2) The groups are generally assertive, clamorous and violent. (An obvious exception is the Amish.) They zealously enter the fray either through legitimate political activity or radically and militantly. The militancy ('terrorism') is most conspicuous in the activities of some Islamists, and the political zealotry in the activities of the American Christian right. Energetic political exertions and extreme violence by fundamentalist groups now proliferate across Asia and Africa and are scattered elsewhere. (As I write, Islamist gunmen, having killed or maimed hundreds of people in a Kenyan shopping mall, are shooting it out with security forces. On the same day Islamists have blown up a Christian church killing scores of people in Pakistan.)

(3) The members of the group are the Elect, the Chosen Ones, the Saved, the Exclusive Brethren. The idea of being a 'chosen people' with a special mission is a concept best known in relation to Jews, but is in fact widespread amongst religious groups. It is not restricted to fundamentalist groups but is a prominent mark of all of them. It appears amongst Ulster Protestants and amongst some Buddhist Sinhalese. A Sinhalese religious nationalist expresses it typically: 'the Sinhalese nation... had come into being with the blessing of Buddha as a "chosen race" with a divine mission to fulfil...' (Ruthven 2004: 184). To be chosen is to be marked for a superior fate; one is marked by virtue of *being* superior. As early as around 60 CE the small Christian community under James 'regarded itself as the prefigurement of the eschatological assembly of the chosen people' (Trocme 1997: 78). On St. Augustine's ferocious doctrine, revived by Calvin, only the Elect ascend to Heaven; the remainder are consigned to everlasting torment. Premillenial Protestants believe that following the imminent return of Christ they, together with 144,000 'righteous Jews', will be 'raptured' into Heaven whilst the unrighteous majority perish.

(4) Superiority and distinction have to be marked publicly, so fundamentalists are obsessed with demarcating between believers and non-believers: skullcaps, turbans, hijab, crosses, markings on the skin, circumcision, initiations, baptisms, rituals, food abstentions, and so on. Marking the group assists in the preservation of distinctive identity, but it is also part of the narcissistic struggle to be considered unique and special. Small differences between similar groups are accentuated and exaggerated because the superiority which is predicated on membership of a special group is threatened most by those who are most similar but excluded. The heretic is more feared than the infidel.

(5)   There is only one true religion and correct way of living, and these must be defended against encroachment by other religions and secularism. Religious pluralism is problematic for the fundamentalist. Judaism, Christianity and Islam, even in their fundamentalist expressions, are universalist in principle, willing to embrace all comers – but only under an exclusive truth. So, in practice, they intensify the differences on which their narcissism feeds. Since there is only one true way, and it is under threat, the world is perceived through Manichaean lenses as a persecutory place: 'you are either with us or against us'. The struggle for religious identity is transformed into a cosmic struggle between truth and error, good and evil, God and the Devil.

(6)   There is a Holy Book, prophet or charismatic leader. They are inerrant, and literal obedience to their word is mandatory. In general, the Holy Books are the word of God. Consequently, the Books are timelessly true and comprehensive. The Book contains the Law prescribing right conduct. Obedience to its dicta leaves no space for uncertainty. Hence, the crazier and more uncertain the world, the more fiercely fundamentalists clutch the letter of the Law.

(7)   Law and authority to rule descend from God. Civic law is either already fully contained in the Holy Book or must be derived from it. God's law always trumps human law. The conception of law animating the active Christian right, for example, is that 'God's law is higher than mere human law, so human law should emulate God's. God's law is revealed in the Bible, so the Bible is the charter for modern lawmakers' (Maddox 2005: 267).

(8)   Fundamentalists are deeply concerned to control sexuality, especially female sexuality, and to draw irrefragable boundaries between male and female. The subordination of women extends over issues of marriage, reproduction, abortion, ordination and access to education. The patriarchal family is the indispensable unit within which sexuality is controlled. Homosexuality is also a major concern for all fundamentalists.[3] Opposition to gay rights and marriage is a major rallying point for fundamentalist Christians, Jews and Muslims without exception.

(9)   Fundamentalism and nationalism engage and unite in complex ways. Prima facie, they appear incompatible since one represents, essentially, the will of people and the other the will of God. But reconciliation is possible. All fundamentalists agree that God alone is sovereign and God's commandments are law. The state or nation must also be under God's law, for the good religious life can be lived only in a society of co-religionists, in a political organisation fashioned along religious lines. Hence the aims of religion and of nation converge in the formation of the religio-nationalist state.

It is striking that the fundamentalist beliefs and dispositions listed here range across religious cultures. Thus, fundamentalist attitudes to the subordination of women, to homosexuality, to the inerrancy of their Holy Books, etc. are fairly constant across Judaic, Islamic and predominantly Christian cultures. Moreover, they tend to cluster in patterns that are significant from the perspective of psychoanalytic psychology, and even predictable. This suggests that there are underlying psychological structures engendering, ordering and sustaining fundamentalist beliefs and dispositions. It suggests the possibility, in brief, of basic character traits expressing themselves in religious forms. In fact, the noted features have a patent affinity with narcissistic character traits: they are concerned with defending individual and group identity, self-esteem, 'specialness' and superiority, with achieving certainty or a kind of omniscience. Their wishful character is scarcely hidden. Because we are focused on the psychology of religion, it is useful to distinguish between religious ideology and religious character (or personality). We can reserve 'fundamentalism' for the side of ideology or belief, and utilise the term 'religiose' for the character which has an affinity with fundamentalism. Whilst not all the religiose (as I am using the concept here) are fundamentalists (they may not have encountered the relevant doctrines), they would be attracted to fundamentalism because it accommodates their psychological dispositions.

7.5 The religiose mind

There is now a substantial body of science concerning the nature of human attachment. It has evolved from psychoanalytic object-relations theory and the original investigations of John Bowlby, who initiated what is now known as Attachment Theory. Bowlby described an innate attachment behavioural system with the basic function of maintaining proximity between infant and a parenting figure who provides the infant with a secure base. The evolutionary advantages of such a system in slow developing primates like us are evident. Suffice to say here that in infancy attachment to an adult protective figure, and later in life to its various incarnations, is amongst the most fundamental of human needs. The psychologist Lee A. Kirkpatrick has drawn attention to the ways in which religious belief provides for attachment needs:

> To achieve the objective of establishing physical proximity, infants engage in a variety of behaviors such as crying, raising arms (to be picked up) and clinging. With increasing cognitive abilities, older children are often satisfied by visual or verbal contact, or eventually by mere knowledge of an attachment figure's whereabouts. This latter observation opens the door to the possibility of a non-corporeal attachment figure with which actual physical contact is impossible. Religious beliefs provide a variety of ways of enhancing perceptions about the proximity of God. A crucial tenet of most theistic religions is that God is omnipresent; thus one is always in 'proximity' to God. God is frequently described in religious literature as always being by one's side, holding one's hand, or watching over one… [V]irtually all religions provide places of worship where one can be closer to God. In addition a diverse array of idols and symbols – ranging from graven images to crosses on necklaces to painting and other art forms – seem designed to continually remind the

believer of God's presence. The most important form of proximity-maintaining attachment behavior directed toward God, however, is prayer...

(Kirkpatrick 1999: 806, 813)

Kirkpatrick assembled extensive survey data which supports a link between attachment needs and religious belief, and there have been many subsequent investigations supporting his claim. Other studies summarised by Kirkpatrick suggest that personal images of God and other supernatural figures are influenced by the vicissitudes of a person's attachment history. As one would expect, individuals may turn to God as a substitute attachment figure if parental figures have been inadequate. 'In a word, God may provide the kind of secure attachment relationship one never had with one's parents or other primary attachment figures' (Kirkpatrick 1999: 813).

The story of the growth of love is complex but there is agreement amongst developmental psychologists and psychoanalysts that attachment to the primary caring figure is the intricate relationship in which love grows, even if they disagree about the exact causes of attachment. Freud had anticipated some rudiments of this conception when he concluded that erotic instinctual drives 'lean upon' the self-preservative drives that first attach to the object (the breast or mother), and he sketched out in patches how attachment is sexualised and rapidly generates the entire assembly of erotic love, jealousy, hatred, guilt, and so on. At a few months of age, the absence of loved or needed figures evokes in the infant intense wishes for their presence, but the older child eventually finds indirect ways of satisfying them: by using substitute objects (dummies, toys, other people), wish-fulfilling phantasies (daydreams, masturbatory phantasies), dramatic play and make-believe. When a child begins to experience herself as a separate person, affections and thoughts that previously had other people as their objects can be experienced reflexively in relation to the self. There is now a dawning capacity to take oneself as an object: to love, hate or fear oneself or aspects of oneself. In addition, if conceptions of supernatural persons such as God, Jesus and angels are introduced vividly to the child, with strong parental endorsement, then the attachment and emotions engendered in interpersonal or in reflexive contexts may be transferred onto the divine figures, who may then to varying degrees substitute for the missed (usually parental) figure, or lost aspects of the self. The divine figures take on meaning, representing missed parents or aspects of the self.

Consider more closely the development of the narcissistic economy of mind which comprises those elements – sustaining self-esteem, suppressing shame, fulfilling wishes for specialness, superiority and so on – so marked in the religiose of our day. From the beginning of mental life the infant wants to feel good, to be free of hunger, pain and anxiety, and he wants his objects (his parents or caretakers, at first usually mother) to be all-good and provident. He wants to live in the circle of an omnibenevolent world. But the world is not omnibenevolent and the fit between the infant's needs and mother's solicitude is never perfect. However, the infant has available to him various means of regulating his internal states and the environment. By splitting off (withdrawing attention from) bad aspects of his experience and projecting it into his objects, or by taking in (introjecting) good aspects of his objects, the infant can, as it were, omnipotently alter the dispensation of pleasure and pain, of good and bad, in his experiential world. Later, he can also identify with objects, either introjectively (the object is in me, and I am like the object) or projectively (I am in the object, and it is like me) (5.3–5.4). This regulation of experience is probably largely achieved through wish-fulfilling (omnipotent) phantasy: when the infant phantasises something, it seems at the time to be true or real. The infant's mental life is under the sway of 'the omnipotence of thought', an aspect of FWT, and this experience of (quasi)omnipotence combines with incidental affirmations of it (3.7). The heightened sense of mastery experienced at the time when he is beginning to walk and talk augments it. Parental solicitude may be felt as an extension of his will. The conjunction of these circumstances elates the infant and reinforces his (illusory) sense of grandeur and omnipotence. Under the impress of omnipotence, the child's need to stay in proximity to mother and monitor her whereabouts may develop into a powerful need for omniscience. At a few months the infant must usually have his mother present in his alert hours and does everything in his power, in his attachment repertoire, to secure it. Later, he must *know* his mother's whereabouts. If the optimal ranges of attachment intimacy and proximity are seriously disrupted, as they usually are in modern societies, the need to know where mother (or the primary caring figure) is may be deformed into a need to know *everything*, which, under the impress of omnipotence, is transformed into the illusion of omniscience. The infant may in phantasy become omniscient, or suffer desperately from the need to be so.

With the formation of a nascent self it becomes appropriate to speak of the reflexive libidinal relation referred to as 'narcissism'. The maintenance of the omnibenevolent world now requires regard to the complex relations one has with oneself. Although at first good states of the self, or primitive self-esteem, depend largely on feeling loved by others, it increasingly comes to depend on the capacity to value and to love oneself. Self-hatred, being a libidinal relationship, is also an important aspect of narcissism. Self-hatred leads to a form of depression, a loss of self-esteem. Where self-esteem cannot be gained through love, either another's or one's own, then the machinery of omnipotent phantasy may be invoked to compel love, to create an illusion of it, or to build a fortress against its absence.

Another important mode of regulating self-esteem is *idealisation*, either of objects or the self.[4] Children invariably try to sustain the belief that parents are omnipotent, especially if they feel persecuted or when parents become a disappointment to them. Figures who are needed for protection, security and love are often idealised by having their 'bad' aspects split off ('decathected') so as to prevent contamination of their desired goodness. The child may then bask in the idealised parents' radiance or, by identifying with them, appear omnipotent and omniscient himself. Sometimes in this process, the child will take the split-off badness upon himself in order to keep the object pure (5.3). This leads to self-hatred and self-abasement before the idealised object. This constellation may be found in romantic love, but also in the religious worshipper's tedious refrain about the greatness of God and the feebleness of humankind.

These are more or less normal transitional processes. But in some circumstances the use of such mechanisms can lead to the creation of unconscious grandiose, god-like conceptions of the self that dominate the entire personality. And it is remarkable, is it not, that the conditions – omnipotence, omniscience and omnibenevolence – so instrumental in the regulation of infantile narcissism and wellbeing are precisely the key perfections attributed to the Abrahamic gods.

I have already noted that if conceptions of supernatural beings are introduced vividly and forcefully to a child then the attitudes appropriate in interpersonal or reflexive contexts may be transferred to the divine figures, who may then partly substitute for the inadequate parental figure, or aspects of the self. If the religious ideas become associated with representations of the parents then they are likely to fuse, and the ideas will seem to have, as Schopenhauer said, the force of innate ideas. Religious teaching about God's omnipotence, omniscience, and goodness are particularly fitted to re-invigorating narcissistic desires and gratifying them, for these are the very properties the child is striving to possess. So, as earlier with parents, he may once again attempt to establish a relationship in phantasy with the omnipotent supernatural figures, much as with a pop star or sporting hero, and bask in their radiance. To have a close relationship with an omnipotent being who loves and forgives certainly heightens self-regard.

Or the child may consciously surrender his self-love but restore it in some measure by unconsciously identifying with God. In that way he can achieve humility on the surface, whilst unconsciously extending his narcissism in loving God (since he is identified with God)[5] and in God's love for him. This strategy may be especially necessary when parents are remote or inadequate, or where narcissism is forcefully extinguished with threats or punishment. Children raised in a cold or crushing atmosphere – and it is often part of religious upbringing to crush the child's natural narcissism (egoism or 'will') – are more likely to depend on supernatural or other substitute imaginary figures to contain their narcissism. Their self-esteem will be precarious and sustained only through unremitting effort – prayer, sacrifice, self-abasement – to stay in emotional proximity to a remote and perhaps punitive, wrathful and vengeful God. If the child has split his self-conception and projected the good into the figure of God (i.e. the images or 'imagos' of God), or if he has split the parental conception and projected the good into God and identified with the bad counterpart, then he is left with an unmoderated all-bad conception of himself. If, as is often the case, there arises a dominant identification with this bad self-image and the attachment to, and identification with, the idealised figure of God fails or is precarious, then the expense of maintaining an image of an all-good, almighty God is to see oneself as sinful, weak, dependent, and suppliant. Worse: underlying this bad self-image is an image of the bad parents with which he has identified – the child feels bad because he feels that he is, or is engulfed by, these internalised bad parents. At bottom, confronting this feature of their inner life may be the most difficult ordeal for people captive to these psycho-religious constellations. To unstitch the fabric of religious belief which has become so enmeshed with internal object relations would expose them to the unbearable image of the bad parent. The image of parents who were experienced in childhood as depriving, hateful or terrifying may seem in the child's, and in the adult's, unconscious mind – like the infusorian under the microscope – a hideous monster, a Satan. For many of the religiose, any perceived assault on their religion threatens this exposure, and is received with murderous fury. One common way of coping with this painful psychic situation is to project the Satanic image onto suitable objects in the external world and reinforce the identification with God. That manoeuvre underlies much of the religious and religio-nationalistic Manichaeism witnessed today. In the worst-case scenario, when the narcissistic organisation has been idealised for its aggression, the images of a wrathful god may be drawn into it as part ideal object, or the destructive, grandiose self may be projected onto the god and re-introjected **(5.6–5.7)**. This terrible god may pass itself off as protector or friend, but is really a god of vengeance and war. It is not difficult to descry this destructive narcissistic organisation, and a god of that ilk, in the arrogance, ambition and destructiveness of some contemporary religious movements.

Finally, a later developing but important strategy for maintaining narcissistic wellbeing is to idealise and identify with the religious group to which one belongs, so that the grandiosity conferred on the group can be claimed for oneself. Identifying with a supposedly superior race or religious group – even a football club or rock band – whose merits are exaggerated and mythologised is a very common way of elevating self-esteem. The wish-fulfilling logic is simple: if the group you belong to is special, you are special. This strategy also has the advantage of appropriating the group's achievements and thus diminishing envy. It also enhances one's power, and the scope for exercising it, in the group's ability to 'throw its weight around', an expression of narcissistic assertion. The strange joy in barracking for a winning sporting team is almost entirely derived from this strategy.

The activities of the religiose are influenced by these phantastic configurations. If the influence is relatively moderate, adequately disguised or channeled into culturally sanctioned activities then it may pass unnoticed. But in some circumstances the configurations may be intensified, and even detach their subject from reality. The lure of the omnipotent self and the religious megalomania with which it may now be joined is especially potent in circumstances of real threat. When people are frightened they idealise and cling. They regress to defensive grandiosity, idealise their leaders, call upon their omnipotent gods and demonise their enemies by projecting their own hated characteristics and aggression. This renders them more vulnerable to humiliation and shame, which sets off a further cycle of idealisation, projection and demonisation.

7.6 Religion as Freudian wish-fulfilment

We can now see how religious ideologies (practices, institutions) can come to fulfil (or pacify) a host of unconscious needs (or wishes) and dispositions in the manner of FWT. There are two main parts to the account. The first is the essentially Freudian argument for FWT set out in this book. We are creatures for whom illusion can supplant reality, for whom the dream, the sexual phantasy or the arts can provide effective, even lasting satisfactions. The central fact of human life is its striving for sustaining relationships in the inner and outer worlds. Most remarkable is the fact that in these strivings we are turned Janus-like to the past and the future, and seek in most of what we do symbolic re-constitution of the past, the world of our child-hood. It would be astonishing if the religious enterprise evaded this universal com-pulsion. The extraordinary feature of religion precisely is its determined, systematic extension of object-relational striving into a supernatural or spiritual dimension. It is extraordinary because there are no supernatural objects meet for relationship; or, at most, we have only the scantiest of reasons for thinking that there are, and pow-erful reasons for thinking that there are not. But the fact (if it is a fact) that super-natural objects do not exist, or that they cannot be experienced sensorially is not an obstacle to seeking relationship with them. That is a lesson of FWT. In most cul-tures supernatural figures have a kind of cultural reality, the reality immanent in shared belief; that reality serves as a screen for the projection of the images of the most important figures of our past. Religion creates a fabric of shared belief that functions somewhat like an objective mass illusion, or delusion, as Freud said. That is partly why the heretic, apostate and infidel are so feared, and often eliminated. They rend the fabric of shared illusion.

The second part of our account has not been as thoroughly investigated as the first, but is just as important. *Religious beliefs and attitudes may enter early into the con-stitution of mind and create some of the very needs that religion satisfies.* Some crucial religious conceptions (e.g. a child's conception of God), as well as being assimilated in the ordinary sense, are introjected, linked with internal objects, identified with and enter into the unconscious matrix of mind. Indoctrination, a form of learning, should be distinguished from introjection as I am using the term here. Prominent atheists such as Richard Dawkins (2006) and Christopher Hitchens (2007) place great store on the notion of indoctrination. They think that religious wickedness is a result of children having the horrid things in the Bible or Koran drummed into them, together with the supine attitude of unquestioning faith. Dawkins (2006: 335) says that suicide bombers and other extremists have been indoctrinated into 'unquestioning faith' and have their minds 'captured by poisonous religious non-sense'. But what kind of conditions are they? It is instructive to ask why one cannot be indoctrinated into geography or horticulture. Why are the religious views of the supposedly indoctrinated immune to rational considerations? Why are the doc-trines held so fervently and tenaciously? The weakness in the indoctrination story is that it doesn't have a conception of being inducted into unquestioning faith or of being captured by nonsense that goes beyond *learning* doctrine. But no matter how inculcation is intensified at this level, it won't yield the quality that resists rational considerations and change of view. The weakness of the indoctrination story points up the strength of the account developed here.

Religious doctrines and teaching 'capture the mind' and are held with 'unques-tioning faith' when they are reinforced and held in place by the type of uncon-scious needs and wishes that they satisfy. What matters critically is the way in which religious doctrine, practices, and institutions are able to satisfy symbolically or substitutively the unconscious wishes formed under the impress of religion and imbricated with internal object-relationships. Religion becomes especially dangerous and violent because of its deep roots in narcissism and omnipotence, in the frustrations and rage of relinquishing narcissism, and in the distorted and uncompromising internalised object-relationships – which may be viewed as relations between personations **(5.6)** – in which these things are consolidated. To surrender a religious idea could then be equivalent to renouncing loyalty to your parents and group, or to losing a part of yourself.

I have already mentioned some of the ways in which religious conceptions and institutions may be wish-fulfilling. There is no space to elaborate on all of the enumerated features of fundamentalism **(7.4)**, so discussion of some of the prominent strategies underlying a few of the features must serve as representative. Recall that the sense of importance, power, and self-esteem that has to be surrendered in infancy may be retrieved by establishing a 'special relationship to God', or, indeed, through identification with images of God and other supernatural figures. Such a (pseudo-) relationship – living in the sight of God, 'having Jesus in one's life' – can, of course, be reassuring and even exhilarating; the wishful phantasy graduates to belief. Since in most instances narcissism is not painlessly relinquished, the divine images (or introjects) may be coloured by the projections of a hurt, angry and deprived child. Especially in punitive homes, the child may identify with God as a controlling, angry aggressor.[6] In certain such cases the relationship may generate grandiosity or religious megalomania of a type with which hospital psychiatrists are familiar.

Belonging to the 'chosen' group, or the Elect, is very gratifying and an effective way of retrieving lost narcissism. The group is idealised and the grandiosity conferred upon it is re-claimed through identification. As we said, if the group you belong to is special, you are special. The group then represents the ideal object (God, the body of Christ, etc.), and the idealised aspects of the self. Consequently, religious group identity is prone to being an instrument of narcissistic assertion and aggression that had to be suppressed in childhood. The aggression is expressed in several ways. Becoming a member of the Elect is in itself a gratifying exclusionary process: being special means being one of the Few, not of the Many. Consigning non-believers to hell, or converting them, is also gratifying, though not of the best elements in human nature. Evangelising and proselytising are doubly rewarding acts. Consciously, there is the pleasing knowledge of bestowing a grace upon another; unconsciously, there is the pleasure of stripping converts of their former identity, aggressively incorporating them into the group and annulling differences by assimilation. It is because assimilation of a group is often experienced unconsciously as an aggressive incorporation (or 'eating') that multiculturalism and religious pluralism, which resist it, are so painful to the (orally incorporative) narcissistic character. Compelling others to think and act as you do not only confirms your faith and eliminates challenges to it, but also nourishes grandiose self-conceptions by testifying to one's power. It affirms the wish-fulfilling special relationship, or partial identification with, God or other divine figures.

It may be objected at this point that *any* group identity can become an instrument of narcissistic assertion and aggression. Why, after all, should aggressive group narcissism restrict itself to expression in religious groups? We have witnessed enough ethnic and racial conflicts and struggles between political ideologies (not to mention sporting teams) to know that patently narcissistic investments, matters of pride or humiliation, ride on the outcome. Certainly, other group identities can serve as vehicles for narcissistic satisfactions: for example, membership of a supposedly superior race or football club. But it does not follow that all groups are equally amenable to becoming instruments of narcissistic aggression. Religions are particularly fitted because their ideological conceptions – commerce with the Supreme Being, membership of an Elect, moral certainty and incorrigible knowledge – both create and feed the lopsided narcissism that needs to assert itself. Most religions, like racial ideologies, provide exceptionally attractive ideological frameworks for organising and satisfying the infantile and pathological narcissistic (and other) needs that generate the sorts of aggression we have been describing.[7]

Because religion is a repository for powerful wishful structures, it frequently takes on a delusional character that conflicts with reason and the deliverance of science. I have already mentioned the religiose need for omniscience. The religiose need to know, but they need to know absolutely, infallibly and quickly: about their place in creation, about an afterlife, whether they are watched over and loved by the creator, and so on. Most people are curious about such 'final' things, but the curiosity of the religiose is desperate because it is animated by the necessity to maintain passionate contact with an attachment figure and the unconscious need to secure the illusion of omniscience. Unfortunately, neither infallibility nor immediacy mark either science or the humane disciplines, and these obstinately refuse to endorse what the religiose wish to posit as knowledge. But *not knowing*, for them, is intolerable; it is like being abandoned. So Reason, the wounded messenger, becomes hateful: it refuses support to religious belief and, indeed, challenges it. At the deepest level, Reason threatens to subvert the cherished relationship to God and the (illusional) omnipotence and omniscience of the self. In the grip of offended narcissism, in precarious identification with God, the eye is plucked out and Reason is abandoned. The religiose cannot say in their hearts 'I just don't know!' So the wishful – one might say, magical – artifices of faith, revelation and supernatural experience are employed to provide what Reason will not.

Herein lays the great resource of the Holy Book. For people who don't know much but must know everything, knowledge of a book which is supposed to contain the most important articles worth knowing is an immeasurable gift. If they grasp and understand the Bible or Quran as the word of God then it seems as if they infallibly *do* know the things they crave, and the Book comes with a bonus: its message is simple and congenial; it is not quantum mechanics. Frequent prayer and converse with the texts means associating with God. One surely cannot be a lowly worm (as Russell once put it), being so close an associate to the Supreme Being. Small samples of the holy texts may be placed near the heart, or on door-posts, or, as with phylacteries, on the forehead and arm. The books may be carried in the van to war or waved around in public demonstrations to warn your enemies: you're not to be messed with, you have the Omnipotent One, Truth and Right on your side. Assiduously studying the word of God is unconsciously like incorporating the mind of God and is a vehicle for identification: to thoroughly internalise the word of God is to *be* God. One is omniscient after all!

Religion shields people from pain and forsakenness and the exposure of ignorance, but it also shields them from self-knowledge and insight. A passage from John Haldane's *An Intelligent Person's Guide to Religion* tells how in paradise the blessed will gaze upon the divine nature and see

> the perfection of every positive quality…[and find] what they have always craved – absolute, unconditional, and everlasting love – their minds are themselves made more loving, but now without prospect of relapse, for the wound from which their darkness and disturbance issued as a consequence of wilful disobedience has now been healed…
>
> (Haldane 2005: 203)

This is a touching picture of the afterlife of the blessed. There is almost nothing of probative value to suggest that this is an accurate representation of post-mortem life (of the Elect) and there are powerful philosophical reasons for supposing that the picture is incoherent. And it is 'a very striking fact' (in Freud's words) that this picture is 'exactly as we are bound to wish it to be'. In fact, it corresponds with the phantasy of the young child reconciled with mother after painful separation or discord. It repairs the final and most terrible separation of all; for the fear of death is separation anxiety, separation from one's self and one's objects. It matches the phantasies universal in childhood: the idealised mother and child joined in harmony, forever.

The reader who has come this far may agree that this religious picture is just an illusion – a composition of wish-fulfilling beliefs – or, indeed, a delusion. But it is not just that. In its religious frame it is also an evasion, for the religious understanding of the picture occludes its origin and true psychological significance. Instead of pointing inwards to what is deep – human love, loss, despair, regeneration – it points to the heavens, to figments that are at best improbable, but most likely incoherent. By giving such phantasies a context in religious ideology, religion denatures them. Opportunities for insight and understanding are caught and wasted in webs of artifice. Religion does not illuminate the things of this world; it obscures them. And in this too, in its defence of the self against intolerable knowledge, we may recognise self-solicitude.

Finally, I want to put to rest an objection to the wish-fulfilment account of religiosity, widely spread amongst evolutionary psychologists, cognitive anthropologists and others and usually considered fatal.

The anthropologist S. E. Guthrie (2007) states that the wish-fulfilling theories of Freud, Abram Kardiner and other psychoanalytically orientated anthropologists are mistaken because many religions 'have features for which no-one is likely to wish. The deities of some are cruel and angry, and often complemented by devils or frightening ghosts. In others the after-life is either absent or fleeting or is a Hades or other unpleasant place' (2007: 288). Another anthropologist, Pascal Boyer, asseverates that many religious ideas are anything but comforting: if 'religious concepts' are 'solutions to particular emotional needs [they] are not doing a very good job. ... A religious world is often far more terrifying than a world without supernatural presence...' (2002: 23); many religions, he adds, do not promise salvation or eternal bliss (2002: 237). Bering (2011), a psychologist, thinks that comfort theories are circular, question-begging and hand-waving. Dawkins says they are only proximate explanations and quotes Stephen Pinker, who says such theories 'only raise the question of why a mind would evolve to find comfort in beliefs it can plainly see are false' (Dawkins 2006: 168). Dennett (2006: 102) says that such theories are not explanatory because there is always a further question about *why* the comforting ideas within them are comforting.

These objections are muddled and superficial. To begin with, wish-fulfilment theories are not circular or question-begging. Suppose someone asks me why I am not hungry and I explain that I have just eaten a hamburger. She could insist that the fact that a hamburger extinguished my hunger raises the further question of why this organism, my person, should be such that hamburgers extinguish its hunger. But it doesn't follow that the hamburger explanation is circular or question-begging. It follows only that *further* questions of a different order may arise. One might reasonably ask Dawkins (and Dennett), for example, why they think that the evolutionary explanations of religious belief are ultimate as opposed to, say, explanations in terms of molecular biology or physics, since the evolutionary explanations obviously raise questions about processes germane to these disciplines. The adequacy of explanation is relative to context. Relative to the context of psychological explanation, wishful, comfort or needs-based explanations are neither circular nor question-begging.

The contention that 'wishful' theories of religion are false because gods are often cruel and religions have nasty features that no-one is likely to wish for is not only ignorant of the psychoanalytic theory it is supposed to refute, but offends adult common sense. People have all manner of wishes, including sadistic, destructive and self-destructive ones, and do quite often harm themselves and enter into masochistic relationships. In the 1930s the psychoanalyst Ronald Fairbairn, working with abused children, found that even the most abused of them will cling to their abusive parents and blame themselves (rather in the way sinners do) as wrongdoers. Fairbairn expressed the motive underlying this behaviour succinctly: it is better to have a bad object than no object. Freud asserted that the need for punishment, suffering in the form of a sense of guilt, entry into sado–masochistic relations (including relations with one's self) are universal in humankind. Subsequent psychoanalytic work has hugely expanded understanding of the terrifying aspects of the inner world which are often externalised or projected into perceived enemies and supernatural beings. In the first place, then, it is obvious that many of the wishes people harbour are for destruction and are pacified in the imagination of destruction or savage religious doctrines or beliefs. Second, it is an unfortunate but common occurrence that the consequences of our wishes fulfilled are neither known to us nor anticipated. It is unsurprising then that the religious enterprise, which in many ways is a continuation of persecutory relationships with internalised parental imagos and with dissociated aspects of the self, generates terrifying scenarios and vicious and vindictive supernatural beings as well as loving and protective ones. The rebuttals of the wish-fulfilment theory advanced by the evolutionary psychologists and anthropologists are lazy and patently fallacious.

I have argued that we must seriously consider the possibility that many people's religious convictions, especially of that large but indeterminate group I labelled 'religiose', supervene principally, not on ignorance or conceptual impoverishment or bad reasoning (though all these things play a part), but on something akin to the delusional: there is a failure to think rationally because at certain points thought is abducted into the service of unconscious wishful processes. Religious beliefs and attitudes at such points are the symbolic expressions or elaborations of unconscious phantasy about needed internalised objects. Most religions provide conceptions of idealised, powerful and protective supernatural figures, representing prototypes formed in infancy, with whom worshippers can continue dependent, oftentimes narcissistic (pseudo)relationships. They also provide doctrines which, through their internalisation and imbrication with early object-relationships, enter into the formation of character and are irresistibly attractive to character types whose unconscious wishes (for superiority, belonging, and so on) they substitutively satisfy. Even in the most abstract, depersonalised and sublimed accounts of the gods, the unconscious significance of their conceptions is probably much the same as in the religions worshipping their personal supernatural cousins. The preoccupation with gods, no matter how abstract the conceptions, is partly an attempt to maintain an unconscious relationship with the early parental and other objects that entered into the construction of the god-imagos. Without these delusory attractions, religions would probably collapse. That they have not, and that they are not likely to but, on the contrary, will in all likelihood flourish in the immediate future, is testament to the ineluctable desire for human relationship and the effectiveness of Freudian wish-fulfilment.

Notes

1 To the charge that he, Freud, may be deluded in his atheism, he responds: 'my illusions are not, like religious ones, incapable of correction. They have not the character of delusion' (1927c: 53).

2 Young-Bruehl (1996) is a brilliant psychoanalytic study of many kinds of prejudice. Michael Levine and others (Levine 2004; Levine and Pataki (eds) 2004; Cox, Levine and Newman 2009) pursue the approach to racism and to politics. I have followed a similar line in relation to some aspects of religion in Pataki (2007, 2010) as I do here.

3 Pataki 2007, chapter 6.

4 It has been said, as by Neville Symington (1993: 63), that 'Freud does not discuss the mechanism by which people rid themselves of their sense of helplessness through

identifying with an omnipotent figure…' This is not quite accurate: it is central to Freud's understanding of group psychology (1921c) that the members of the group identify with its idealised leader, who may be regarded as more or less omnipotent. Freud does not venture to affirm that the members of a church may identify with God, but he does say that they may identify with Christ. What seems to be lacking in Freud's treatment is an appreciation of the extent to which the object of worship is narcissistically idealised (i.e. idealised by projection of the ideal self, not through defensive splitting) in order to serve narcissistic functions. Freud does, however, make some passing remarks on narcissistic aspects of the relation to God. He notes that circumcised peoples feel exalted by it (1939a: 29). This is explained in the Jewish context as a mark of specialness or chosenness, or at least equivalence with the Egyptians who practised it. Freud notes that Moses inspired in the Jewish people the notion that they were God's chosen: 'they believe that they stand especially close to Him' (1939a: 106). Mosaic religion, Freud says, increased Jewish self-esteem because (a) it allowed the people to take a share in the grandeur of the new idea of God; (b) it asserted that this people had been chosen by this great God and were destined to receive evidences of his special favour; and (c) it forced upon the people an advance in intellectuality (1939a: 123). This third factor is explained as the consequence of a renunciation of instinct followed by superego approval. In relation to the first factor Freud says specifically that 'the pride in God's greatness fuses with the pride in being chosen by him' (1939a: 112). These sources of self-esteem appear to be narcissistic in a broad sense, if it is considered that all sources of self-esteem or self-regard are narcissistically mediated (e.g. if X feels special or has her self-esteem elevated when loved by Y, that is because Y's love enables X to love herself better.) The second factor is unambiguously narcissistic, even in a narrower sense, and if we interpret the idea of 'sharing' in God's grandeur and power as involving a projective identification so that the relationship to God is partially a reflexive one then the other two may be as well. But it is not clear that Freud had that in mind; and there is no mention whether the characteristics of omnipotence and so on, as these are experienced by the worshipper, derive from the worshipper's idealised projections or are merely the cultural givens with which any initiate is endowed.

5 Ernest Jones: 'An unconscious phantasy in which they identify their personality with that of God… is not at all rare, and possibly occurs here and there in all men' (Jones 1913: 245).

6 Many Christian pedagogues still recommend beatings, other harsh chastisement and breaking of the child's will. James C. Dobson's books *Dare to Discipline* and *The New Strong-Willed Child* are best-sellers. The motivation for the discipline they recommend is to convince the child that they are being beaten out of love and that the parent is doing God's will, imposed in love. The aftermath of the beating and tears is supposed to provide an opportunity for parent and child to come together in recognition of the parent's love for the child and service to God. The punitive attitudes in the religious household which sees corporal punishment as Biblically endorsed certainly make an impression: children who believe in a personal, punitive God are more likely to incorporate an image of God as punitive and uncaring, their pleading to be spared going unanswered. It has often been noticed that Protestant Christians who advocate harsh physical punishment are often also intensely apocalyptic (Capps 1995). For the child an impending beating looms as a catastrophe, the end of the world. And, of course, where punishment and the affectation of parental love are intertwined, children are more likely to repeat offences and keep the cycle of sin and punishment in motion. Donald Capps (1995) contends that religious ideas may be as abusive as physical punishment. The doctrine of hell and eternal punishment, the aversive attitudes towards natural sexual feeling, the breaches between friends occasioned by religious labelling and segregation cause great emotional torment to a child. Religions often make people think abjectly of themselves. Capps makes a persuasive case. He argues that physical punishment and emotional abuse operate traumatically

in much the same way as childhood sexual abuse. Consequent to trauma there is (a) a repression of the traumatic experience which leads to the splitting or dissociation of part of the self which is intricated in the experience; (b) a withdrawal of feeling or affect; and (c) the frequently observed loss of confidence in his own judgement that the victim suffers. So, in some victims, abusive ideas linked to the trauma tend to 'get split off from the rest of their thought processes and are not incorporated into them' (1995: 52–3). Hence, Capps observes, people who can think independently and well about politics, science, etc. become unexpectedly bland, uncritical and deferential about religion. These are good observations: the dissociation that follows sexual abuse and the dissociation following corporal punishment and emotional abuse are persuasively coordinated.

7 See discussion in Pataki 2007, ch. 5 and Pataki 2010. My point is not that all members of religious groups exhibit narcissistic assertion and aggression. Clearly they do not. It is rather that the structures of religion and the developmental paths that are outlined in the chapter dispose people brought up in a religiose atmosphere to such assertion and aggression.

Chapter 8

Writing as redemption

Because of these shortcomings, and for no other fault, we are lost, and only so far afflicted that without hope we live in longing.

Dante, *Inferno*, Canto IV

8.1 Exhibits of loss

Although the discussion in this chapter probably bears on several areas of creative endeavour, it seems to me wise to restrict it to what I know best: some forms of creative writing. For although there are obvious affinities between many of the arts from the psychological perspective we have adopted, there are also vast differences that cannot profitably be investigated here. Consider, then, the act, or acts, of writing fiction. The writer inscribes words, renders scenes, depicts character, instructs and entertains, expresses philosophical ideas or reflections, exorcises personal demons, prods the community, earns a living, wastes paper, and so on. There are many true descriptions of the action events which constitute the physical process of writing, and under some of these descriptions the action events are intentional, under others not.[1] Thus the writer may be intending to entertain an audience, but non-intentionally, perhaps unconsciously, be exorcising personal demons. Or it may go the other way: the writer believes that the act is therapeutic, that it may lay the past.

The ontology of fiction is difficult, but it seems possible to divide the various descriptions of the action events which constitute its production into the following three groups. Such things as producing sentences and framing paragraphs could be said to be *for*, or to go towards, the making of the work. Others, like having Mrs Dalloway throw a party or hanging Tess, are things done *in* the work. Making money or affronting the community are things done *with* or through the work. This classification is rough, and of course it is possible to classify the activities according to other types, but it will serve our purposes here.

I want to discuss a number of unusual processes which are aspects of writing, most of which are things done through the work. I will suggest that writing can involve intricate, unconscious, wish-fulfilling transactions that we have with ourselves, and which make use of the text as an object whose content may be only obliquely relevant to the success of the transaction. I think that these transactions are not essentially linguistic and that they are, in a certain sense, pre-cultural: although they may depend on the use of language, they are not themselves linguistic acts, and they are processes so primitive as to be independent of culture, of any particular culture, which is to say that they appear in all cultures. But even if I am wrong about the non-linguistic and pre-cultural character of these processes, their investigation remains of great interest. They offer hope of a kind of redemption, but fall short of it.

The investigation also has a subsidiary, controversial interest. There are a number of diverse tendencies in contemporary philosophical and critical thought which are united in seeking to diminish in one way or another the complexity, depth and self-reflective capacity of the self. In some views the self is an artificial construction of culture or a hollow, trammelled thing invaded by culture. Another view insists on the complete dependence of thought on language and so exposes thought, the self's most private possession, to all the exigencies of publicity. Cognitive and neuroscience explore mechanisms in which the self cannot recognise itself. In much contemporary literary criticism a kind of linguistic Idealism has all but exiled the individuality of the author. We are all at the mercy of language – are, in fact, said by some to be 'constituted' by language. There are many related ideas in this vicinity. They are large ideas and some of them have large consequences for the study of literature and writing: they affect the way in which authorial responsibility for literary work is appraised; they affect the way in which literary criticism is performed; and they affect the way literature and criticism are taught. Many of the ideas I touched on are associated with Lacan, Foucault, Derrida and others. I believe that they are profoundly misleading. Be that as it may, investigation of the sorts of processes I mentioned at the outset challenge some of these ideas by recalling the unconscious pre-linguistic activity of the author in an unusual way. I do not think that the sort of exercise undertaken here carries us far in literary criticism but it does reveal, I think, something of real import in the act of creation.

Here is the first exhibit.

> It would concern the reader little, perhaps, to know how sorrowfully the pen is laid down at the close of a two years imaginative task; or how an Author feels as if he were dismissing some portion of himself into the shadowy world, when a crowd of the creatures of his brain are going from him for ever. Yet, I had nothing else to tell; unless, indeed, I were to confess (which might be of less moment still), that no one can ever believe this Narrative, in the reading, more than I believed it in the writing.
>
> (Dickens 1970: v)

We should be puzzled by some of the things Dickens says here. Why is the pen retired 'sorrowfully'? Why not delight or relief at the completion of a masterpiece? Sorrow doesn't answer to the circumstances. It is true that for two years the author has laboured on this extraordinary imaginative task, surrounded by the ghostly company of wonderful characters – 'creatures of his brain'. But he is not really losing them. He's set them alive in an immortal book, and he knows it. Yet he evidently feels that he's losing something, and losing it forever. Why the sense of irretrievable loss?

There is a similar sense in the second and third exhibits.

> I have often noticed that after I had bestowed on the characters of my novels some treasured item of my past, it would pine away in the artificial world where I had so abruptly placed it. Although it lingered on in my mind, its personal warmth, its retrospective appeal had gone and, presently, it became more closely identified with my novel than with my former self, where it had seemed to be so safe from the intrusions of the artist.
>
> (Nabokov 1969: 95)

> It is perfectly true that she obsessed me, in spite of the fact that she died when I was thirteen, until I was forty-four. Then one day walking round Tavistock Square I made up, as I sometimes make up my books, *To the Lighthouse*, in a great apparently involuntary, rush. One thing burst into another. Blowing bubbles out of a pipe gives the feeling of the rapid crowd of ideas and scenes which blew out of my mind, so that my lips seemed syllabling of their own accord as I walked. What blew the bubbles? Why then? I have no notion. But I wrote the book very quickly; and when it was written, I ceased to be obsessed by my mother. I no longer hear her voice; I do not see her. I suppose that I did for myself what psychoanalysts do for their patients. I expressed some very long felt and deeply felt emotion. And in expressing it I explained it and then laid it to rest. But what is the meaning of 'explained it'? Why, because I described her and my feeling for her in that book, should my vision of her and my feeling for her become so much dimmer and weaker? Perhaps one day I will hit on the reason...
>
> (Woolf 1989: 81)

In these extracts, too, there seems to be a difficult parturition followed by something like a faint echo of remorse. In each case, emotionally significant objects are experienced as being lost to the self, and the process is felt to be sad or painful. Notice that the separation and pain recorded in these passages is not fictional separation and pain; they are not things that occur *in* the novels, but through them. The pain is not of a kind with that which afflicts Copperfield when he discovers that Steerforth is a cad, or with Angel Clare when Tess is hanged. Nor is it of a kind, I think, with Hardy's rage and grief at the unbearable fate of Tess, or with Dumas' when he emerges from his atelier, crying 'I have killed my Porthos'. Hardy and Dumas are reacting to events they have engineered in the narrative of their novels, whereas in the exhibits there seem to be powerful emotional reactions to the process of writing itself, not to particular fictional events.

In the extract from *Moments of Being* there is a kind of enervation or sadness, not explicitly stated, but conveyed as a mixture of manic triumph in achievement, in forcefully expelling what seems to be a persecutory presence, and an uncertain sombre regret at having done so. There is a very vivid account of evacuation or externalisation of charged ideas and a progressive distancing – 'my feeling for her has become so much dimmer and weaker' – between the author and the images of her mother, and you might with justice wonder why, given the concentrated engagement of the creative process, the careful picking over of every ligament that bound Virginia to her mother, things did not go the other way. Nabokov is less intense in recollection and less curious about the process, but he too senses his writing as consigning treasured items of his past to 'pine away in an artificial world'. Dickens also dismisses 'some portion of himself into the shadowy world', forever.

8.2 Some psychoanalytic approaches to loss in art

Notwithstanding the plentiful use of psychoanalysis in contemporary criticism, it seems to me a hazardous adventure to subject pieces of fiction – as opposed to fiction writers – to its (applied) methods; and it is perhaps only a little less risky to apply those methods to the self-analytical reflections of the writers themselves. Nevertheless I think that the exhibits I presented justify the attempt. It is baffling why these writers react to their work as they do. The concrete language, the unexpected and anomalous character and intensity of the writers' emotions seem impenetrable to ordinary understanding, and it is precisely this sort of anomaly which invites psychoanalytic explanation. Why psychoanalysis and not another discipline with a bearing on the explanation of such anomaly, say some branch of cognitive psychology or neuroscience? Even if there were no other reason for invoking psychoanalysis (or its kin), this reason would be enough: these other disciplines have hardly begun to deal with the sorts of experience which the vignettes describe; they have as yet nearly nothing on offer.

There is a considerable body of psychoanalytic theory that sheds light on our material, and of course I can only touch on a fraction of it. Heinz Kohut has advanced the idea that the work of art is an extension of the self, more specifically of the perfect or ideal self. The idea can be understood like this. We create for ourselves idealised representations of how we would like to be, using the material of admired or envied others, and elaborate them in phantasy. Such representations, because they are often radically incompatible with reality, are largely unconscious, but nevertheless play a very important part in the regulation of self-esteem. Falling short of the ideal self in appearance, action or virtue causes depression and suffering; approaching it enhances self-esteem and the sense of wellbeing. It is important that these representations can be identified with in several different ways (5.3). As we have seen, it is not at all uncommon to encounter people with inflated self-esteem or delusional megalomania – of which they may be quite unconscious – based on identification with an ideal self or object or a fusion of them (7.5). It may also be observed how other people or objects are sometimes mistaken for the ideal self and are then loved or admired as if they were that part of the self; or, rather, they are not loved at all but become instruments in the business of loving oneself.

Kohut says of the unhappy writer Aschenbach, in *Death in Venice*, that he became

> capable of providing himself with the needed experience of psychological per-
> fection and wholeness ie. the experience of basic self-esteem - through the
> creation of works of art. Extensions or duplications of the self were now avail-
> able which he could invest with narcissistic libido: he could give them formal
> perfection.
>
> (Kohut 1978a: 821)

But Aschenbach eventually collapses:

> The artist is aging, and his power to create replicas of the perfect self is waning.
> On the way to total disintegration, however... we see the revival of the sexual-
> ised precursor of the artistic product: the beautiful boy (though frail and already
> marked for destruction) who is the symbolic stand-in for the core of the still
> unaltered childhood self which craves love and admiration.

The second passage makes clear that Tadzio, the beautiful boy in the story, represents the sexualised precursor of Aschenbach's artistic work. But it is initially not the
boy who represents the perfect or ideal self; as the first passage makes clear, that is
the work of art itself. The replica of the perfect self is not something *in* Aschenbach's
work, but the work itself. (Similarly, we might conjecture, the *character* Tadzio does
not represent Thomas Mann's ideal self; *Death in Venice* does that.) The work as a
whole, with the order, harmony and beauty wished for by a disordered self, becomes
(in phantasy) the ideal self, and the creation of such a work is felt as fusion with it.
Becoming the creator of such beautiful things thus enlarges and irradiates the self.
However, with regressive decomposition the writer reverts to yearning for a personal relationship or, rather, for a relationship with someone who represents an
aspect of himself – Tadzio. For Aschenbach the narcissistic regression is fatal. It is
possible that this pathological constellation was a prefiguring of something that also
afflicted Thomas Mann, but in a more benign form. With him, however, there seems
to be an intermediate phase, not identified in Aschenbach, in which the various
transformations of Tadzio in his novels mark first a sublimation and then, in his old
age, his deterioration (Dolimore 2001: ch. 19).

This account of the work of art as an extension or enlargement of the writer's
self captures the intricate intimacy between writer and work expressed in the
exhibits, but it does not answer well to that additional experience of loss described
by Dickens, Nabokov and Woolf. Although they are clearly preoccupied with
boundaries, with containing and losing things to the 'outside', with being depleted,
the core emphasis in the cited passages is not so much on the work of art as part of
the self, but as a container of precious but insecurely situated internal objects. The
Kleinian analyst Hanna Segal considers the distinction between inflating (extending?) the self and reconstructing or restoring the self's internal objects and lost parts.
She distinguishes manic reparation, in which the self is precariously restored in

phantasy by denial or other pseudo-creative ways, from 'genuine' artistic creation in which, through the fictional reconstruction of lost real objects, the corresponding internal objects are eventually reconstituted in the self. She quotes the narrator in *A la recherche du temps perdu*:

> I had to recapture from the shade that which I had felt, to reconvert it into its psychic equivalent. But the way to do it, the only one I could see, what was it - but to create a work of art?... And indeed it was not only Albertine, not only my grandmother, but many others still from whom I might have assimilated a gesture or a word, but whom I could not even remember as distinct persons. A book is a vast graveyard where on most of the tombstones one can read no more the faded names.
>
> (Segal 1981: 189)

Segal then comments:

> In the last volume of his work Proust describes how at last he decided to sacrifice the rest of his life to writing. He came back after a long absence to seek his old friends at a party, and all of them appeared as ruins of the real people he knew – useless, ridiculous, ill, on the threshold of death. Others he found had died long ago. And on realising the destruction of a whole world that had been his, he decided to write, to sacrifice himself to the recreation of the dying and the dead. By virtue of his art he can give his objects an eternal life in his work. And since they represent his internal world too, if he can do that, he himself will no longer be afraid of death. What Proust describes corresponds to a situation of mourning: he sees that his loved objects are dying or dead. Writing a book for him is like the work of mourning in that gradually the external objects are given up, they are reinstated in the ego, and recreated in the book... Melanie Klein has shown how mourning in grown up life is a reliving of the early depressive anxieties; not only is the present object in the external world felt to be lost, but also the early objects, the parents; and they are lost as internal objects as well as in the external world. In the process of mourning it is these earliest objects which are lost again, and then recreated. Proust describes how this mourning leads to a wish to recreate the lost world. ... It is when the world within us is destroyed, when it is dead and loveless, when our loved ones are in fragments, and we ourselves in helpless despair – it is then that we must recreate our world anew, reassemble the pieces, infuse life into dead fragments, recreate life.

Creative work on this account is a kind of mourning, a working through of the depressive position. The artist recreates a lost world and at the same time reinstates in the self once-loved but now lost and ruined internal objects and aspects of the self. This is not an easy doctrine but its general drift should be fairly clear. It has much to recommend it, especially when considered against the backdrop of works of redemption like *To the Lighthouse* and *A la recherche du temps perdu*, but it would be amazing if, as Segal thinks, all creative endeavour in the arts springs from attempts at resolution of the depressive constellation. However, let that pass.[2] Segal's thesis is confronted with other instructive difficulties.

One of these emerges most clearly when she criticises Freud's well-known (and much criticised) account of art as wish-fulfilment. Freud wrote:

> The artist, like the neurotic, had withdrawn from an unsatisfactory reality into this world of imagination; but, unlike the neurotic, he knew how to find a way back from it and once more to get a firm foothold in reality. His creations, works of art, were the imaginary satisfactions of unconscious wishes, just as dreams are; and like them they were in the nature of compromises, since they too were forced to avoid any open conflict with the forces of repression. But they differed from the asocial, narcissistic products of dreaming in that they were calculated to arouse sympathetic interest in other people and were able to evoke and to satisfy the same unconscious wishful impulses in them too.
>
> (Freud 1925d: 64–5)

In this view the artist sits in the camp of the daydreamer and the neurotic. But Segal insists that art is not daydream or play or, in her term, omnipotent wish-fulfilment; it is an expression of the constructive working through of depressive anxieties, loss and pain. She denies, in other words, that art is a member of the class of FWTs. The daydreamer and the neurotic seek to avoid conflict and shun reality by phantasying or omnipotent wish-fulfilment; but good artists, she continues, never lose their sense of reality, they do not attempt manically to inflate the self and create an illusion of invulnerability to loss and despair; they confront their conflicts and work through and resolve them in creation (Segal 1991: 82).

This is a nice attempt to distinguish artists from their more sickly cousins, but it won't do. The trouble is that there is no robust sense in which writers – to revert now to the narrower focus – directly resolve their depressive problems through their work; though of course such problems can be represented and resolved *in* the work (think, for example, of Humbert's terrible awakening to his destruction of Lolita's childhood, or of the narrator's growth during the glorious threnody on the death of Albertine). In the first place, it is evident that if you want (the dead) Albertine back, writing about her, even if you can write like Proust, isn't going to do the trick. Obviously, writing does not revive the dead, though it may sometimes seem that it does, especially to the writer. It creates only semblances of them. But nor do writers appear to work through and resolve their problems in any clinically recognised sense: for example, in the sense that problems are recognised for what they are, assimilated and placed in perspective, that the pathological object attachments which underlie them are relinquished, that alternatives to the satisfaction of ineluctable desires are made available, and so on. It does not seem as if the writer succeeds even in the restitution of internal objects. For one of the striking things about (most) good writers is their productivity. By and large, good writers cannot let things be and *they go on*. This suggests either that they have many more depressive problems than everybody else or that they never really allay the sources of their artistic animation, or at least do not do so in a way that lasts. Aschenbach's creativity fails him, and as he can no longer produce work which represents to him an ideal self, his desire for an ideal self reverts to the image of the beautiful and loveable boy he wished to be. That shows that his need to sustain and to merge with an ideal self was *not* resolved by his creative work; it was postponed. The creative act appears to have more the character of an illusion than a cure. And if we recall the unhappy fates of the aged Thomas Mann, of Dickens, Proust or Woolf, and a good many others, we will find some support for this objection.

8.3 Illusion and the internal audience

Well, what if art – some art – really is a species of illusion? Many thinkers from Plato to Freud have thought so, though they did not think of illusion in quite the same way or make the equation for quite the same reasons. Freud is once again the most interesting for our purposes. As previous chapters and the passage quoted directly above show, he thought that art, like its congeners the dream, phantasy, hallucination, delusion, neurotic symptoms and religion, is an instrument for the substitutive satisfaction of repudiated or unconscious wishes. Unlike Plato he did not think that art involves malign illusion: art does not seek to supplant or distort reality, as do, for example, hallucination and religion. Art presents itself *as* illusion and asks to be valued in despite. And, unlike Plato, Freud was more interested in the effect of the work of art on the artist than on the audience. Previous chapters have (I think) resolved some formidable problems with Freud's conception of wish-fulfilment. To rehearse them in the present context: how can the manufactured semblance, the work of art, be mistaken for the original object of desire? How can it evoke a response as if it were the real thing? How can the semblance representing real and internal objects, the artist's own creatures, not be known to be so? To come to our present concern, how can the writer, using the writer's art, dupe the writer? Formidable difficulties, but not insuperable. After all, we *know* that semblances can seem real because we dream and because we really do weep for Tess, and if we do not exactly grieve for Albertine we do something very much like it. We know that we can, in a way, satisfy our own desires with the stuff of illusions because we enjoy erotic and compensatory daydreams which we ourselves author. We have seen how symptoms, apparently unwanted, can be the fulfilments of wishes. Couldn't the writer also be illusionist and audience to her own illusions in the manner of FWT?

In 1940 the British psychoanalyst John Rickman suggested, in a very interesting paper, that the artist works primarily for, and attempts to influence, an *internal audience*. That audience, according to Rickman, is a compound superego of art school and mentors, the cultured audience for the particular art and, at its core, the internalised parental objects. How is this to be understood? The superego, you will recall (5.3), is an aspect of the self, organised around internalised parental attitudes and the experience of parents and later parent-like figures. I argued that the superego, like many other internal or virtual objects, is best conceived as a personation or role that one can adopt with unassimilated perspectives on oneself and the world. It is most conspicuous when in disharmony with the rest of the self. In such cases a common clinical picture is that of the superego – of the agent personating the role of internalised, often harsh, figures – criticising and threatening, perhaps actively injuring the agent, accompanied with a reaction of depressive, persecutory or suicidal feeling. But the superego can be a less conspicuous and demanding actor in the economy of self. I once read in an autobiography extracts from a diary that the author kept as a boy. It was the diary of a very good boy. It recorded all the things that good, regular boys did and nothing that bad boys did. It was obviously very selective and reassuring and had a kind of tendentious innocence. It all pointed in one direction, though the whole truth about the boy, as the rest of the autobiography shows, was not in that direction and the young diarist probably knew that. So why would someone produce such a one-sided document? Well, the diary narrative was intended to propitiate or mollify a very exacting audience: it seemed to say: 'Look what a good boy I am. You have nothing to fear from me – and, so, I hope, I won't have anything to fear from you'. But the diary was not intended for other people's eyes. It seems likely that the young diarist was in fact placating an internal audience, an aspect of himself, though he was not fully conscious of that. Things like that happen. There are people who write letters to themselves, and enjoy them as much as if they came from others. That such things happen certainly implies dissociations of a kind, milder versions of those explored in **Chapter 5**.

A vivid illustration of the placation of the internal audience is provided in Kohut's reading of Thomas Mann:

> Like the artist-hero in one of his last novels, *Doctor Faustus* (1947), who sells his soul to the devil and accepts disease and early death in return for a measure of active living in artistic productivity, Thomas Mann, too, seems to have to assure the threatening father that he has not really succeeded, and that his sublimations are breaking down. Aschenbach in *Death in Venice* and Leverkuhn in *Doctor Faustus* allowed Mann to spare himself, to live and to work, because they suffer in his stead.
>
> (Kohut 1978a: 130)

Here, it appears, the internal audience mistakes events that occur in the novels, the various sufferings of Aschenbach and Leverkuhn, for what could be real events, the suffering it desires of Mann. We are invited to imagine the writer as creating a wish-fulfilling illusion for the internal audience – the internalised threatening father – which, in the strange manner of FWT, gratifies its wishes to see the writer fail. But, of course, that incarnated illusion, the novel, also becomes the intended instrument of the writer's survival and triumph. It is truly extraordinary that such marvellous nets of illusion can be cast in the depths of the mind.

In the last two examples the wish-fulfilling transactions the writers have with themselves, using the work as an instrument, supervene on the representational content of the work. The specific content of the diary, of the novel, is crucial. But not all the wish-fulfilling transactions found in the process of writing supervene on representation, on what happens *in* the work. They may supervene on what happens *through* the work. Return to the early exhibits. We were struck then by the concrete descriptions provided by the writers themselves of the projection into their work of emotionally charged objects or ideas. Recall Dickens 'dismissing some portion of himself into the shadowy world'; the treasured items of Nabokov's past pining away in the artificial world where he had abruptly placed them; and Woolf's 'rapid crowd of ideas and scenes which blew out of [her] mind'. It is clear that these fragments of descriptions are not conceits, and sincerely render complex experiences of an unusual kind. And those experiences of projection (or ejection) in turn mobilise reactive, vaguely depressive, but deep core feeling in the writers.

Melanie Klein's descriptions of the process of projective identification (1975b) seem most apposite in explaining the phenomena which surprised Dickens, Woolf and Nabokov, and much else associated with creative activity. At its simplest, projective identification is a process in which parts of the self and of internal objects are projected – are phantasised as being externalised – into external objects with which they are then identified. More complex forms of the process involve this phantasy together with the induction in the target object of emotions and thoughts, using non-verbal and often amodal means of proto-communication.[3] And there are further elaborations of this (now somewhat nebulously conceived) mechanism which describe how the invaded object is subjected to various forms of control.

Now, if the exhibits do indeed describe the operation of projective identification, they describe a complex and remarkable use of it. It is complex because the writing of a novel, of a poem, is usually a prolonged process – a thousand acts pointing in the same direction – and the projection must therefore involve the subordination of these acts, over time, to the one over-arching purpose. And it is remarkable in that the highest creative endeavours are subordinated to adventitiously serve or, alternatively, to be put in the strategic service of such primitive motives as those which animate projective identification. But if we can accept that (at least some of) the conscious ideas, memories and fantasies described by the writers, and deposited in their work, are in fact representatives or expressions of internal objects and aspects of the self then, though the projective identification is indeed both complex and remarkable, its contours are clearly discernible. It becomes a plausible supposition that a significant, perhaps decisive, motive in the writing we are examining is the expulsion of unconscious figures, or parts of them, into literary work with which they then become partially identified. Thus it may be that a decisive motive in Woolf's writing *To the Lighthouse* was the need to expel her internalised mother, to feel freed of her and able to control her, and this was achieved by writing, over a period of time, that luminous novel. In other words, the work is engendered by these unconscious aims. But another possibility is that no such strategic aims operate, that the writing is motivated by other forces, but is nonetheless experienced adventitiously as an externalisation of the appropriate kind. Here the writing still serves projective identification but is not motivated by it. The case is the same with

Dickens and Nabokov. They appear to succeed in projecting internal objects and unconscious parts of themselves into their work. The projective identification supervenes on their writing, and it may be an adventitious consequence of the writing, or it may be an efficacious motive which utilises the writing to achieve its ends.

In speculating on the employment of projective identification for the purpose of FWT in the creative process, one more motive, perhaps another aspect of projective identification, requires brief attention. That motive is the need to communicate deep feeling and emotion, to pass on, to have another feel what the writer feels. That need is very fundamental and links art, non-trivially, to the earliest cries that infants utter. In such cases, we may conjecture, the written work, itself the object of projective identification, becomes an instrument of projective identification into the reader. Reminiscing on an adolescent love, Nabokov writes:

> The summer evenings of my boyhood when I used to ride by her cottage speak to me in that voice of hers now. On a road among fields, where it met the desolate highway, I would dismount and prop my bicycle against a telegraph pole. A sunset almost formidable in its splendor, would be lingering in the fully exposed sky. Among its imperceptibly changing amassments, one could pick out brightly stained structural details of celestial organisms, or glowing slits in dark banks, or flat, ethereal beaches that looked like mirages of desert islands. I did not know then (as I know perfectly well now) what to do with such things – how to get rid of them, how to transform them into something that can be turned over to the reader in printed characters, to have him cope with the blessed shiver – and this inability enhanced my oppression.
>
> (Nabokov 1969: 210)

An important feature of these wish-fulfilling projective processes in writing may now be noticed. Although language is used to achieve the projective identifications, the latter are not themselves linguistic acts. Readers feel deeply what Nabokov wished them to feel, but the entire process initiated by Nabokov's need – recalling memories and loss of objects, mourning them, and so on – is not a linguistic act either. It may perhaps be trivial to point out that much goes on in writing, and in the reaction to writing, that is not semantic processing.

Finally, it is appropriate to notice how little of art is illuminated by this discussions of this sort. The need for consoling illusion or the need to expel the painful or persecutory, though they may be very potent motives initiating Freudian wish-fulfilment, are just points of departure for long journeys. The pearl is not the grain at its centre. Perhaps Aschenbach and Leverkuhn had to die to pacify the persecutory father in Mann who would not weaken his grip; this is an important insight, and could have been a gift for Mann. But it does not tell us terribly much about his work. It does not tell how his characters should die, or whether they should love or be enchanted, or how they should discourse on life, time and art. Still, the writer can throw a rude effigy to the *erinys* and get on, for a while. And knowing that is something.

Notes

1 Recall I am using the Davidsonian (1980) way of individuating actions.
2 One significant difficulty with the thesis has to do with that characteristic, already noticed, that there is pain in the creative parturition. Why should reparation occasion pain? Segal does address this question and says that reparation always involves letting the object go – finishing the work – and such separation is always painful. But the separation here seems bogus, for the internal objects have, if all has gone well, been reconstituted in the self, and the work of art (which has in an unexplained way facilitated that reconstitution) is, after all, not lost.
3 Proto-communication because there may be no intention to communicate, though communication is the result, and is the forerunner of communication proper. The cry of the neonate is not intended as a communication, though it may very quickly be harnessed for that purpose. It seems that the infant experiences at first amodally or globally, and that we retain this capacity in projective transactions (Kumin 1996).

Chapter 9

The insanity defence

Actus non facit reum, nisi mens sit rea [The act does not make the crime, unless the intention is criminal.]

9.1 Intention and excuse

In most systems of criminal law a determination of criminal responsibility has required that the 'physical aspects' of the offending act – the *actus reus* – must originate in culpable 'subjective conditions' or states of mind referred to as *mens rea*. Historically, the most important of these conditions – at least in principle, if not always in effect – has been the culpable intention, intent or will to bring about the criminal act.

Intentional action, it is generally held, presupposes that there are reasons for and from which an agent acts, conventionally understood to comprise desires or wishes that the agent tries to satisfy, together with instrumental beliefs or knowledge about how to satisfy them **(1.4)**. In typical cases intentional action would also seem to require knowledge or awareness of what is being done at the time that it is being done, at least under the description that the act is intended. For example, a person intentionally waving to a friend, or trying to get to the cinema, wants to do these things and knows that she is doing them; if, in some unusual circumstance, she does not know, and therefore cannot monitor her actions while they are being performed, her intentions are likely to fall short of their targets.[1]

Culpable intent, as I noted, has been regarded in principle as the most important component of *mens rea*, but in practice has been curiously neglected in formulations of the insanity defence. The reasons for that neglect are interesting, and are connected with the complexities of unconscious motivation that we have been progressively unravelling. In this chapter I want to show (amongst other things) how some of the considerations in earlier chapters concerning unconscious motivation can restore absence of culpable intent as the core condition of absence of *mens rea*.

Other elements of *mens rea* are concerned less directly with the intentional structure of the offending act. They focus on degrees of circumstantial knowledge and the absence of knowledge: on such things as what an agent knows, ignores or should know of distal consequences and general norms regarding the act. These elements include such things as recklessness, advertent or culpable ignorance or negligence and inadvertent negligence. For example, recklessness may involve ignoring the possibility of an act's harmful consequences, and some forms of negligence involve not knowing matters that one is obliged to know. (There are other circumstances in criminal law where mere knowledge of an act, even when it is not one's own act, can render an agent culpable, but such cases won't concern us.)

Most contemporary systems of law recognise a range of *justifications* and *excuses* and (which is different) *mitigating circumstances* for putatively criminal acts. It may be said in general that justifications – lawful self-defence is an example – negate the criminality of the act; that mitigating circumstances, such as abnormal states of mind not amounting to insanity – a mind in the throes of passion, for example – do not negate responsibility but may diminish it; and that excuses, while not rendering the offending act lawful, negate or qualify criminal responsibility by appealing to absence of *mens rea*. The excuses are a mixed bag. Absence of culpable intent, non-culpable ignorance, duress or compulsion, necessity or certain kinds of mistake or circumstantial ignorance may be invoked (though ignorance of the law, where the law is clear, may not). In these cases the *actus reus* is conceded but *mens rea* is denied. The excuses typically find application in cases involving the ignorant, the misled, the coerced, the insane and the intoxicated. It has also been argued that there is another kind of excuse or, rather, a kind of foreclosure of responsibility, which is specific to the insane and children. It is claimed to be predicated not on absence of *mens rea* but on the absence of the status as a rational being that is presupposed in any judgement of legal responsibility.[2] I will return to this view below.

9.2 Mental illness and excuse

The understanding that some types of mental illness should relieve a defendant of criminal liability is very old in western thought. The dominant approach has been to identify insanity as those forms of mental illness which excuse the agent from criminal (and other legal) liability. In this view, it is *because* legal insanity is characterised by the absence of one or more material elements of *mens rea* that it excuses, and is therefore akin to defence in law.[3] Of course, the types of mental illness are many, and the excuses relatively few. So it unsurprising to see most of the diverse insanity tests formalised, from the time of *McNaughtan*, as attempts to retain the traditional framework of excuses by selecting only those features of mental illness which exemplify or can be translated into that legal framework. Thus, in relevant circumstances, a psychotic delusion may be understood as (causing) a mistake of fact, or ignorance of some fact, material to the offending act; impulsive or compulsive behaviour may be interpreted on a model of 'internal' duress or compulsion; psychotic confusional states may be understood as causing ignorance of the nature of the act or inability to appreciate its wrongfulness; and so on.

Given its irreducibly normative character, its foundation in common-sense understanding of norms of behaviour and the values attached to them, it is hard to see how else the law could proceed on such fundamentals. That is not to say, of course, that there is no further scope for analytical refinement within the recognised excuses or that the legal process always succeeds in selecting only those features from the immensely variegated range exemplified in mental disorders which do in fact excuse on traditional grounds. Nor is it to suggest that the law is immune to conceptual shifts that may eventually attenuate its reliance on that mainstay of the law, the reasonable man. Since the eighteenth century, developments in philosophy and science, most recently and dramatically in neuroscience and psychiatry, have been straining those very conceptions that constitute the normative foundations of law. Increasingly, the major mental disorders are being conceptualised in neurobiological and therefore deterministic terms which, on the surface anyway, have nothing of the normative in them. This issue obviously impinges on the subject at hand, but in this chapter I will continue to take the view (a) that where there *is* understanding of the mental disorders the best understanding we have is still largely, though not exclusively, in terms of the extended common-sense or Intentional psychology, of which much of the clinical language of psychoanalysis is a compartment, and (b) even if a comprehensive neurobiological understanding of the major psychotic disorders or of psychopathy was available (and there is nothing like that at present), because of its essentially normative character the judicial understanding of insanity will always require the 'translation' of neurobiological psychiatric characterisations of mental disorder into the Intentional idiom, and will strain out what it can in terms of excuses, mitigations and the rest.

Before proceeding I wish to insert a parenthesis to dispose of the influential approach to insanity represented by Fingarette (1972) and Moore (1984), mentioned above. Both authors oppose the supposition that if insanity exculpates it must be assimilable to one of the standard forms of excuse. The criminally insane in their view are neither innocent nor guilty: they are fundamentally irrational, and therefore do not have responsibility status under law. They do not, says Moore, have the status of persons (1984: 65). He writes: 'the insane, like the very young, are not sufficiently rational to be fairly blamed or punished. If this is so, then lawyers should give up the attempts to define legal insanity in a way that collapses into some traditional excuse. Crazy people are not responsible because they are crazy, not because they always lack intentions, are ignorant, or are compelled' (1984: 223). On Moore's account, to be mentally ill is to be a *very* bad practical reasoner: a person who accepts irrational beliefs and desires as the premises of his practical syllogisms and, presumably (though Moore doesn't spell this out), is unable to draw valid practical conclusions; that is, to form appropriate intentions or proceed to apt actions. 'To be mentally ill is to be very seriously irrational' (1984: 244).

Fingarette's definition of criminal insanity is in accord: 'The individual's mental make-up at the time of the offending act was such that, with respect to the criminality of his conduct, he substantially lacked capacity to act rationally (to respond relevantly to relevance so far as criminality is concerned)' (1972: 211). So both philosophers appeal fundamentally to *irrationality*. But then how is *that* to be characterised? Fingarette says that 'we have to do with the observed pattern of incapacity for rational conduct in the individual's life history. The specific issue faced by the trier of fact is not a causal one but is one of practical judgement in assessing a person. The question is whether it is fitting to view the offending act as belonging to such a pattern of irrational conduct' (1975: 247). Moore is in substantial agreement: 'we predicate "mentally ill" of a person whenever we find his pattern of past behaviour unintelligible in some fundamental way' (1984: 196).

The trouble with this approach, with appealing to antecedent patterns of behaviour to illuminate irrationality, is that a pattern of conduct is not interpretable as either rational or irrational unless we know beforehand the agent's motivating desires, beliefs, intentions – those conditions which reveal *what* is being done intentionally, and what not. Otherwise the pattern remains opaque. I do not know why you raised your hand, I do not know what you are doing in raising your hand, unless I know your reasons, intentions, objectives in raising your hand. I cannot assess the rationality or otherwise of your behaviour without such knowledge. But these precursors of action are precisely what the triers of fact in a court will be considering in coming to a judgment about a defendant's state of mind, and are *nothing other than the material of the traditional tests*. Moreover, the philosophers' views suggest that what should be tried in court is not the criminality of the offence but the character of the defendant, and not just his state of mind at the time of the offence but his state overall, as this may be revealed by a larger pattern of conduct. I agree that the insane are irrational, in a sufficiently catholic sense, but for that notion to advance our understanding it has to be unpacked in terms of, amongst other things, irrational beliefs, desires and the formation of intentions.

I return now to the main thread of the argument. Culpable intent, I said at the outset, is in principle the central element of *mens rea* and it could be expected that its absence would be the foundation of legal defence on grounds of insanity. Historically the expectation has not been borne out. Michael Moore, summarising the history of insanity tests, states that the earliest tests for insanity were based on analogies with children and animals, and that from the time of *McNaughtan* there have been 'basically two kinds of traditional insanity tests: those based on ignorance of the mentally ill accused person; and those based on some notion of his being compelled to act as he did' (1984: 221). I am not sure that this is an accurate historical appreciation but in any event it is easy to see why absence of culpable intent could be seen as taking a back seat in defences based on insanity: it seems obvious that in most relevant cases culpable intent *is* present – that the sequence of action-events that constitute the *actus reus* are organised around a goal (sometimes over an extended period of time), and are patently not in the same category of agency as sleepwalking, epileptic attack or neurological disease. Moreover, defendants themselves will frequently avow an intention which is criminal and on which they genuinely believed they acted.

Notwithstanding the appearances, I will argue that although many intentions and reasons for acting, some of them perhaps criminal, may indeed be present in the minds of some defendants at the time of the alleged offences, it is far from evident that the *efficacious or motivating* intentions or reasons – those reasons for which, and those intentions with which, the agent actually acted – are in fact criminal. I want to show that in at least some relevant cases there is indeed intention that can account for the characteristics of intentionality in the defendant's actions, but that the primary, *efficacious intention* is unconscious and non-culpable, and therefore not criminal – not criminal *both* because it is unconscious *and* because, in most cases, it is in itself not a culpable intention. If the argument can be sustained then the emphasis in determining absence of *mens rea* in some cases of insanity should shift from what the agent didn't know or was compelled to do to what she intended – a position which seems more aligned with procedure in the ascertainment of legal responsibility elsewhere in the law. A sketch of some relevant stages of judicial thought on this matter will shed some light, I hope, on an argument that is not easy.

9.3 A very brief history of intention in insanity

The idea that intention is a primary factor in determining guilt and assessing liability is very old in western legal thought. Draco, in the seventh century BCE, distinguished two categories of crime, the intentional and the unintentional, with instances of the latter constituting lesser offences.[4] Four centuries later, Demosthenes elevated the distinction to natural law:

> Among other people I find this sort of distinction universally observed. If a man has gone wrong wilfully, he is visited with resentment and punishment. If he has erred unintentionally, pardon takes the place of punishment... The distinction will be found not only embodied in our statutes, but laid down by nature herself in her unwritten laws and in the moral sense of men.
> (quoted in Kelly 1992: 34)

In the thirteenth century a leading authority, Bracton, expressed the idea succinctly: 'Remove will and every act will be indifferent. It is your intent that differentiates your acts, nor is a crime committed unless an intention to injure exists; it is will and purpose which distinguish *maleficia*' (quoted in Robinson 1998: 100). The centrality of criminal intent is reaffirmed in this recent, representative statement, but in a significant muddying of the waters, which by this time has considerable historical precedent, it fails to explain whether the concepts of cognition and volition which are introduced beside intention are parts of its analysis or additional new elements.

> The precise words of any formulation on criminal responsibility are not particularly important. The important thing that we must remember is that *mens rea*, criminal intent is the center of it. That is the inquiry the law is making, and any test or any formulation is adequate if it is based upon the concept of cognition, that is, recognition of the nature of the act and its wrongness, and volition or capacity to control conduct... If [the standard] doesn't have those elements, it breaks continuity with all of the law of the past.[5]

Coming now specifically to the role of intent in insanity, we find that ancient Greek and Roman law gave considerable statutory attention to the competence and legal standing of the insane. The general tendency was to regard insanity as a condition legally akin to infancy. The standard model for the insane appears to have been the *furioso*, the man who is so crazed or frenzied that he doesn't know what he is doing, what he is purposing, what he's about. There certainly are people who are like that, at least some of the time, and they ease the judge's task; however, the ancient records also show more flexible and accommodating discriminations.[6] Like infants, such people do not have the capacity to fulfil the duties of citizenship. They are irrational in that they are incapable of forming rational intentions and acting on them – rationally entering into contracts, for example – in ways for which they can be held accountable. Medieval Christianity added little to Roman (and Germanic) law overall, but because it assimilated crime to sin and taught that madness was voluntary possession by demons, and a sin, the relatively humane treatment of the insane afforded by the ancients was considerably diminished where these elements of Christian teaching took hold.

In 1724 Edward Arnold shot and wounded Lord Onslow. Justice Tracy directed the jury.

> That he shot, and that wilfully [is proved]: but whether maliciously, that is the thing: that is the question; whether this man hath the use of his reason and sense? If he was under visitation of god, and could not distinguish between good and evil, and did not know what he did, though he committed the greatest offence, yet he could not be guilty of any offence whatsoever; for guilt arises from the mind, and the wicked will and intention of the man. If a man be deprived of his reason, and consequently of his intention, he cannot be guilty. … [I]t is not every kind of frantic humour or something unaccountable in a man's actions, that points him out to be such a madman as is to be exempted from punishment: it must be a man that is totally deprived of his understanding and memory, and doth not know what he is doing, no more than an infant, than a brute, or a wild beast…
>
> (quoted in Robinson 1998: 134)

Tracy enunciates the ancient principle that guilt arises from wicked will or intention and, on one reading, seems to suggest – though perhaps obscurely – the proposition that a person who does not know what he is doing can't be intending it – that seems to be a natural understanding of the final two sentences taken together. And this proposition is surely a fact. On a narrower reading of 'a man be[ing] deprived of his reason, and consequently his intention', Tracy's madman seems incapable of even forming intentions. In both cases the primacy of wicked intent is affirmed. But the final summing up does not mention intention, only a radical ignorance or impoverishment of which even children and brutes could scarcely be examples. There is here an evident tension, and by the time of the classic *McNaughtan* case (1843), which resulted in the well-known eponymous test, culpable intention as a separate element drops out of the picture, explicitly at least. The main part reads:

> To establish a defence on the grounds of insanity, it must be clearly proven that, at the time of committing the act, the party accused was labouring under such

a defect of reason, from disease of the mind, as not to know the nature and quality of the act he was doing; or if he did know it, that he did not know he was doing what was wrong.

(quoted in Moran 1981: 191)

9.4 McNaughtan

Why has the well-tried excuse of absence of criminal intent disappeared explicitly from this test of insanity, and indeed from most of those that followed? Well, contemporary conceptions of mental illness influenced the tests: the judges who fashioned the *McNaughtan* tests had a conception of mental illness as delusion foremost in mind. More recently notions of inner compulsion, loss of control and various other psychodynamic and neuroscientific conceptions have been influential. Further, as we have seen, the excuses involving ignorance or absence of relevant knowledge can absorb some instances of absence of culpable intent. A person who doesn't know what they're doing can hardly be said to be doing it intentionally. It may erroneously be supposed that ignorance can absorb all instances. Finally, as previously noted, the presence of culpable intent seems all but indubitable in the majority of cases that get to trial; absence of culpable intent is a tough test to pass. We can see that from some comments Michael Moore makes *a propos McNaughtan*. In the course of arguing that *none* of the traditional elements of excuse capture the characteristic that relieves the insane of criminal responsibility, he says:

> First of all M'Naghten (sic) had the *intent* required for murder in England: He shot the gun with the purpose of killing another human being. True, he thought he was killing Prime Minister Peel when in fact he was killing Peel's secretary, Drummond. But such mistakes about the identity of the intended victim never excuse in law, as the doctrine of 'transferred intent' has long established. In every ordinary legal sense of the word, M'Naghten (sic) *intended* the death of another. Similarly he knew the 'nature and quality of his act'; he knew its wrongfulness; he 'appreciated its criminality.' He made no *mistakes* about what he was doing – he knew he was shooting, and he knew that he was killing – nor was he ignorant of the moral and legal prohibitions against killing. Finally there is no persuasive case for saying that M'Naghten (sic) was *compelled* to do what he did.
>
> (Moore 1984: 223)[7]

All of this I do believe, but only because I am persuaded by Richard Moran's investigations which reveal McNaughtan as a rational, paid assassin, albeit one evidently less motivated by money than by political aims and hatred of the Tories. McNaughtan was clearly a troubled man but he probably was not mad; it suited Peel's government, however, to have him believed to be so. But if McNaughtan *was* the mad being that subsequent legal history has portrayed, then Moore's assertions appear to me less than certain. In particular, the conviction with which Moore imputes conscious intentionality to McNaughtan's act seems unwarranted.

Daniel McNaughtan shot and killed Edmund Drummond, mistaking the secretary for the Prime Minister, Robert Peel, who was evidently the intended target. When asked to plead at his arraignment McNaughtan said only: 'I was driven to desperation by persecution'. Recounting the details of the crime at an earlier examination, one of the arresting officers recalled that on the way to the stationhouse the suspect said that 'he' or 'she', the officer was uncertain, 'shall not destroy my peace of mind any longer'. The officer also recalled McNaughtan saying after the arrest, 'I know what I'm about'. At that examination McNaughtan made a statement:

> The Tories in my native city have compelled me to do this. They follow, perse-
> cute me wherever I go, and have entirely destroyed my peace of mind. They
> followed me to France, to Scotland… they follow me wherever I go. I cannot
> sleep nor get no rest from them. … I believe they have driven me into a con-
> sumption. I am sure I will never be the man I was. I used to have good health
> and strength but I have not now. They have accused me of crimes of which I am
> not guilty, they do everything in their power to harass and persecute me; in fact,
> they wish to murder me. It can be proved by evidence. That's all I have to say.
>
> (abridged from Moran 1981: 10)

His comportment at the trial, much of the evidence presented there and the considerations adduced by Richard Moran suggest that McNaughtan was not insane. But let us assume that he was, as the defence argued, suffering delusional insanity.

9.5 Intention in madness

It is understandable that McNaughtan's own account of his persecution and the constructions the defence based on it should have been taken at face value by his contemporaries. It is very strange that many of *our* contemporaries should accept it as a transparent account of what animated McNaughtan. We have, of course, no confirmable idea of the structure of McNaughtan's motivation, but we may suspect from a psychoanalytic perspective that his consciously contrived story cannot be the whole of it. Let's hypothesise a schematic psychodynamic account. It will be hopelessly simple and incomplete but its truth is not the main thing for our purposes here, only the possibility of something essentially like it being true. Suppose then that McNaughtan felt intolerably persecuted by an internal object, an aspect or 'part' of himself identified with an object that had been internalised and was experienced as being persecutory, or had in the course of time become so: the sort of entity referred to as the 'superego' or more generally, as in **5.6**, a personation. Suppose further that McNaughtan's defence against this persecution was to externalise the object, to project and identify it with the despised man who was head of a government enforcing what McNaughtan believed to be, and was in fact, cruel, persecutory policy. Killing *that* thing, which happened to be Peel, would then, in McNaughtan's mind, amount to ridding himself of his tormentor. Something like that could have formed part of the unconscious dynamics that motivated

McNaughtan, if indeed he really was mad in the alleged way. (Projective identification is at issue: see **8.2**).

Although McNaughtan did not state that he had intended to murder Peel, much of what he did say before the trial, and his planned and determined conduct, would seem to imply it. But if something akin to the hypothesised unconscious dynamics obtained, then space for a radically different possibility opens up: *McNaughtan did not intend to kill Peel; he only thought that he did.* What he intended was to destroy the object persecuting him which, through the mechanism of projective identification, happened to be apprehended as the man, Peel. He may have known – almost surely he did – that he was killing a man whom he thought was Peel, but it doesn't follow that he intended to kill that man. We do not, *pace* Jeremy Bentham, intend all the known consequences of our acts **(4.5)** or, to put it another way, an act is not intentional under all the descriptions we know it under. This can be seen clearly if we formalise some relations between intention and knowledge noticed earlier: where 'A' designates an act-event, then (a) 'If a person is intentionally doing A then he knows that he is doing A' is true (even where the intending and the knowing are both unconscious).[8] And (a) implies (b), 'If a person doesn't know that he is doing A then he can't be intentionally doing A', but (a) does *not* imply (c) 'If a person knows that he is doing A then (necessarily) he is intentionally doing it' – (c) is in fact false, and it is important to see that it is.

When I go running I know that I will erode the heels of my runners. 'Running' and 'eroding the heels' are different descriptions of the one act – what *I do.* But I do not wish, will, want or intend to erode the heels. There is a sense in which the act of heel-erosion is *voluntary*: I permit it, I could halt it if I wanted to. But though voluntary, it is not intended: there are no reasons which are *my* reasons for performing the act of wearing down the heels; I form no practical syllogism with a major premise stating a desire for the heel-erosion and a conclusion that is an intention, decision or action to do so. Where there are no reasons which I have made my *reasons for* performing an act, I cannot be performing it intentionally.[9] There are, in fact, several other kinds of action that are voluntary but not intentional. Shivering with cold is not actively willed or done intentionally, but it is usually something that could be halted by an act of will, and so is partly subject to will or *passively voluntary*, in the sense that it is permitted to continue. There is a large class of *expressive* actions such as laughing, smiling with pleasure, clenching one's fists in anguish, which are passively voluntary, and not actively willed or intended. Indeed, when one tries to do them at will or intentionally they immediately lose their expressive force **(3.3)**.

So McNaughtan may have known that he was killing (the man he thought was) Peel without intending to do so, though of course he believed that he intended to do so and believed that he had good reason to do so. We are then confronted with a number of puzzles. The act that can be described as 'the supposed killing of Peel' (or 'the pulling of the trigger', etc.) has many of the purposeful characteristics of intentional action, which suggests that it was intentional under at least one description. There was planning and deliberation. The description under which

McNaughtan avowed an intention was 'killing this man' (Peel, as he thought). How could McNaughtan go wrong about his intention? And if he was wrong, what exactly *did* McNaughtan do intentionally which lends the act its intentional character? Finally, even if McNaughtan did not kill this man intentionally, it appears that he still knew that he was killing the man he thought was Peel, so why should his responsibility for the killing be negated or diminished? 'Knowing the nature and quality of the act he was doing' is, after all, precisely what the McNaughtan test specifies for culpable acts.

It is necessary to show that an act can be intentional without its agent consciously knowing that it is, and so without knowing *what* exactly she is doing. That happens when the intention with which the act is being done and the reasons for it are unconscious. That there are such 'unconscious intentional actions', actions motivated by reasons or intentions consciously unknown to the agent, we have already shown in **Chapter 4**. Recall the obsessive ritual of Freud's bedstead girl that Freud interpreted as a 'magical' attempt to keep her parents separated and to ward off anxieties connected with the birth of a competitor. The ritual seemed to be an intentional enactment but the girl could provide no reasons for doing it and, initially, found her own actions unintelligible. Under the description 'separating bedstead and pillow' there seemed to be no reasons rendering her acts intentional; that is, not only causing her acts but rationalising them. True, she would have felt a strong, irresistible urge to separate these items, but there was no clear belief about what her acts could achieve and no background of further desires or beliefs that could rationalise the urge: her compulsive act was not vulnerable to conscious considerations in the way intentional action usually is. But the same act-event, we saw, could be intentional under other descriptions. It was possible to construct several different practical syllogisms, reflecting unconscious deliberation, that concluded with the required action. For example, if she was unconsciously under the sway of (Segalian) symbolic equations **(4.5)** between the furniture and her parents then one such practical syllogism, incorporating a mad belief but rendering her actions intentional, would be:

Girl wants to prevent the conception of a baby-competitor.
Girl believes that by keeping her father=bedstead and her mother=pillow apart she could prevent that conception.

Girl separates bedstead and pillow.

This was but one of several possible unconscious structures that seemed necessary to make sense of the girl's compulsive ritual as an (unconsciously) intentional act.

I think we can now see how McNaughtan's actions can be provided with an unconscious aetiology of the hypothesised kind. McNaughtan's aim, in the hypothesis, was to destroy a persecutory object which he identified with Peel, or believed was in some magical way associated with Peel, or something like that; in any case, he apprehended the killing of Peel as the destruction of the persecutory object. This understanding is supported by the peculiar fact that McNaughtan appeared to have believed killing Peel would end his persecution, a most improbable outcome even on McNaughtan's own understanding of his situation. His unconscious intentions may have included, as well as the intention to destroy the object, the intention to end the persecution, to defend himself, and so on, and each of these intentions was the conclusion of a piece of unconscious reasoning whose premises may have included one or another mad belief, trading, perhaps, on an equation of Peel and the internal persecutor. If that is right and McNaughtan did set out on some such unconscious but intentional project, then to the observer, the sequence of actions that followed would have appeared no different than if they had been motivated by a conscious intention to murder Peel.

But McNaughtan's case is different from the bedstead girl's in important respects. The girl has unconscious reasons for separating her parents but no supportable conscious reason for separating the bedroom furnishings. McNaughtan not only appeared to have conscious reasons for killing Peel but appeared to have formed an intention to do so, and seemed to avow that he acted on it. Doesn't that entirely undermine the relevance of the story about unconscious intent? I think it does not.

To begin with, first-person avowal indicates a certain kind of immediacy and privileged access to our own mental states, but it is not immune to error. We are not infallible guides to the content of our intentions, motives, beliefs and attitudes. Particular instances of these states are frequently confabulated, distorted or revised to achieve consonance with past actions and with other associated states of the agent. Examples of confabulated reasons being given for acting out directions under hypnosis are commonplace. The prevalence of self-deception is uncontested. Studies of 'cognitive dissonance' show the remarkable extent to which even in fairly ordinary situations we erroneously revise and invent reasons and attitudes in attempting to maintain consistency between our attitudes, beliefs and actions. Most extraordinary are the cases that fall into the category of anosognosia or unawareness of deficit following serious right hemisphere brain damage:

> In its extreme form, this symptom presents as a near-delusional disavowal of illness, even in the face of the most obvious contradictory evidence – such as Babinski's (1914) seminal collection of cases in which densely hemiplegic patients insisted that they could walk without difficulty, or in Anton's (1899) classical study in which cortically blind patients insisted they could see normally.
> (Kaplan-Solms and Solms 2000: 150)

Other patients with paralysis of a limb and neglect may confabulate inventive accounts of why they do not wish to move the limb, or deny the limb is theirs, and so on (2000: 151ff). Kaplan-Solms and Solms are able to show that the patients unconsciously *are* aware and can attend to the damage, but repress the knowledge of it (4.2).

Given the unreliability of first-person avowal about one's mental state, then, it is quite possible that McNaughtan's avowals were founded on what were only apparent, confabulated or factitious states of mind. A preponderance of such irrational phenomena is, after all, a mark of serious mental disorder. One can think of McNaughtan's *conscious* intentions as delusional, not in the sense that they were caused by a delusional process and really existed, but in that they were only apparent, not intentions at all.

What if it is insisted that this hypothesis is far-fetched, mistaken; that McNaughtan *did* have a real intention to kill Peel. Perhaps. But even if that were so, it doesn't establish *mens rea*. To establish *mens rea* would require a demonstration not just of the presence of intention but of the presence of an *efficacious* intention, one on which the agent actually acted. Our hypothesis about McNaughtan's illness suggests that his unconscious motives were sufficient for the act to take place, and that implies that the avowed conscious intention had no necessary instrumental role. It is as if the act interpreted in terms of the avowed motives was just the shadow cast by the reality, like those shadows cast by puppeteers whose motives are, of course, quite different from those of the characters their shadow puppets portray.

But now it may be pressed that McNaughtan did have an *efficacious* intention to kill Peel. One can accept some version of the story about unconscious dynamics and still insist that conscious culpable intentions were present and had an instrumental role. Intentions generate other intentions. It can be argued plausibly that although McNaughtan unconsciously intended to destroy a persecutory object (or had some similar intention), his targeting of Peel resulted from the emergence of fresh intentions created by his unconscious intentions through the prism of the projective or symbolic activities that we discussed earlier **(4.5)**. The unconscious intention to destroy the persecutory object generates the conscious intention to destroy Peel. There is, I think, a genuine question about whether intentions that have been, as it were, injected into consciousness in this way, and not *made* intentions in the light of the agent's overall aims and deliberations, are really the agent's intentions. For something to *be* a conscious intention or reason for an agent, it has to be formed or taken up by the agent and endorsed in a particular way. But leaving that difficult consideration aside, some such process of generation certainly seems possible. It is not, however, an objection to the argument being advanced here. I have been contending only that such conscious intentions are not *necessary* to explain McNaughtan's conduct and that unconscious intentions, much like the bedstead girl's, may be sufficient.

This contention implies that only in the case of the injected conscious intention to kill Peel, a mental state whose agential role I have suggested is problematic, does the question of culpable intent and criminal responsibility arise. In the cases where the conscious intention is either confabulated or inefficacious, and where the unconscious intention suffices for action, no culpable responsibility exists. In the case of conscious confabulated and inefficacious intention there is an absence of efficacious culpable intent; in the case of efficacious unconscious intention, there is no responsibility because actions performed while unconscious, or for reasons or intentions that are unconscious, do not (in general) attract legal liability. 'Criminal law and the law of torts', writes Moore, 'have consistently held that sleepwalking, posthypnotic and similar acts are examples of nonaction. Case law, model codes and commentary uniformly classify unconsciously directed behaviour, or behaviour engaged in while unconscious as nonaction' (1984: 73). The person who doesn't know why he acts doesn't know the main thing that he is doing, and is not able to morally assess what he is doing, and is therefore not accountable for *that* act (the act-event under a description of which he is unaware.)

But may he not be responsible for his actions known to him under other descriptions: 'Killing *this* man', for example? If Bentham is right, that we intend all those actions which we know we are performing – that is, that our actions are intentional under all the descriptions that we know them – then the matter is easily settled. There would be intent and, therefore, responsibility. But we have seen that that is a mistake. A person can know that they are doing something without intending to do it. And that raises a further interesting question for the hypothetical model of McNaughtan's madness – and those cases which may be significantly similar to it. Even if McNaughtan didn't intend to kill Peel, he still knew that he was killing a man. He did not attempt to stop himself. His act was, as it seems, *passively volitional*. A person who knows that they are doing something but does not have access to the reason for doing it is in a very strange situation. The bedstead girl was in this situation. McNaughtan was not quite in this situation because he had reasons or, rather, confabulated reasons: it's a fair surmise, indeed, that the reasons were confabulated precisely to fill this gap between the actions he observes himself performing and the want of real (conscious) reasons for performing them.

This strange situation suggests some concluding remarks. First, once we see that an agent's knowledge of an act of his does not imply that he intended it, the case for imputing strict criminal liability becomes less compelling. Other considerations of excuse or mitigation may well come to the fore. And that thought is reinforced by another. Situations of being, as it were, an observer of one's own actions without having access to the real reasons for which one performs them suggest a degree of alienation or dissociation very much of a kind with those serious forms of irrationality which many commentators have identified with legal insanity. They are very reminiscent of the circumstances of dissociation of the self we discussed in **5.7**. They are aspects of insanity partly unpacked. It may be that in practice juries will decide the guilt of defendants on more or less indefinite notions of intelligibility and gross departure from accepted norms of rationality. But that should not exempt us (nor the judicial process) from trying to identify in the particular instance precisely if, where and how rationality breaks down – and indeed where our understanding of it breaks down, as when the passenger just grabs the wheel for no discernible motive.

Notes

1 I am as usual using Davidson's (1963) approach to individuating actions. A single act event – moving an arm – may be intentional under some descriptions and not others. So in the example, the waving to friends is intentional, while casting shadows and alarming

the pigeons, though these are the very same act-events under different descriptions, are not – assuming these are not things the person wants to do. It may seem that a person could perform an act intentionally and not know whether they are performing it. For example, a person rings a doorbell with the intention of alerting the residents of a house but does not know whether she is alerting the residents, though in fact she is. Intuitions in this sort of case differ. Mine is that although the person has an intention to alert the residents she is only trying to alert them, and is intentionally alerting them only if she knows that she is succeeding. In any case, in the text I am requiring only that the agent knows what she is trying to do, not that she is succeeding.

2 Influentially, by Fingarette (1972) and Moore (1984). Fingarette writes: 'Insanity and childhood both preclude responsibility status, and they therefore preclude moral judgements and legal judgements of criminality. In these conditions, questions of knowledge and appreciation of what one is doing or of its wrongness, or questions of voluntariness, self-control, or intent become beside the point' (1972: 141).

3 Chief Justice Weintraub: 'although we sometimes speak of insanity as a defense, it is not a separate defense, as we lawyers use that concept, to a case that the state has otherwise established but, rather, it is essentially a denial of the state's main case, a denial of *mens rea*' (cited in Fingarette 1972: 130).

4 I have relied principally on Robinson (1998) and Kelly (1992).

5 Warren Burger, *Proceedings 10th Circuit, Appellate Court, District of Columbia, 1962*, cited in Fingarette (1972: 130).

6 Robinson (1998: 28ff). Of course, the introduction of anti-psychotic medication has done much to mitigate the manifestations of such states.

7 Similarly, Fingarette on another classic case:

> It is clear that in a plain and natural sense of the words Hadfield knew that he was attempting a kind of murder that is legally and morally condemned with peculiar intensity, namely, high treason... [H]e was engaged, at his own leisure and without compulsion, in a complex course of conduct which he himself planned and executed; he had a well-formed and specific intent, indeed a plainly criminal intent if one takes the words at their everyday face value. Thus, in any plain and straightforward use of language, he was not acting under an 'irresistible impulse' nor was the 'governing power of his will destroyed.' What we have is irrational conduct, true enough, and based on an irrational belief. But the act was not involuntary, nor was Hadfield unaware of what he was doing.
>
> (Fingarette 1972: 138–9)

8 The conception of unconscious knowledge or belief is, of course, essential to psychoanalytic understanding and demonstrable clinically. Particularly interesting is Karen Kaplan-Solms and Mark Solms, *Clinical Studies in Neuro-Psychoanalysis* (Karnac: 2000), ch. 8.

9 Even if a necessary connection between the having of reasons and intention is rejected (as discussed in **3.8**), it is clear that no intention to erode the heels is entailed by my knowing that the heels are being eroded.

Chapter 10

A word on psychiatry

Vain is the word of a philosopher which does not heal any suffering of man.

Epicurus

Let me discuss two of the underlying themes in this book, from a rather high and trying altitude, and their relation to psychiatry.

I have tried in these pages to provide a wide-ranging account of Freudian wish-fulfilment (FWT) using only Intentional concepts, the concepts of an augmented common-sense psychology. I argued that there are several types of FWT, and that they constitute a distinctive compartment within a theory of action that can elucidate some of the causal structure of many forms of pathology, irrational action and belief-formation and illusions (in Freud's sense) such as religion and art. In fact, FWT is a distinctive mode of explanation uncovered by psychoanalysis. The scope of FWT, the range of phenomena falling under it, is (we saw) very wide, but the question of its limits, whether for example it is present in all psychotic conditions, was left open. FWT was, I showed, central to Freud's theorising, though its character and scope have been obscured in later developments within psychoanalysis.

In the biological psychiatry descending from Griesinger, and certainly in the contemporary neo-Kraepelinian orthodoxy, FWT is, of course, unknown and uncountenanced. Griesinger asserted that all mental illness was due to morbid action of the brain, and Kraepelin later tried heroically to prove that (major) mental illness stemmed exclusively from hereditary and biological causes. FWT is part of a scheme of Intentional, and rather unmedical, concepts which neurobiological explanation is intended to replace.

Intentional concepts are not incompatible with most of the concepts used in cognitively orientated clinical psychology or, indeed, the broader range of concepts employed in social psychology or most other areas of psychology that have a self-image as more scientific than psychoanalysis. Many of these concepts are extensions of Intentional psychology or depend for their meaningfulness on being cashed out in Intentional terms. To my knowledge, the idea that pathological conditions can be explained as instances of FWT plays no more part in the aetiological constructions of cognitively orientated clinical psychology than it does in biological psychiatry. I believe this applies to neurotic symptoms and personality disorders as well as the major psychotic disorders. But it is not only FWT that is missing from these disciplines; also absent is any serious consideration of the pathology of desire.

This neglect, on the face of it, is passing strange. Think of *desire* in the broad sense as including wanting, longing, wishing, and so on. In humankind, infant needs soon graduate to wants or desires (and strictly speaking, to wishes, when desire is forsaken – see **1.1**). FWT consists of processes and strategies for containing or regulating ineluctable desires, usually directed at other people, and very often of a sexual or aggressive kind. The will or desire to satisfy or pacify these desires, ultimately arising from exigent basic needs, is among the most potent motives to action we know. Surely, to take one instance, this is so with sexual desire. 'Th' expense of spirit in a waste of shame/ Is lust in action… /All this the world well knows…'[1] Well, no. The desiderative sources of action are scarcely mentioned even in some of the best recent theoretical literature on psychiatry and cognitively oriented clinical psychology. Richard Bentall, for example, complains that although *emotions* play a pivotal role in human nature, they are 'not usually considered to be important features of some of the extreme forms of mental suffering' (2004: 205), a neglect he intends to remedy. He clearly hasn't been reading the psychoanalytic literature. In any case, his interest in emotions does not tarry and attention quickly turns to cognitive concerns, to beliefs and appraisals. Object relations receive only a curt nod (2004: 204), but he is at least prepared to consider that emotional dynamics in the family may have pathogenic consequences (2004: 436ff). There was a scent that desire, with its motivational associations to emotions, may receive attention, but in the event it is ignored almost altogether. 'Sexual feeling' is mentioned once in a very big book, and destructive dispositions not at all. This is, of course, but one example; yet it is representative of a still dominant perspective that is partly a reaction to Freudian conceptions of unconscious thought and instinctual drive theory (or wishful motivation). It is animated as well by narrow and quite naive notions of scientific methodology – of the heterogeneity of scientific investigation – in the human sciences and something that looks for all the world like Puritanism.

The disappearance of desire is one major point of contention in the contest between cognitive behavioural therapy and psychodynamic psychotherapy for the theoretical and clinical high ground. However, it does now seem likely, with the rapid development of affective neuroscience, that the cognitively orientated models of motivation will be eclipsed by affective and drive motivational models. That will mean a resurgence of interest in desire (and wish) and the neurobiological systems that may constitute its neural realisers or correlatives – and from that may follow renewed interest in Freudian wish-fulfilment (Hopkins 2012, 2013) which, as I remarked earlier, is a means of coping with ineluctable desire, that is, an aspect of self-regulation or self-solicitude.

Perhaps, though, Intentional concepts such as *desire* or *wish* have no place in biological or biomedical psychiatry?[2] Certainly the aspiration of biological psychiatry since the 1980s has been to provide *complete* neurobiological explanations of the major mental disorders diagnosed along descriptive Kraepelinian lines. If that *were* possible, then it would seem that Intentional concepts would indeed be redundant. The program of Intentional psychology, and for finding a place in it for FWT, would seem futile. But is it possible?

Why would anyone think that a mental disorder could be given a complete neurobiological characterisation? Well, if you thought that the mind was identical with the brain, then it would seem to follow that a disordered mind entailed a disordered brain. In fact, this does not follow.[3] A useful and straightforward analogy has been proposed. In a computer, the software may malfunction or glitch without any corresponding fault in the hardware. The mind can go awry without the brain doing so. Or look at it this way. Pathogenic beliefs (or something very much like them) are obviously implicated in mental illness. From the perspective of the brain, all beliefs are on the same level. Supposing an identity theory according to which beliefs could be tokened by some kind of neural state, *as beliefs* there is nothing that marks out pathogenic beliefs at the neural level. An adolescent's belief that her parents will survive her leaving them is no different on the neural plane than the belief that the parents won't survive her leaving them. Yet we know that in certain circumstances the latter belief can be intensely pathogenic, guilt-inducing and inhibitive.

The mistake has already been made before the argument got underway. The mind is not the brain. The mind is not some *thing* for which 'brain' is another name. A human creature with a mind has specific thoughts, dispositions, susceptibilities, beliefs, desires, fears, and so on. And these things, or at least some of these things, cannot be given full neurobiological descriptions, as we shall see in a moment.

A psychiatrist might say: drop the metaphysics; there is good empirical evidence for believing that in every case of serious mental disorder there is a damaged or broken brain, some tangible indication of neurobiological malfunction. This is doubtful. The putative evidence comes from several main sources: from genetic studies, brain-imaging and neurochemical investigations. Some of these investigations suggest that there are differences between normal brains and the brains of those suffering from a mental disorder, in at least some forms of pathology. In fact, the data from these investigations is the subject of much contention and differing interpretation. There is now consensus that environmental factors can induce gross anatomical and neurophysiological changes in the brain; indeed, that they affect gene expression. Abnormal neurophysiological features that are *constant* across the various major disorders have not been found. The evidence for broken brains in most mental disorders, even in the psychotic disorders, is in fact rather thin: it remains unclear whether such neurobiological abnormalities as have been identified (and they are by no means consistent) are causes of the illness or manifestations or consequences of it. Such considerations tend to undermine the hard neurobiological view that mental disorders are (as Graham expresses it) not only disorders *in* the brain but also *of* the brain.[4] Rather than trying to still further compress and assess this material, however – for which I have neither the space nor the qualifications – let me quote expert opinion on one source of the evidence, genetic involvement (which, of course, being realised physically would suggest neurobiological aetiology).

Arthur Kleinman, a Harvard professor of psychiatry writing in the late 1980s, said: 'The genetic theory of schizophrenia, which up until several years ago seemed well established, is now in considerable disarray... There is still after more than 30 years of intensive biological investigation, no clear-cut understanding of the biology of schizophrenia' (1988: 188). Moreover, 'the leading researchers in the field now have impressive data that there is no such thing as depression that occurs solely from biological causes. Endogenicity is refuted by the most recent research studies' (1988: 73). He adds, tellingly, that contemporary studies had shown that cognitive psychotherapy and psychodynamic treatments are as effective as antidepressant drugs – a consideration which, if true, must throw at least some doubt on overriding genetic or biochemical involvement. In case this seems like old hat, here are the psychiatrists Kenneth Kendler and Carol Prescott in their major study, *Genes, Environment and Psychopathology*:

> Our findings provide substantial support for the hypothesis that genetic factors – expressed of necessity through biological mechanisms – are an important risk factor for all major forms of adult psychopathology... Despite this our results do not support the 'hard' reductionist position that psychiatric and substance use disorders can be entirely understood within a neurobiological and molecular framework... For example, we found that SLEs [significant life events] predicted the onset of episodes of MD [major depression]. When we attempted to characterize the important dimensions of these events, we found that those that involved both loss and humiliation were especially depressogenic. It is hard to conceive of a more classical mental construct, or one that would be harder to reduce to biological phenomena, than that of humiliation. These results strongly suggest that how we humans experience and interpret the psychological and social world around us alters our risk of illness.
>
> (2006: 350)

This position is not very different from the *complemental series* that Freud enunciated more than 100 years ago (1905d), in which mental illness resulted from a combination of constitutional and environmental factors. Except in the psychoses, Freud leaned towards environmental factors. And indeed, the genetic risk factors Kendler and Prescott refer to, even in the psychoses, are fairly modest.

Now, why can't the Intentional concepts (such as *humiliation*), as Kendler and Prescott notice, be reduced to neurobiological concepts, or, alternatively, the Intentional idiom be replaced by the language of neurochemistry, neuroanatomy and so on? If the brain *is* broken in mental illness than surely it is possible to give a complete description of the broken brain in neurobiological terms indicating the cause or realisation of the mental illness. Well, there certainly are conditions – Parkinsonism, Alzheimer's and various neurological disorders – that can be so described, or will eventually be so described. But they *are* neurological conditions, and though they may still appear as mental disorders in the Psychiatric Diagnostic Manuals, they shouldn't.[5] Mental disorders are not akin (or not close kin) to these neurological afflictions. The evidence for radical reduction, as we said, is thin, but some degree of neurobiological damage in at least some cases can be conceded. The chief issue, however, is not whether there can be *any* neurobiological involvement, but whether neurobiological description can provide *complete* or exhaustive characterisations of mental disorder.

The case for neurobiology falling short must of necessity be made here swiftly and a little loosely. *Mental* disorders are characterised essentially by their irrationality: recall the anxious scientist, the bedstead girl and the exhibitionist. Where there is irrationality there are norms that are transgressed and rational behaviour; where there is rational behaviour there are reasons, beliefs, desires, fears and intentions – the Intentional concepts from which we have constructed our account of Freudian wish-fulfilment. There are strong arguments to the conclusion that at least many of these concepts cannot be reduced to or replaced by neurobiological ones, so a description in terms of the latter will always be incomplete.

On one plausible line of thought (referred to in philosophy as 'mental externalism'), Intentional content is at least partly determined by conditions which lie outside the brain; so every description of the brain, no matter how detailed, will fall short of capturing their content. Let me abridge and alter slightly a famous thought experiment owed to Donald Davidson (1987). D is in a swamp when struck by lightning. A tree next to him is transformed into a perfect, molecule-for-molecule, replica of D. This is the swampman. The swampman decides to go home, D's home. Can he recognise D's house? No, he can't. In order to re-cognise the house he would have to have cognised it in the first place. But the swampman has never set his eyes on it. One lesson, not the only lesson, that can be drawn from this example is that mental content (so-called wide content) cannot be ascribed on the basis of neural conditions alone. The swampman's neural condition is identical to D's. D can recognise his house, but the swampman can't. Hence, though neurally identical, their mental content differs. We need not conclude with Davidson that the swampman can have no Intentional states at all; it suffices to see that at least some mental content cannot be caught in descriptions of the brain, no matter how complete. We can't describe what is in the mind without having to refer to what is outside the brain, at least sometimes. Some mental content is wide, and most content of interest in psychiatry (recall *humiliation*) appears to be wide. It follows that the Intentional idiom is indispensable for a complete characterisation of mental states and therefore of the irrational mental states encountered in mental illness. So goes one compelling line of thought; there are others arriving at the same end.

Is the Intentional idiom *sufficient* to characterise mental illness, the major disorders, at least? Mostly philosophers have thought not. George Graham (2010), for example, has argued persuasively for the necessity of Intentional characterisation and rejected reductive 'neuralism'. But he also insists that a full explanation requires reference to the intrusion of brute, a-rational neural causes or mechanisms. That is what 'gums up the works' and renders the disorder involuntary and unintended, and the patient 'unreason-responsive' (2010: 47). Graham develops a 'mixed theory' of mental disorder: 'the gum or disorder of disorder... consists (in part) of non-rational/a-rational/mechanical/brute neural forces irrupting into the space of a person's reasons or Intentionality and being partly responsible for the truncation or impairment in reason and rational control that helps constitute a disorder' (2010: 126). In other words, the brain is only a little bit broken.

The evidence for the brain being a little bit broken is about the same as it is for it being a lot broken; good for some disorders in some people, bad in others. Graham offers few hints, references to neurochemical imbalances and the like figure in the slight discussion of this issue **(6.5)**. It is surely problematic for his view that there are cases of people suffering schizophrenia, florid delusions and major depression in which there is no evidence of their brains being even a little bit broken. Still, his 'mixed' way is probably the right way, at least for the most serious of symptoms at the psychotic end of the spectrum; but no further. His reasons for adopting it, however, appear to be determined less by the evidence from neurobiology than by the philosophical rejection of unconscious motivation and dirempted selves.

Non-Intentional (and non-intentionalist) views dominate the current philosophical understanding of mental illness and other irrational phenomena. I have tried to show in this book how much can be achieved using only Intentional concepts, drawing upon psychoanalytic theory and an extended role for unconscious intentionality, in explaining the large class of phenomena that Freud a long time ago brought under the rubric of wish-fulfilment.

Notes

1 William Shakespeare, 'Sonnet CXXIX', available online at http://www.poetryfoundation. org/poem/174374 (accessed 24 January 2014).
2 The phrase 'biomedical' seems to me a misnomer since neo-Kraepelinian nosology, based largely on descriptive criteria, on classes of syndromes or traits, and ignoring almost altogether aetiological considerations, is scarcely medical. A more accurate term for the modern orthodoxy might be *psychopharmacological psychiatry*, since the influence of the availability of drug treatments on nosology, treatment and aetiological understanding has been utterly penetrating and profound. See e.g. Bentall 2004, 2010; Graham 2010; Healy 2008; Lane 2007.
3 Leibniz's law breaks down for relational properties. The Evening Star (Venus) is worshipped by some people; the Evening Star is the Morning Star, but the latter is not worshipped – not on *de dicto* constructions anyway.
4 Bentall (2004) marshals a huge array of sceptical evidence against the neurobiological view. See also Fonagy *et al.* 2004: ch. 3; Healy 2008; Kleinman 1988; Lane 2007; Graham 2010.
5 Graham (2010) is excellent on this issue.

Bibliography

Alexander, F. and Selesnick, S. (1966) *The History of Psychiatry*, New York: Mentor Books.

APA (American Psychiatric Association) (1994) *Diagnostic and Statistical Manual of Mental Disorders* (4th ed.), Washington DC: APA.

Ambrose, Alice (1970) 'Philosophy, language and illusion' in Hanly, C. and Lazerowitz, M. (eds) *Psychoanalysis and Philosophy*, New York: International Universities Press.

Anscombe, G. E. M. (1957) *Intention*, Oxford: Basil Blackwell.

Armstrong, D. M. (1973) *Belief, Truth and Knowledge*, London: Cambridge University Press.

Bacon, Francis (1854 [1620]), *Novum Organum*, in Montague, B. (ed.), *The Works, Vol. 3* (pp. 343–71), Philadelphia, PA: Parry & Macmillan.

Baker, L. R. (1995) *Explaining Attitudes*, Cambridge: Cambridge University Press.

Bennett, M. R. and Hacker, P. M. S. (2003) *Philosophical Foundations of Neuroscience*, Malden, MA: Blackwell.

Bentall, R. P. (2004) *Explaining Madness: Psychosis and Human Nature*, London: Penguin.

Bentall, R. P. (2010) *Doctoring the Mind*, London: Penguin.

Bering, J. (2011) *The God Instinct*, London: Nicholas Brearley Publishing.

Bion, W. R. (1984 [1967]) *Second Thoughts*, London: Karnac.

Blackford, R. and Schuklenk, U. (eds) (2009) *50 Voices of Disbelief*, Oxford: Wiley-Blackwell.

Boag, S. (2005 [2001]) 'Addressing mental plurality: justification, objections and logical requirements of strongly partitive accounts of mind' in Mackay, N. and Petocz, A (eds) *Realism and Psychology* (pp. 727–54), Boston: Brill.

Bollas, C. (1987) *The Shadow of the Object*, New York: Columbia University Press.

Bonett, W. (ed.) (2010) *The Australian Book of Atheism*, Melbourne: Scribe.

Bowlby, J. (1971 [1969]) *Attachment: Attachment and Loss, Vol. 1*, Harmondsworth: Penguin.

Bowlby, J. (1998 [1980]) *Loss: Sadness and Depression, Vol. 3 Attachment and Loss*, London: Pimlico.

Boyer, P. (2002) *Religion Explained*, London: Vintage Books.

Brakel, L. A. W. (2009) *Philosophy, Psychoanalysis, and the A-rational Mind*, Oxford: Oxford University Press.

Brook, A. (2003) 'Kant and Freud' in Chung, M. C. and Feltham, C. (eds) *Psychoanalytic Knowledge* (pp. 20–39), London: Palgrave Macmillan.

Burkert, Walter (2004) *Babylon Memphis Persepolis: Eastern Contexts of Greek Culture*, Harvard, MA: Harvard University Press.

Capps, D. (1995) *The Child's Song*, Louisville: Westminster John Knox Press.

Carhart-Harris, R. L. and Friston, K. J. (2012) 'Free-energy and Freud' in Fotopoulou, A., Pfaff, D. and Conway, M. A. (eds) *From the Couch to the Lab: Trends in Psychodynamic Neuroscience* (pp. 219–29), Oxford: Oxford University Press.

Cassidy, J. and Shaver, P. R. (eds) (1999) *Handbook of Attachment,* New York: Guildford Press.

Cavell, M. (1993) *The Psychoanalytic Mind,* Cambridge, MA: Harvard University Press.

Cavell, M. (2006) *Becoming a Subject,* Oxford: Clarendon Press.

Chung, M. C. and Feltham, C. (2003) *Psychoanalytic Knowledge,* London: Palgrave Macmillan.

Clarke, G. S. (2006) *Personal Relations Theory,* London: Routledge.

Collins, A. W. (1979) 'Could our beliefs be representations in our brains?', *The Journal of Philosophy* LXXVI: 225–243.

Cox, D., Levine, M. and Newman, S. (2009) *Politics Most Unusual,* Basingstoke: Palgrave Macmillan.

Damasio, A. (1999) *The Feeling of What Happens,* San Diego: Harcourt.

Dante, A. (2013) *Inferno,* London: Sovereign.

Dawkins, R. (2006) *The God Delusion,* New York: Houghton Mifflin Company.

Davidson, D. (1975) 'Thought and talk' in S. Guttenplan, *Mind and Language* (pp. 7–23), (ed.) Oxford: Oxford University Press.

Davidson, D. (1980 [1963]) 'Actions, reasons and causes' in *Essays on Action and Events* (pp. 3–20), Oxford: Clarendon Press.

Davidson, D. (1980 [1967]) 'The logical form of action sentences' in *Essays on Action and Events* (pp. 105–21), Oxford: Clarendon Press.

Davidson, D. (1980) *Essays on Action and Events,* Oxford: Clarendon Press.

Davidson, D. (1982a) 'Paradoxes of irrationality', in Wollheim, R. and Hopkins, J. (eds) *Freud: A Collection of Critical Essays* (2nd ed.) (pp. 289–305), New York: Anchor.

Davidson, D. (2001 [1982b]) 'Rational animals' in Davidson, D. *Subjective, Intersubjective, Objective* (pp. 95–106), Oxford: Clarendon Press.

Davidson, D. (1987) 'Knowing one's own mind' in Cassam, Q. (ed.), *Self-Knowledge* (pp. 43–64), Oxford: Oxford University Press.

Dennett, D. C. (1989) *The Intentional Stance,* Cambridge, MA: MIT Press.

Dennett, D. C. (2006) *Breaking the Spell,* Harmondsworth: Penguin.

Descartes, R. (1972 [1642]) *Meditations on First Philosophy,* in Anscombe, E. and Geach, P. T. (eds) *Descartes' Philosophical Writings* (pp. 59–124), London: Nelson 1972.

De Sousa, R. (1976) 'Rational homunculi', in Rorty, A. (ed.) *The Identities of Persons* (pp. 217–38), Berkeley: University of California Press.

Dickens, Charles (1970) 'Introduction', in *David Copperfield (*pp. xix–xx), London: *Heron Books.*

Dodds, E. R. (1951) *The Greeks and the Irrational,* Berkeley: University of California Press.

Dolimore, J. (2001) *Death, Desire and Loss in Western Culture,* New York: Routledge.

Eagle, M. (1984) *Recent Developments in Psychoanalysis,* Cambridge, MA: Harvard University Press.

Eagle, M. (2011) *From Classical to Contemporary Psychoanalysis,* New York: Routledge.

Ellenberger, H. F. (1970) *The Discovery of the Unconscious,* New York: Basic Books.

Epicurus (n.d.) *Fragments.* Available online at http://www.epicurus.info/etexts/fragments.html (accessed 21 January 2014).

Fairbairn, W. R. D. (1931) 'Features in the analysis of a patient with a physical genital abnormality' in *Psychoanalytic Studies of the Personality* (pp. 197–221), London: Routledge-Kegan Paul.

Fairbairn, W. R. D. (1976 [1952]) *Psychoanalytic Studies of the Personality,* London: Routledge-Kegan Paul.

Fenichel, O. (1945) *The Psychoanalytic Theory of Neurosis,* New York: W. W. Norton.

Ferenczi, S. (1956 [1909]) 'Introjection and transference' in *Sex in Psychoanalysis* (pp. 30–79), New York: Dover.

Ferenczi, S. (1956 [1913]) 'Stages in the development of a sense of reality' in *Sex in Psychoanalysis* (pp. 181–203), New York: Dover.

Fingarette, H. (1972) *The Meaning of Criminal Insanity*, Berkeley: University of California Press.

Fonagy, P., Gergely, G., Jurist, E. and Target, M. (2004) *Affect Regulation, Mentalization, and the Development of the Self*, New York: Other Books.

Fotopoulou, A., Pfaff, D. and Conway, M. A. (eds) (2012) *From the Couch to the Lab: Trends in Psychodynamic Neuroscience*, Oxford: Oxford University Press.

Freud, S. (1892–93) 'A case of successful treatment by hypnotism'. SE, I.

Freud, S. (1894a) 'The neuro-psychoses of defence'. SE, III.

Freud, S. (1895d) (with Joseph Breuer) *Studies in Hysteria*. SE, II.

Freud, S. (1900a) *The Interpretation of Dreams*. SE, IV,V.

Freud, S. (1901b) *The Psychopathology of Everyday Life*. SE, VI.

Freud, S. (1905d) *Three Essays on the Theory of Sexuality*. SE, VII.

Freud, S. (1907b) 'Obsessive actions and religious practices'. SE, IX.

Freud, S. (1908a) 'Hysterical phantasies and their relation to bisexuality'. SE, IX.

Freud, S. (1908e) 'Creative writers and daydreaming'. SE, IX.

Freud, S. (1909a) 'Some general remarks on hysterical attacks'. SE, IX.

Freud, S. (1909d) 'Notes upon a case of obsessional neurosis'. SE, X.

Freud, S. (1910c) *Leonardo Da Vinci and a Memory of His Childhood*. SE, XI.

Freud, S. (1911b) 'Formulations on the two principles of mental functioning'. SE, XII.

Freud, S. (1911e) 'The handling of dream interpretation in psychoanalysis'. SE, XII.

Freud, S. (1912f) 'Contributions to a discussion on masturbation'. SE, XII.

Freud, S. (1912g) 'A note on the unconscious'. SE, XII.

Freud, S. (1912–13) *Totem and Taboo*. SE, XIII.

Freud, S. (1913j) 'The claims of psychoanalysis to scientific interest'. SE, XIII.

Freud, S. (1914c) 'On narcissism; an introduction'. SE, XIV.

Freud, S. (1915c) 'Instincts and their vicissitudes'. SE, XIV.

Freud, S. (1915e) 'The unconscious'. SE, XIV.

Freud, S. (1916–17) *Introductory Lectures on Psychoanalysis*. SE, XV-XVI.

Freud, S. (1917d) 'A metapsychological supplement to the theory of dreams'. SE, XIV.

Freud, S. (1921b) 'Introduction to Varendock, *The Psychology of Daydreams*'. SE, XVIII.

Freud, S. (1921c) *Group Psychology and the Analysis of the Ego*. SE, XVIII.

Freud, S. (1922b) 'Neurotic mechanisms in jealousy, paranoia and homosexuality'. SE, XVIII.

Freud, S. (1923b) *The Ego and the Id*. SE, XIX.

Freud, S. (1923c) 'Remarks on the theory and practice of dream interpretation'. SE, XIX.

Freud, S. (1924b) 'Neurosis and psychosis'. SE, XIX.

Freud, S. (1924e) 'The loss of reality in neurosis and psychosis'. SE, XIX.

Freud, S. (1925d) *An Autobiographical Study*. SE, XX.

Freud, S. (1925i) 'Some additional notes on dream interpretation'. SE, XIX.

Freud, S. (1926d) *Inhibitions, Symptoms and Anxiety*. SE, XX.

Freud, S. (1926f) 'Psychoanalysis'. SE, XX.

Freud, S. (1927c) *The Future of an Illusion*. SE, XXI.

Freud, S. (1927e) 'Fetishism'. SE, XXI.

Freud, S. (1928c) 'On humour'. SE, XXI.

Freud, S. (1930a) *Civilization and its Discontents*. SE, XXI.

Freud, S. (1933a) *New Introductory Lectures on Psychoanalysis*. SE, XXII.

Freud, S. (1937c) 'Analysis terminable and interminable'. SE, XXIII.

Freud, S. (1939a) *Moses and Monotheism*. SE, XXIII.

Freud, S. (1940a) *An Outline of Psychoanalysis*. SE, XXIII.

Freud, S. (1950a [1887–1902]) *The Origins of Psychoanalysis*. SE, I.

Gardner, S. (1991) 'The unconscious' in Neu, J. (ed.) *The Cambridge Companion to Freud* (pp. 136–60), Cambridge: Cambridge University Press.

Gardner, S. (1993) *Irrationality and the Philosophy of Psychoanalysis*, Cambridge: Cambridge University Press.

Ghaemi, S. N. (2007) *The Concepts of Psychiatry*, Baltimore, MD: John Hopkins University Press.

Gill, M. and Holzman, P. (eds) (1976) *Psychology versus Metapsychology*, New York: International Universities Press.

Glymour, C. (1991) 'Freud's androids' in Neu, J. (ed.) *The Cambridge Companion to Freud* (pp. 44–85), Cambridge: Cambridge University Press 1991.

Goldman, A. I. (1970) *A Theory of Human Action*, New Jersey: Prentice-Hall.

Graham, G. (2010) *The Disordered Mind*, New York: Routledge.

Griesinger, W. (1867) *Mental Pathology and Therapeutics*, London: The New Sydenham Society.

Grotstein, J. S. (2009) *But at the Same Time and on Another Level*, London: Karnac.

Grunbaum, A. (1984) *The Foundations of Psychoanalysis*, Berkeley: University of California Press.

Guntrip, H. (1973 [1961]) *Personality Structure and Human Interaction*, London: Hogarth.

Guntrip, H. (1977 [1968]) *Schizoid Phenomena, Object Relations and the Self*, London: Hogarth.

Guthrie, S. E. (2007) 'Anthropological theories of religion' in Martin, M. (ed.) *The Cambridge Companion to Atheism* (pp. 283–99), Cambridge: Cambridge University Press. 2007.

Haldane, John (2005) *An Intelligent Person's Guide to Religion*, London: Duckworth.

Hampshire, S. (1974) 'Disposition and memory' in Wollheim, R. (ed.) *Freud: A Collection of Critical Essays* (pp. 113–31), New York: Anchor Books.

Hanly, C. and Lazerowitz, M. (1970) (eds) *Psychoanalysis and Philosophy*, New York: International Universities Press.

Hartmann, H. (1958 [1939]) *Ego Psychology and the Problem of Adaptation*, New York: International Universities Press.

Hartmann, H. (1947) 'On rational and irrational action' in *Essays in Ego Psychology* (pp. 37–68), New York: International Universities Press.

Hartmann, H. (1948) 'Comments on the psychoanalytic theory of instinctual drives' in *Essays in Ego Psychology* (pp. 69–89), New York: International Universities Press.

Hartmann, H. (1964) *Essays in Ego Psychology*, New York: International Universities Press.

Hartmann, H., Kris, E. and Loewenstein, R. (eds) (1964) *Papers on Psychoanalytic Psychology*, New York: International Universities Press.

Healy, D. (2008) *Mania: A Short History of Bipolar Disorder*, Baltimore, MD: John Hopkins University Press.

Hitchens, Christopher (2007) *God is not Great: How Religion Poisons Everything*, London: Allen and Unwin.

Holmes, Jeremy (2010) *Exploring in Security*, Hove: Routledge.

Holt, R. R. (1976) 'Drive or wish?: A reconsideration of the psychoanalytic theory of motivation' in Gill, M. and Holzman, P. (eds) *Psychology versus Metapsychology* (pp. 158–97), New York: International Universities Press.

Holt, R. R. (1989) *Freud Reappraised*, New York: Guildford Press.

Hook, S. (1959) *Psychoanalysis, Scientific Method and Philosophy*, New York: New York University Press.

Hopkins, J. (1982) 'Introduction: Philosophy and psychoanalysis' in Wollheim, R. and Hopkins, J. (eds) *Philosophical Essays on Freud* (pp. vii–xlv), Cambridge: Cambridge University Press.

Hopkins, J. (1988) 'Epistemology and depth psychology' in Clark, P. and Wright, C. (eds) *Mind, Psychoanalysis and Science* (pp. 33–60), Oxford: Blackwell.

Hopkins, J. (1994) 'The unconscious' in Guttenplan, S. (ed.) *A Companion to Philosophy of Mind* (pp. 598–607), Oxford: Blackwell.

Hopkins, J. (1995) 'Irrationality, interpretation and division' in McDonald, C. and McDonald G. (eds) *Philosophy of Psychology* (pp. 409–32), Oxford: Blackwell.

Hopkins, J. (2012) 'Psychoanalysis, representation, and neuroscience: The Freudian unconscious and the Bayesian brain' in Fotopoulou, A., Pfaff, D. and Conway, M. A. (eds) *From the Couch to the Lab: Trends in Psychodynamic Neuroscience* (pp. 230–65), Oxford: Oxford University Press.

Hopkins, J. (2013) 'Understanding and healing: Psychiatry and psychoanalysis in the era of neuroscience', in Fulford, K. W. M., Davies, M., Gipps, R., Graham, G. Sadler, J., Stanghellini, G. and Thornton, T. (eds) *Oxford Handbook of Philosophy and Psychiatry* (pp. 1264–92), Oxford: Oxford University Press.

Hunt, H. T. (1989) *The Multiplicity of the Dream*, New Haven: Yale University Press.

Huysmans, J.-K. (1959) *Against Nature*, London: Penguin.

Isaacs, S. (1952 [1948]) 'The nature and function of phantasy', in Riviere, J. (ed.) *Developments in Psychoanalysis* (pp. 67–121), London: Hogarth.

James, W. (1950 [1890]) *The Principles of Psychology*, New York: Dover Books.

James, W. (1971 [1901–2] *The Varieties of Religious Experience*, London: Fontana.

Jaspers, K. (1997 [1913]) *General Psychology*, translated by J. Hoenig and M. W. Hamilton, Baltimore, MD: John Hopkins University Press.

Johnston, M. (1988) 'Self-deception and the nature of mind' in Rorty, A. and McLaughlin, B. P. (eds) *Perspectives on Self-Deception* (pp. 63–91), Berkeley: University of California.

Jones, E. (1913 [1974]) 'The God complex' in *Psycho-Myth, Psycho-History* (pp. 244–65), New York: Stonehill Publishing Company.

Kaplan-Solms, K. and Solms, M. (2000) *Clinical Studies in Neuro-Psychoanalysis*, London: Karnac.

Kelly, J. M. (1992) *A Short History of Western Legal Theory*, New York: Oxford University Press.

Kenny, A. (1963) *Action, Emotion and Will*, London: Routledge and Kegan Paul.

Kendler, K. S. and Prescott, C. A. (2006) *Genes, Environment and Psychopathology*, New York: The Guilford Press.

Kernberg, O. F. (1966) 'Structural derivatives and object-relationships', *International Journal of Psychoanalysis* 47, pp. 236–53.

Kernberg, O. F. (1975) *Borderline Conditions and Pathological Narcissism*, New York: Jason Aronson.

Kirkpatrick, Lee A. (1999) 'Attachment and religious representations of behaviour' in Cassidy, J. and Shaver, P. R. (eds) *Handbook of Attachment* (pp. 803–22), New York: Guildford Press.

Kitcher, P. (1992) *Freud's Dream*, Cambridge, MA: MIT Press.

Klein, M. (1930) 'The importance of symbol formation in the development of the ego' in *Love, Guilt and Reparation* (pp. 219–32), London: Hogarth.

Klein, M. (1975a [1929]) 'Personification in the play of children' in *Love, Guilt and Reparation* (pp. 199–209), London: Hogarth.

Klein, M. (1975b [1952]) 'Some theoretical conclusions regarding the emotional life of the infant' in *Envy and Gratitude* (pp. 61–93), London: Hogarth.

Klein, M. (1975c) *Love, Guilt and Reparation*, London: Hogarth.

Klein, M. (1975d) *Envy and Gratitude*, London: Hogarth.

Kleinman, A. (1988) *Rethinking Psychiatry*, New York: The Free Press.

Kneale, W. (1968) 'Intentionality and intensionality', *Proceedings of the Aristotelian Society* 73, pp. 73–90.

Kohut, H. (1978a [1948]) '*Death in Venice* by Thomas Mann: A story about the disintegration of artistic sublimation' in *The Search for the Self* (pp. 107–30), New York: International Universities Press.

Kohut, H. (1978b [1976]) 'Creativeness, charisma, group psychology' in *The Search for the Self* (pp. 793–843), New York: International Universities Press.

Kris, E. (1952) *Psychoanalytic Explorations in Art*, New York: Schocken Books.

Kumin, I. (1996) *Pre-object Relatedness*, New York: Guildford Press.

Lane, C. (2007) *Shyness: How Normal Behaviour Became a Sickness*, New Haven, CT: Yale University Press.

Lear, J. (1995) 'The heterogeneity of the mental', *Mind*, 104 (416), pp. 863–79.

Lear, J. (1998a) 'Restlessness, phantasy and the concept of mind' in *Open Minded* (pp. 80–122), Cambridge, MA: Harvard University Press.

Lear, J. (1998b) *Open Minded*, Cambridge, MA: Harvard University Press.

Levine, M. (ed.) (2000) *The Analytic Freud*, London: Routledge.

Levine, M. (2004) 'Philosophy and racism' in Levine, M. and Pataki, T. (eds) *Racism in Mind* (pp. 78–96), Ithaca, NY: Cornell University Press.

Levine, M. and Pataki, T. (2004) *Racism in Mind*, Ithaca, NY: Cornell University Press.

Libet, B. (2004) *Mind Time*, Cambridge, MA: Harvard University Press.

Locke, J. (1968 [1706]) *An Essay Concerning Human Understanding*, London: Dent and Sons.

McDougall, J. (1986) *Theatres of the Mind*, London: Free Association Books.

Mackay, N. and Petocz, A. (eds) (2011) *Realism and Psychology: Collected Essays, Leiden: Brill*.

McLaughlin, B. P. (1988) 'Exploring the possibility of self-deception in belief' in McLaughlin, B. P. and Rorty, A. O. (eds) *Perspectives on Self-Deception* (pp. 29–62), Berkeley: University of California Press.

McLaughlin, B. P. and Rorty, A. O. (eds) (1988) *Perspectives on Self-Deception*, Berkeley: University of California Press.

McTaggart, J. M. E. (2012 [1906]) *Some Dogmas of Religion*, London: Forgotten Books.

Maddox, M. (2005) *God Under Howard*, Crows Nest: Allen and Unwin.

Mahler, Margaret S. (1968) *On Human Symbiosis and the Vicissitudes of Individuation*, New York: International Universities Press.

Makari, G. (2008) *Revolution in Mind: The Creation of Psychoanalysis*, Melbourne: Melbourne University Press.

Marshall, G. (2000) 'How far down does the will go' in Levine, M. (ed.) (2000) *The Analytic Freud* (pp. 36–46), London and New York: Routledge.

Martin, M. (ed.) (2007) *The Cambridge Companion to Atheism*, Cambridge: Cambridge University Press.

Martin, R. and Barresi, J. (2006) *The Rise and Fall of Soul and Self: An Intellectual History of Personal Identity*, New York: Columbia University Press.

Maze, J. (2009) *Psychologies of Mind*, London: Continuum Books.

Mele, A. (1987) 'Recent work on self-deception', *American Philosophical Quarterly* 24 (1), pp. 1–17.

Mele, A. (2009) *Effective Intentions: The Power of Conscious Will*, Oxford: Oxford University Press.

Mill, J. S. (1865) *An Examination of Sir William Hamilton's Philosophy*, London: Longman, Green, Longman, Roberts & Green.

Mitchell, S. A. (1993) *Hope and Dread in Psychoanalysis*, New York: Basic Books.

Moore, M. (1984) *Law and Psychiatry*, Cambridge: Cambridge University Press.

Moran, R. (1981) *Knowing Right from Wrong: The Insanity Defense of Daniel McNaughtan*, New York: Free Press.

Nabokov, Vladimir (1969) *Speak, Memory: An Autobiography Revisited*, Harmondsworth: Penguin.

Neu, J. (ed.) (1991) *The Cambridge Companion to Freud*, Cambridge: Cambridge University Press.

Nietzsche, F. (1966 [1886]) *Beyond Good and Evil*, in Kaufmann, W. (ed.) *Basic Writings of Nietzsche* (pp. 179–436), New York: The Modern Library.

Nietzsche, F. (1994 [1878]) Human, *All Too Human, Lincoln*, London: Penguin Books.

Newberry, G. (2010) 'Drive theory reconsidered (again)' in Mackay, N. and Petocz, A. (eds) *Realism and Psychology* (pp. 839–71), Leiden: Brill.

Ogden, T. H. (1993 [1986]) *The Matrix of the Mind*, Northville, NJ: Jason Aronson.

O'Shaughnessy, B. (1980) *The Will: A Dual Aspect Theory*, Cambridge: Cambridge University Press.

Panksepp, J. (1998) *Affective Neuroscience: The Foundations of Human and Animal Emotions*, New York: Oxford University Press.

Panksepp, J. and Biven, L. (2012) *The Archaeology of Mind: Neuroevolutionary Origins of Human Emotions*, New York: W. W. Norton.

Pataki, T. (1996a) 'Psychoanalysis, psychiatry, philosophy', *Quadrant* 40 (4), pp. 52–63.

Pataki, T. (1996b) 'Intention in wish-fulfilment', *Australasian Journal of Philosophy* 74 (1), pp. 20–37.

Pataki, T. (1997) 'Self-deception and wish-fulfilment', *Philosophia* 25 (1–4), pp. 297–322.

Pataki, T. (1998) 'Review of *Irrationality and the Philosophy of Psychoanalysis* (Gardner 1993) and *The Psychoanalytic Mind: From Freud to Philosophy* (Cavell 1993) in *Australasian Journal of Philosophy* 76 (4), pp. 644–47.

Pataki, T. (2000) 'Freudian wishfulfilment and subintentional explanation' in Levine, M. (ed.) *The Analytic Freud* (pp. 49–84), London: Routledge.

Pataki, T. (2003) 'Freud, object relations, agency and the self' in Chung, M. C. and Feltham, C. (eds) *Psychoanalytic Knowledge* (pp. 157–80), Houndmills: Palgrave.

Pataki, T. (2004a) 'Psychoanalysis, racism, and envy' in Levine, M. and Pataki, T., *Racism in Mind* (pp. 179–208), Ithaca, NY: Cornell University Press.

Pataki, T. (2004b) 'Introduction to *Racism in Mind*' in Levine, M. and Pataki, T., *Racism in Mind* (pp. 1–26), Ithaca, NY: Cornell University Press.

Pataki, T. (2006) 'Intention, excuse and insanity' in Mason, T. (ed.), *Forensic Psychiatry: Influences of Evil* (pp. 67–88), Totowa, NJ: Humana Press.

Pataki, T. (2007) *Against Religion*, Melbourne: Scribe Publications.

Pataki, T. (2009) 'Some thoughts on why I am an atheist' in Blackford, R. and Schuklenk, U. (eds), *Voices of Disbelief* (pp. 204–10), London: Blackwell.

Pataki, T. (2010) 'Religion and violence' in Bonnet, Warren (ed.), *The Australian Book of Atheism* (pp. 385–402), Melbourne: Scribe 2010.

PDM Task Force (2006) *Psychodynamic Diagnostic Manual*, Silver Spring, MD: Alliance of Psychoanalytic Organizations.

Pears, D. (1984) *Motivated Irrationality*, Oxford: Clarendon Press.

Pereira, F. and Scharff, D. E. (eds) (2002) *Fairbairn and Relational Theory*, London: Karnac.

Perner, J. (1991) *Understanding the Representational Mind*, Cambridge, MA: MIT Press.

Petocz, A. (1999) *Freud, Psychoanalysis and Symbolism*, Cambridge: Cambridge University Press.

Plato (1966) *Republic*, Cambridge: Cambridge University Press.

Plato (2009) *Protagoras*, Rockville, MD: Serenity.

Post, J. M. (2007) *The Mind of the Terrorist*, London: Palgrave Macmillan.

Price, H. H. (1975 [1954]) 'Belief and will' in Dearden, R., Hirst, P. and Peters, R. (eds) *Reason* (pp. 198–217), London: Routledge-Kegan Paul.

Radden, J. (2011) *On Delusion*, New York: Routledge.

Ramsey, F. P. (1931) *The Foundations of Mathematics, and Other Logical Essays*, London: Routledge.

Rappaport, D. (1971) *Emotions and Memory*, Topeka, KS: International Universities Press.

Rickman, J. (1940) 'On the nature of ugliness and the creative impulse', *International Journal of Psychoanalysis* 21, pp. 294–313.

Robinson, D. N. (1998) *Wild Beasts and Idle Humours: The Insanity Defense from Antiquity to the Present*, Harvard, MA: Harvard University Press.

Ronningstam, E. F. (2000) *Disorders of Narcissism*, Northvale, NJ: Jason Aronson Inc.

Rorty, A. (1988) 'The deceptive self: liars, layers and lairs' in McLaughlin, B. P. and Rorty, A. (eds) *Perspectives on Self-Deception* (pp. 11–28), Berkeley: University of California Press.

Rorty, A. and McLaughlin, B. P. (eds) (1988) *Perspectives on Self-Deception*, Berkeley: University of California Press.

Rosenfeld, H. (1987) *Impasse and Interpretation*, London: Tavistock.

Russell, B. (1921a) 'Introduction' in Wittgenstein, L., *Tractatus Logico-Philosophicus* (pp. 4–39), London: Routledge and Kegan Paul.

Russell, B. (1921b) *The Analysis of Mind*, London: George Allen and Unwin.

Ruthven, M. (2004) *Fundamentalism*, Oxford: Oxford University Press.

Rycroft, C. (1979) *The Innocence of Dreams*, London: Pantheon Books.

Sandler, J. (1976) 'Dreams, unconscious fantasies and "identity of perception"', *International Review of Psychoanalysis* 3 (1), pp. 33–42.

Sandler, J. and Sandler, A. M. (1978) 'The development of object-relationships and affects', *International Journal of Psychoanalysis* 59 (2), pp. 285–96.

Sandler, J. and Sandler, A. M. (1998) *Internal Objects Revisited*, London: International Universities Press.

Sartre, J-P. (1969) *Being and Nothingness*, London: Methuen.

Schafer, R. (1976) *A New Language for Psychoanalysis*, New Haven, CT: Yale University Press.

Schore, A. (1994) *Affect Regulation and the Origin of the Self*, Hillsdale, NJ: Lawrence Erlbaum Associates.

Schore, A. (2003) *Affect Regulation and the Repair of the Self*, New York: W. W. Norton.

Schroeder, T. (2004) *Three Faces of Desire*, New York: Oxford University Press.

Schopenhauer, A. (1966 [1844]) *The World as Will and Representation, Vol. II*, New York: Dover Books.

Segal, H. (1964) *An Introduction to Melanie Klein's Work*, London: Hogarth.

Segal, Hanna. (1986 [1957]) 'Notes on symbol formation', reprinted in *Delusion and Artistic Creativity and Other Essays* (pp. 49–65). London: FreeAssociation Books 1986.

Segal, H. (1986) *Delusion and Artistic Creativity and Other Essays*, London: FreeAssociation Books.

Segal, H. (1986 [1981]) 'A psychoanalytic approach to aesthetics' in *Delusion and Artistic Creativity and Other Essays* (pp. 185–205), London: Free Association Books.

Segal, H. (1991) *Dream, Phantasy and Art*, London: Tavistock Routledge.

Shope, R. K. (1967) 'The psychoanalytic theories of wish-fulfilment and meaning', *Inquiry* 10 (1–4), pp. 421–38.

Shope, R. K. (1970) 'Freud on conscious and unconscious intentions', *Inquiry* 13, 149–59.

Smith, D. L. (2003) '"Some Unimaginable Substratum": A contemporary introduction to Freud's philosophy of mind' in Chung, M. C. and Feltham, C. (eds) *Psychoanalytic Knowledge* (pp. 54–75), London: Palgrave Macmillan.

Snelling, D. (2000) 'Subject, object, world: Some reflections on the Kleinian origins of mind' in Levine, M. (ed.) *The Analytic Freud* (pp. 101–18), London: Routledge 2000.

Solms, M. and Turnbull, O. (2002) *The Brain and the Inner World*, New York: Other Press.

Solms, M. and Zellner, M. R. (2012a) 'Freudian drive theory today' in Fotopoulou, A., Pfaff, D. and Conway, M. A. (eds) *From the Couch to the Lab: Trends in Psychodynamic Neuroscience* (pp. 49–63), Oxford: Oxford University Press.

Solms, M. and Zellner, M. R. (2012b) 'Freudian affect theory today' in Fotopoulou, A., Pfaff, D. and Conway, M. A. (eds) *From the Couch to the Lab: Trends in Psychodynamic Neuroscience* (pp. 133–44), Oxford: Oxford University Press.

Sorabji, R. (2006), *Self: Ancient and Modern Insights about Individuality, Life and Death*, Chicago: University of Chicago Press.

Spillius, E. B., Milton, J., Garvey, P., Couve, C. and Steiner, D. (2011), *The New Dictionary of Kleinian Thought*, New York: Routledge.

Spitz, R. (1965) *The First Year of Life*, New York: International Universities Press.

Steiner, J. (1982) 'Perverse relationships between parts of the self', *International Journal of Psychoanalysis* 63 (3), pp. 241–51.

Steiner, J. (1993) *Psychic Retreats: Pathological Organizations in Psychotic, Neurotic and Borderline Organizations*, London: Routledge.

Stern, D. N. (2000 [1985]) *The Interpersonal World of the Infant*, New York: Basic Books.

Stoller, R. J. (1979) *Sexual Excitement*, New York: Simon and Schuster.

Strawson, Galen (2009) *Selves*, Oxford: Clarendon Press.

Sulloway, F. J. (1992) *Freud, Biologist of the Mind: Beyond the Psychoanalytic Legend*, Harvard, MA: Harvard University Press.

Symington, N. (1993) *Narcissism: A New Theory*, London: Karnac.

Tauber, A. I. (2010) *Freud: the Reluctant Philosopher*, Princeton, NJ: Princeton University Press.

Thalberg, I. (1974) 'Freud's anatomies of the self' in Wollheim (ed.) *Freud: A Collection of Critical Essays* (pp. 147–71), New York: Anchor Books.

Thomson Jnr, J. Anderson (2011) *Why We Believe in Gods*, Charlottesville, VA: Pitchstone Publishing.

Tomasello, M. (1999) *The Cultural Origins of Human Cognition*, Cambridge, MA: Harvard University Press.

Trivers, R. (2011) *Deceit and Self-Deception*, London: Penguin Books.

Trocme, Etienne (1997) *The Childhood of Christianity*, London: SCM Press.

Weiss, J. and Sampson, H. (1986) *The Psychoanalytic Process*, New York: International Universities Press.

Wegner, D. (2002) *The Illusion of Conscious Will*, Cambridge, MA: MIT Press.

Whisner, W. (1992) 'Self-deception and other-person deception: A new conceptualization of one central type of self-deception', *Philosophia* 22 (3–4): pp. 223–40.

Wilshire, B. (1982) *Role Playing and Illusion*, Bloomington: Indiana University Press.

Winnicott, D. W. (1965) *The Maturational Process and the Facilitating Environment*, London: Hogarth Press.

Winnicott, D. W. (1988) *Human Nature*, London: Free Association Books.

Wisdom, J. (1969) *Philosophy and Psychoanalysis*, Oxford: Basil Blackwell.

Wisdom, J. O. (1953) *The Unconscious Origin of Berkeley's Philosophy*, London: Hogarth.

Wittgenstein, Ludwig (1958 [1953]) *Philosophical Investigations, Oxford: Basil Blackwell.*

Wittgenstein, L. (1967) *Zettel*, Berkeley: Basil Blackwell and University of California Press.

Wittgenstein, Ludwig (1980) *Culture and Value, Oxford: Basil Blackwell.*

Wollheim, R. (1974a) 'Identification and imagination' in Wollheim, R. (ed.) *Freud: A Collection of Critical Essays* (pp. 172–95), New York: Anchor Books.

Wollheim, R. (ed.) (1974b) *Freud: A Collection of Critical Essays*, New York: Anchor Books.

Wollheim, R. (1979) 'Wish-fulfilment' in Harrison, R. (ed.) *Rational Action: Studies in Philosophy and Social Science* (pp. 47–60), Cambridge: Cambridge University Press.

Wollheim, R. (1984) *The Thread of Life*, Cambridge: Cambridge University Press.

Wollheim, R. (1991 [1971]) *Freud*, London: Fontana.

Wollheim, R. (1993a) 'Desire, belief, and Professor Grunbaum's Freud' in *The Mind and its Depths* (pp. 91–111), Harvard, MA: Harvard University Press.

Wollheim, R. (1993b) 'The bodily ego' in *The Mind and its Depths* (pp. 64–78), Harvard, MA: Harvard University Press.

Wollheim, R. (1993c) *The Mind and its Depths*, Harvard, MA: Harvard University Press.

Wollheim, R. and Hopkins, J. (eds) (1982) *Freud: A Collection of Critical Essays* (2nd ed.), New York: Anchor.

Woolf, Virginia (1989) *Moments of Being* (2nd ed.), London: Grafton Books.

Young-Bruehl, E. (1996) *The Anatomy of Prejudices*, Cambridge, MA: Harvard University Press.

Index

Nabokov, Vladimir 169, 175–6
narcissism: 'destructive narcissistic
    organisation' 116; of childhood 104;
    development of 154–5; and group
    identity 159–60; and idealisation 157;
    and identification with God 156, 157,
    159, 160, 161; Leonardo da Vinci's 105;
    and omnipotence of thoughts 70–1
nationalism 152
'neuralism', Graham 78, 196–7
neuroscience 17, 26n4, 41, 76, 124n14,
    180, 193–4
neurosis 10, 49, 137, 145
Nietzsche, F. 13, 24
non-intentionalism 54–5; enactment 66–9;
    omnipotence of thought 69–72;
    problems with 55–61; wish-fulfilment
    and 'belief-like' representations 64–6;
    wish-fulfilment without belief 61–4
non-intentionalist approaches 55–6

object relations 14–15, 23, 93–4, 106–7;
    see also external object; internal object
Ogden, T. H. 112
omnibenevolence of God 156
omnipotence: of gods 156, 157; of parents
    155; of thought 69–73, 80–1, 155
omniscience 153, 155, 156, 160
Onslow, Lord, shooting of 183
O'Shaughnessy, Brian 18, 51n11, 51n13, 56

Panksepp, Jaak 26n4, 17
parents, omnipotence of 155
partition 21–2, 23, 29, 99, 113; and
    delusions of self-observation 103;
    divided self 12, 15, 99–101
Pears, David 21, 94–5, 101, 123n4
Peel, McNaughton's attempted
    assassination of 184–9
personations 116–18, 122
personhood, Locke 112–13, 115
Petocz, Agnes 29n20, 91, 96n13, 124n12
phantasy 73–6, 109–10, 112; belief and
    46–7; and delusion 137, 139, 141; DNO
    experienced in 122, 136; Hopkins on
    79–80; intentional 60; omnipotent 7,
    80, 155; projective and introjective 135;
    self-consoling 121; see also wishful
    phantasy
philosophy of psychoanalysis 16–19
plasticity of instinct 67
Plato 99–100, 173

play 46–7, 72
Popper, Karl 77
preconscious attention 39, 52
preoccupation 38–40
Prescott, Carol 195
Price, H.H., belief and will 78n2
primitive man 70–1
projective identification 175–6
promissory materialism, Popper 77
psychiatry 192–7; neglect of FWT by
    76–7
psychoanalysis of philosophy 24–6
psychotic disorders/symptoms 77, 136,
    137, 140, 179, 180
punishment: need for 103–4, 162–3;
    religious ideas 164–5

Ramachandran, V. 40–1
Ramsey, F. P. 45
the Ratman 18–19, 69, 70, 81n21
reality 3, 4; and art 169, 172, 173; and
    delusion 137, 138, 140; disavowal of,
    religion 145, 158; double denial of 42;
    equation, psychic equivalence 36; and
    hallucination 34; reality principle 46;
    and sleep 34–5
reason/Reason: and action 17–18, 66–9,
    74–5, 80n14; loss of, insanity defence
    183–4; and personations 116–17; Plato's
    100; and religious belief 160; and
    subintentionalism 133
regression 33–4
rejective object (RO) 111
religion(s) 147–8; Freud on 144–7; as
    wish-fulfilment 157–63
the religiose 153–7; and fundamentalism
    150–3
religious identity 149, 159
religious vs. religiose people 149–50
repression 38–9, 41, 56
Rickman, John 173–4
Romantic age 12, 13
Rosenfeld, H. 116, 117–18, 121–2, 136,
    140
Russell, Bertrand 44
Ruthven, Malise 150
Rycroft, Charles 53n20

Sampson, H. 53n20, 85–6, 93
Sandler, A. M. 20
Sandler, Joseph 20, 97
Sartre's censor argument 22, 94–5